JUL    2008

# A PARENT'S
# GUIDE
# SPECIAL TO IAL
# EDUCATION

# A PARENT'S GUIDE TO SPECIAL EDUCATION

Insider Advice on How to Navigate the System
and Help Your Child Succeed

**Linda Wilmshurst, Ph.D., ABPP**
**& Alan W. Brue, Ph.D., NCSP**

**AMACOM**
American Management Association
New York • Atlanta • Brussels • Chicago • Mexico City • San Francisco
Shanghai • Tokyo • Toronto • Washington, D.C.

*This publication is designed to provide accurate and authoritative information in regard to the subject matter covered. It is sold with the understanding that the publisher is not engaged in rendering legal, accounting, or other professional service. If legal advice or other expert assistance is required, the services of a competent professional person should be sought.*

*Library of Congress Cataloging-in-Publication Data*

*Wilmshurst, Linda.*
  *A parent's guide to special education : insider advice on how to navigate the system and help your child succeed / Linda Wilmshurst, & Alan W. Brue.*
      *p.   cm.*
  *Includes bibliographical references and index.*
  *ISBN-10: 0-8144-7283-4 (pbk.)*
  *ISBN-13: 978-0-8144-7283-5 (pbk.)*
  *1. Special education—United States.   2. Special education—United States— Law and legislation.   I. Brue, Alan W.   II. Title.*

*LC3981.W55   2005*
*371.9—dc22*

                                                                    *2005006169*

*Printing number*

*10   9   8   7   6   5   4*

# Contents

# Acknowledgments

The authors wish to give special thanks to the following organizations for granting permission to use their forms and information in our book to assist us in providing parents with a better understanding of the special education process.

Lake County Schools
Student Services, Howey-in-the-Hills, Florida
Jay Marshall, Director of Student Services, and
Janice Tobias, chairperson of the Section 504 Manual Development
  Committee.
  - Comparison Chart of IDEA and Section 504 of the Rehabilitation Act of 1973 (Chapter 5)
  - Lake County Schools Section 504 Accommodation Plan (Appendix B)

Thank you for allowing us to add this helpful information on understanding and implementing Section 504 accommodations in the schools.

Dr. Mary Beth Klotz, Director of Technical Assistance
National Association of School Psychologists
Bethesda, Maryland

Thank you for your technical assistance.

American Diabetes Association

Thank you to the American Diabetes Association for allowing us to include a copy of your Section 504 Plan in Appendix B.

Paulding County School District
Dallas, Georgia
Trudy Sowar, Superintendent
LaVerne Suggs, Director, Exceptional Students Educational Programs

Thank you for allowing us to include copies of your IEP forms in Appendix E.

I would like to thank my mom, Jean, and my children, Luke and Rachel, who continue to inspire me to be the best that I can be. To Fred, for his continued support, and to Alan, my coauthor, who has taught me how collaboration can make a project twice as rewarding. To Lake County (FL) School District, my colleagues and friends, and ultimately to the parents and children for whom this book was written . . . may our words inspire and our information help you to make today's challenges stepping stones to increased success tomorrow.

—Linda Wilmshurst

To my family—my mother, Doris, my sisters, Laura and Jennifer, and in memory of my father, William, and my brother, Warren—for their love and support. To Terri Tangeman for her love, support, and assistance. To Dr. Thomas Oakland, a mentor and a friend, whose work ethic is inspiring. To my friends and colleagues at the National Association of School Psychologists, at Capella University, and at the Paulding County (GA) School District. My thanks to Linda Wilmshurst, a wonderful and creative collaborator. Most importantly, I would like to thank the school personnel and parents (and especially their children) with whom I have worked. Their hard work and dedication underscore the importance of education in the lives of children.

—Alan W. Brue

# A PARENT'S GUIDE SPECIAL TO EDUCATION

# Introduction to Special Education:
# A New Territory

**Did you know?** The biggest complaint many parents of children in special education have about the process is trying to obtain information in the early stages concerning the types of services that are available for their child. Furthermore, in one survey of parents of children in special education, an overwhelming 70 percent of those surveyed reported the belief that children lose out if parents are unaware of what their children are entitled to (Johnson & Duffett, 2002).

Although most parents would agree that it is important to be informed about their child's education, accessing information about special education can be a difficult task. One reason is that the federal laws supporting special education and related services can be difficult to understand and interpret. Not only is the language unclear, but there are also frequent changes to the laws. It can be difficult to determine which law is the most recent. Furthermore, different states have interpreted the federal laws in different ways, so learning how your particular state has interpreted these laws can also be an important part of the process.

An important question that parents may ask is:

*"How many children in the United States currently might be eligible for Special Education Services?"*

**According to the U.S. Department of Education, Office of Special Education Programs,** more than 6 million children in the United States age 3 to 21 receive special education services under IDEA, the Individuals with Disabilities Education Act.

We believe there is a great deal that you can learn about special education by asking the right questions. *However, if you do not know the right questions to ask, then it is virtually impossible to get the right answers.* As school psychologists who have worked in public education for a number of years, we have prepared this book to help you navigate a system that can be difficult and, at times, seemingly inaccessible. To get you started, in this chapter we will address the *Who, What, Where, When, Why,* and *How* of the special education process and provide direction as to where you can access important information on several topics presented throughout this book.

- *Who* is responsible for deciding when a concern becomes a problem.
- *What* the complex educational laws and rules that regulate the special education process mean to your child.
- *Where* to go for information, support, and assistance in the early stages of early intervention.
- *When* the education process should intervene and adjust to your child's special needs and the degree to which intervention is necessary. When to ask for an assessment and how to understand what the results mean.
- *Why* it is important to know what services are available and the amount of assistance your child will be receiving.
- *How* to advocate on behalf of your child. Understand your rights and the fine arts of negotiation and mediation.

To assist you in navigating this difficult system, we have organized information in this book in a way that we feel will be most helpful. The book is organized in three parts, around three different but connected themes:

- **Introduction:** Welcome and introduction to special education: an overview of what to expect and how to find it.
- **Part I**: Walking Through the Process: This section reviews important and recent changes in federal laws; provides insight and understanding concerning disabilities and assessment; and information that will increase understanding of the special education process, service delivery, and procedural safeguards.
- **Part II**: Helpful Hints for Positive Parenting: resources for parents in several areas, including parent-teacher communication; behavior and discipline; increasing self-esteem; and reducing stress.

## Introduction: Welcome to Special Education—A New Territory and a New Language

In this Introduction, we present an overview of our book that can serve as a guide to help you locate specific information.

## Part I: Walking Through the Process

In Part I, we will walk you through the special education process, one step at a time.

> **What is special education?** Special education refers to educational instruction that is specifically designed to meet the needs of a child with a disability.

**Step One:** In the first three chapters, you will become familiar with how special education services originated and the changing nature of federal laws that have been developed to support services for children with disabilities.

### How Special Education Began

Special education for children with disabilities was first initiated in 1975 with the passing of Public Law 94-142, then called the Education of All Handicapped Children Act (EHA), which legislated grants to states specifically for the education of children with disabilities. The law has been amended several times since then and was renamed the Individuals with Disabilities Education Act (IDEA) in 1990. The law was reauthorized in 1997, and after considerable debate, Congress passed the most recent reauthorization, titled the Individuals with Disabilities Education Improvement Act of 2004, in November 2004. President George W. Bush signed the new bill into law on December 3, 2004. The law, which will be referred to as IDEA 2004 throughout this book, became effective on July 1, 2005.

### Special Education and Federal Laws

Chapter 1 contains valuable information about IDEA 2004, the federal law that provides funding for special education and related services, plus recent reforms that have been included in the newly reauthorized version of this law. In addition to discussing how changes in the law will have an impact on eligibility requirements for special education and related services, this chapter will also highlight how IDEA 2004 differs from previous versions of the law.

Children with disabilities may also receive protection under Section 504 of the Rehabilitation Act, which prohibits discrimination against persons with disabilities. You will learn more about Section 504 in Chapter 2 and access actual 504 Plans that have been developed by a school district and the American Diabetes Association. Finally, in Chapter 3, you will have an opportunity to look at the similarities and differences between IDEA 2004 and Section 504, a discussion that will help to increase your understanding about these federal laws and which law may be most appropriate to support your child's needs. Chapter 3 also provides a brief look at No Child Left Behind (NCLB) and the Elementary and Secondary Education Act of 1965, the country's main education laws that were not written especially for children with disabilities. However, significant energy has been devoted in IDEA 2004 to align itself more closely with NCLB, both in matters of funding, as well as addressing qualification standards for special education teachers, and the necessary accommodations that should be made for disabled students taking state and district-wide assessments. We will discuss NCLB and the critical provisions of that law that influenced the reauthorization of IDEA 2004.

**Step Two:** In order to qualify for services under IDEA 2004, children with disabilities must meet certain eligibility criteria. Most of the information about a child's eligibility is provided by a comprehensive assessment, of which the psychological assessment is a major component.

Based on our experiences as school psychologists in the public school system and as university trainers in several school psychology graduate programs, we will walk you through the stages involved in the comprehensive assessment process, helping you to gain a better understanding of what is involved and what to expect. You are given an overview of the assessment process in Chapter 4, with particular attention given to the types of psychological assessments that might be conducted and how to understand the psychological report that will summarize the results of your child's assessment. Chapter 5 is devoted to the assessment of intelligence so that you will become familiar with different aspects of IQ scores and how this information can be used to predict academic expectations. In Chapter 6, you will learn how to interpret scores from academic tests, processing tests, and tests of emotional and behavioral functioning. The focus of Chapter 7 concerns the concept of disability under IDEA 2004 and gives you a more comprehensive understanding of the psychological foundations of your child's disability, as well as the types of interventions that can be developed to increase your child's opportunities for success at home and at school.

**Step Three:** The final step in understanding the special education process is addressed in three chapters that cover controversial topics such as *labels* (Chapter 8) and how parents can be more proactive partners in developing their child's Individualized Education Program (Chapter 9). This section of the book will also talk about the delivery of special education and related services.

Special education instruction may differ from regular education in areas of content, delivery, or the location where the instruction takes place. Instruction may occur in the regular education classroom or in one of two special education classroom settings, such as a resource room in which children can receive specialized help for brief parts of the day (generally one or two academic areas) or a self-contained room, where children remain for the majority of their day. Specialized instruction is developed and documented in an IEP. It is important that you understand these differences in service delivery so that you can be a more effective advocate for your child when his IEP is developed and reviewed each year.

In Chapter 10, you will learn what to expect once your child is deemed eligible for special education services. This chapter will provide you with information about annual reviews, reevaluations, and transition plans. IDEA 2004 has made several changes to the IEP process to reduce paperwork and meeting times. Recommendations include merging IEP meetings and reevaluation meetings, and including parents in the process through conference calls and video conferencing. When a child reaches 14 years of age, IDEA 2004 requires that the IEP must include a statement of *transition service needs* that will bridge services between the middle school and high school. After this time, annual reviews will include increasing emphasis on statements concerning goals for successful transition from high school to postgraduation plans, whether this includes preparation for employment, technical training, or higher education. A student who reaches 18 years of age, under IDEA 2004, may have the option of developing a comprehensive three-year IEP, which will serve as the final transition plan.

Also in Chapter 10, you will learn the limits of protection for children with disabilities under IDEA 2004 and Section 504, if your child violates school rules or the law. Important changes to the procedural safeguards, under IDEA 2004, will also be discussed in this section. You will be given an overview of your rights and your child's rights under IDEA 2004, and advice concerning mediation, due process hearings, and appeals.

## Part II: Helpful Hints for Positive Parenting

The final portion of our book provides you with much-needed information and assistance in several important areas, such as improving parent-teacher communications and what to expect at school meetings (Chapter 11). This section also addresses reducing parent and child stress (Chapter 12); improving your child's self-esteem (Chapter 13); and child behavior management and discipline (Chapter 14). In Appendix F, you will find Web sites, addresses, and telephone numbers for organizations that can further support your ability to access more information about disability awareness, support groups, and legislative bodies. Finally, in the Glossary you will find 101 acronyms that are commonly used in the educational system. Educational terminology includes jargon and abbreviations that can be overwhelming to people unacquainted with them. Therefore, as a start, just having access to these acronyms can be a helpful resource, and can minimize the confusion and overwhelming feelings associated with many three- and four-letter abbreviations. For example, you might hear something like:

***"We have discussed your child's IEP at the SAT meeting and would like to obtain your permission to conduct an FBA and***

***develop a BIP to address the high number of ISSs he has had
recently."***

You will be able to translate this sentence into meaningful communication after
reading the Glossary, which covers educational acronyms. (By the way, what the
statement really says is: "We have discussed your child's Individual Education
Program (IEP) at the Student Assistance Team Meeting (SAT) and would like to
obtain your permission to conduct a Functional Behavioral Assessment (FBA) and
develop a Behavioral Intervention Plan (BIP) to address the high number of in-
school suspensions (ISS) he has had recently.")

Throughout our book, we have referred to the child as a male child (he) to
avoid the necessity of referring to he/she on a repetitive basis. Although the majority of children with disabilities are male, parents who have daughters with disabilities are encouraged to substitute "she" when reading these sections.

We believe that we have developed a helpful book that provides you with *insider advice* rarely found in other parent books about special education. *A Parent's
Guide to Special Education* will provide you with the necessary information to
make informed decisions to increase your child's opportunities for educational
success.

# PART I

# WALKING THROUGH THE PROCESS

# STEP ONE:

Federal Law and

Your Child's Education

# The Individuals with Disabilities Education Improvement Act of 2004: What a Great IDEA!

In this chapter, we will discuss a brief history of how IDEA came to be and how this law specifically mandates special education and related services for children with disabilities. This chapter also introduces IDEA 2004, which became law on July 1, 2005.

## A Brief History of IDEA

Special education for children with disabilities was first initiated in 1975 with the passing of Public Law 94-142, then called the Education of All Handicapped Children Act (EHA), which legislated grants to states specifically for the education of children with disabilities. The law has been amended several times since that time, and in 1990 the law was renamed the Individuals with Disabilities Education Act, which has come to be known as IDEA. This law sets guidelines regarding how schools should deliver special education and related services to students with disabilities. The law has been changed many times, with more regulations and procedures being added with each successive change. Congress last reauthorized IDEA in November 2004, with the passing of the Individuals with Disabilities Education Improvement Act of 2004, which President George W. Bush signed into law on December 3, 2004. Prior to this time, the last revision of the act was in 1997. (The entire contents of the congressional report can be accessed at http://www.ed.gov/policy/speced/guid/idea/idea2004.html.) In our discussion, we will include the section numbers (such as Sec. 614) to indicate which portion of the law to access for additional information.

IDEA 2004 is a federal law that was developed to protect the rights of students with disabilities. It defines a disability as "a natural part of the human experience" (Sec. 601). The act seeks to equalize educational opportunities for individuals with disabilities. IDEA 2004 lists thirteen specific categories of disabilities children may experience that are mandated under the act, including children with the following needs:

- Having mental retardation, hearing impairments (including deafness), speech or language impairments, visual impairments (including blindness), serious emotional disturbance (hereinafter referred to as emotional disturbance), orthopedic impairments, autism, traumatic brain injury, other health impairments, or specific learning disabilities
- Requiring special education and related services as a result of their disability

We will discuss the thirteen categories at greater length in Chapters 7 and 8.

In addition to these thirteen categories of disabilities, IDEA 2004 also states that *at the discretion of the state and the school district,* children age 3 through 9 *(or any subset of that age range, including ages 3 through 5),* may also receive special education and related services, if the child is experiencing developmental delays. It is important to understand, however, that under IDEA 2004, states are not mandated to provide services for children with developmental delays, and if they do, they may chose to serve a more limited age span. We will discuss this at greater length when we focus on how the act applies to school-age children (Part B of IDEA 2004).

The major goal of IDEA 2004 is to improve educational results for children with disabilities to ensure that they have the same opportunities for participation, independent living, and economic self-sufficiency as their nondisabled peers. Specifically, the legislation strives to:

- Ensure that children with disabilities have access to a Free Appropriate Public Education (FAPE) that includes special education and related services when these services are required to address the child's individual learning needs
- Ensure that undiagnosed disabilities do not prevent children from obtaining a successful educational experience
- Ensure that public schools provide the necessary services for children with disabilities to have a FAPE
- Protect the rights of children with disabilities and their parents
- Ensure that funds are available to support states, local school districts, and agencies to provide special education and related services
- Monitor the effectiveness of educational programs in meeting the needs of children with disabilities

The law has four main parts:

- *Parts A and B.* These sections cover eligibility procedures, regulations, and required services for children between the ages of 3 years and 21 years.
- *Part C.* This section of the law pertains to services for infants and toddlers with disabilities, under 3 years of age.
- *Part D.* The final section discusses national activities that have been promoted to enhance educational services for children with disabilities.

**Did you know?** Under IDEA 2004, infants and toddlers with disabilities and developmental delays can receive *intervention services* as part of their Individualized Family Service Plan (IFSP). Also, children with disabilities between the ages of 3 and 21 can receive *special education and related services* that are part of their *Individualized Education Program (IEP)*.

According to IDEA 2004, improving educational success for children with disabilities can only be achieved in an environment that supports:

- High expectations for success and meeting developmental goals with maximum access to the general curriculum.
- Increased parent participation in their child's educational program.
- Coordinating efforts of IDEA 2004 with other educational laws, such as the Elementary and Secondary Education Act of 1965 (ESEA), as amended by the No Child Left Behind Act of 2001 (NCLB), to increase the emphasis on children with disabilities having the same opportunities for education as their nondisabled peers. IDEA 2004 includes more than sixty references to ESEA/NCLB, importing terms directly from these laws, such as references to achievement in the "core academic subjects"; discussing qualifications for special education teachers related to standards for "highly qualified teachers" noted in NCLB; and references to "homeless children," which were not cited in previous versions of IDEA.
- Supporting the regular curriculum with special education and related services when required.
- Supporting the development and use of technology to maximize access to education.
- Increased effort to reduce mislabeling and high dropout rates of minority children with disabilities. IDEA 2004 requires states to develop policies and procedures to minimize the overidentification of students from racially and ethnically diverse cultures.

## IDEA 2004: Part C—The Infants and Toddlers with Disabilities Program: (Age Birth to 2)

Although the majority of information in this chapter will discuss special education and related services for children between the ages of 3 and 21, we will provide a brief explanation of how IDEA 2004 addresses intervention services for children from birth to the end of the child's second year.

Under Part C of IDEA 2004 (Sec. 631), financial assistance is provided to each state to:

- Develop multidisciplinary, interagency systems to provide early intervention services for infants and toddlers with disabilities and their families.

- Encourage expansion of opportunities for children under 3 years of age who would be at risk of having substantial developmental delay if they did not receive early intervention services.

- Identify, evaluate, and meet the needs of all children, particularly minority, low-income, inner city, and rural children, and infants and toddlers in foster care. According to IDEA 2004, *early intervention services* include those services that may be required to assist in the identification and remediation of problems for infants and toddlers with identified developmental delays or may offer services to those at risk of developmental delays that could have a negative influence on a child's ability to learn. IDEA 2004 uses the term *at-risk infant or toddler* to refer to a child under 3 years of age who would be at risk of being substantially delayed, if early intervention services were not provided. IDEA uses the term *developmental delay* (Sec. 635) to refer to a delay of:

  - 35 percent or more in one of the developmental areas described next.

  - 25 percent or more in two or more of the developmental areas.

  Delays (Sec. 632) may be evident in one of five developmental areas:

  1. How the child learns (cognitive development)

  2. Physical development (motor skills)

  3. Communication skills (speech and language development)

  4. Social or emotional development

  5. Adaptive functioning

Adaptive functioning can include daily living and self-help skills, such as a child's ability to dress or feed himself. Parents who believe that their infant or toddler may be eligible for intervention services should contact the agency in their state that is responsible for early intervention programs.

IDEA 2004 also mandates services for infants and toddlers who have a diagnosed physical or mental condition that has a high likelihood of resulting in a developmental delay.

Congress has allocated funds to help states develop early intervention services. If the state chooses, it can also use these funds to develop programs for children who are at risk of developing disabilities. For children under 3 years of age, services are provided by several different agencies. In some states, the department of education may be responsible for programs for children of all ages; however, in other states, other agencies, such as the health department, may be responsible for programs designed for infants and toddlers. When multiple agencies are involved, a lead agency will be established and a service coordinator selected from that agency to oversee the intervention services. These agencies differ from state to state but can be located for your state by visiting the National Dissemination Center for Children with Disabilities (NICHCY) Web site at www.nichcy.org and logging on to the State Resources fact sheet to search for "Programs for Infants and Toddlers with Disabilities." It is also possible to contact NICHCY directly by telephone to inquire about *early intervention services* in your area by using the contact information provided in Appendix F.

## How Will I Know If My Child Needs Intervention Services?

In order to determine whether a child is eligible for intervention services, according to IDEA 2004, an evaluation is provided at no cost to parents to determine whether a child meets eligibility criteria for services. Information is collected by the intervention team. It is a *multidisciplinary team* that might include a social worker, school psychologist, speech and language pathologist, physical therapist, and/or occupational therapist.

## What Types of Information Are Required?

The intervention team will evaluate eligibility for intervention services based on information collected from a group of professionals who are familiar with the child. Information may be obtained from:

- Family social history, including developmental milestones (when the child sat, walked, talked, and so forth)
- Medical history and physician's reports
- Results of developmental tests (cognitive, language, motor functioning)
- Observations of the child by intervention team members

## What Types of Intervention Services Are Provided?

Under IDEA 2004, infants and toddlers with disabilities and developmental delays who are eligible for services can receive intervention programs designed to target specific areas of delay:

- Physical
- Cognitive
- Speech and language (communication)
- Social, emotional/behavioral
- Adaptive functioning

Once it is determined that a child is eligible for intervention services, a *service coordinator* is assigned to the family and will assist the family in locating the appropriate resources that are available in the community. The service coordinator assists the family until the child either no longer requires services or the child turns 3 years of age. At this time, the coordinator will assist the family in the transition to appropriate services for children 3 years and older.

### Who Pays for the Intervention Services?

Although the evaluation is free for families, some parts of the services may be charged to parents, depending on state policies and regulations. Most services, if not free of charge, will be allocated on a sliding scale based on income. Some services may fall under Medicaid or other health insurance plans.

**Individualized Family Service Plan**   In the spirit of IDEA 2004, the family is seen as the child's foundation for support, and as such, the services are built around a plan that has family at the core. This plan is called the Individualized Family Service Plan.

Under Part C of IDEA 2004 (Sec. 636), each infant or toddler with a disability, and the infant's or toddler's family, are entitled to:

1. A multidisciplinary assessment of the child's strengths and individual needs, and the identification of services appropriate to meet these needs
2. A family-based assessment to determine the family needs (resources, concerns) and available community resources and services to assist the family in meeting the child's developmental needs
3. An IFSP written by the multidisciplinary team and parents outlining the needs, resources, and appropriate transition services for the child

Although IDEA 2004 outlines the goals for the family service plan, each state determines specific guidelines concerning how the plans are to be developed. While these plans can differ in some ways from state to state, most family service plans include some or all of the following:

- Current levels of functioning
- Services required, and who will provide the services
- Expected outcomes
- Where the services will be provided, with emphasis on services within the natural environment

- When services will be initiated and the length, duration, and frequency of the services
- Identification of the service coordinator
- Transition plans for other programs

IDEA 2004 mandates that parent permission must be obtained prior to the provision of early intervention services described in the IFSP. Only those services that have parental consent can be provided. Although IDEA 2004 determines that the IFSP is to be evaluated annually, the family will receive a review of the plan at six-month intervals (or more often, if needed).

IDEA 2004 stresses the importance of *developing an effective transition plan* to assist in providing a smooth and effective transition from interventions covered under Part C (Infants and Toddlers with Disabilities) to preschool programs existing under Part B (Education of All Children with Disabilities). IDEA 2004 mandates that by the child's third birthday, an IEP or an IFSP must be developed and implemented. The service coordinator is responsible for arranging a conference and inviting the school district to participate in the transition planning process.

## IDEA 2004: Part B—Special Education Programs and Services: Preschool (Age 3 to 5)

Under Part B of IDEA 2004, all public schools must provide free special education services for eligible children with disabilities once the child turns 3 years of age. With the introduction of IDEA, special education preschool programs were mandated for eligible children with disabilities who were between 3 and 5 years of age.

### How Will I Know If My Child Is Eligible for a Special Education Preschool Program?

According to IDEA 2004, children can become eligible for special education services if they meet the following three criteria:

1. They have received an individual evaluation (as set out in the regulations).
2. The evaluation has confirmed the existence of a disability (in one of thirteen specified areas).
3. The disability interferes with the child's ability to learn.

A comprehensive discussion of the various types of individual evaluations that may be conducted and how to interpret and understand the results of the assessment is presented in Chapters 4, 5, and 6. An in-depth look at the specific categories of disabilities listed by IDEA 2004 can be found in Chapters 7 and 8.

## Children "At Risk" of Developing Disabilities and Children with Developmental Delays

Prior to the 1997 reauthorization of IDEA, the law stipulated that preschool-age children (3 to 5 years of age) who demonstrated *developmental delays* could be eligible for special education services, if the child demonstrated significant developmental delays determined through a comprehensive initial evaluation. However, the developmental delay classification was to be removed prior to the child's sixth birthday. At that time, further evaluation would be conducted to determine whether the child would continue to receive services under one or more of the thirteen categories of disabilities, or whether the child was no longer eligible to receive services under IDEA.

With the 1997 reauthorization of IDEA, the age range for consideration of developmental delay was expanded from 3 to 5 years to the age range of 3 through 9 years. Under IDEA 2004, this expanded age range of 3 through 9 is retained and now the phrase "including the subset of ages 3 through 5" has been added to the age description. Children with identified delays in one of the five developmental areas (physical development, cognitive development, communication development, social or emotional development, or adaptive development) *may be granted* access to special education and related services, at the discretion of the state, if these services are deemed necessary. However, as noted previously, IDEA 2004 did not change the discretionary nature of this service, and states are not mandated to provide special education and related services for children with developmental delays.

The controversy regarding whether the expanded age should be adopted has resulted in wide variations in age criteria for the developmental delay category among the states. Proponents in favor of extending the age of classification believe that standardized tests are not as reliable in early childhood and could possibly lead to misdiagnosis. Furthermore, the need to have children meet criteria for one of the thirteen disability categories might also lead to inappropriate diagnoses or ineligibility for services at a time when increased services might have the most impact.

Those who are not in favor of increasing the age span are concerned with the overidentification of children eligible for special education services.

## Special Education Services for School-Age Children (Age 3 to 21)

According to IDEA 2004, if a child (age 3 to 21) has a disability that interferes with his ability to learn, he is legally entitled to a FAPE in the *least restrictive environment* (LRE). Special education and related services (such as special transportation, speech and language, assistive technology) must be available from the child's third birthday until receipt of a high school diploma or the end of the school year of the student's twenty-first birthday, whichever is earlier. However, under

IDEA 2004, it has been more clearly noted that schools are not required to conduct an exit evaluation to terminate special education services when the child graduates with a standard diploma or is no longer eligible for services due to age (22 years of age).

## Who Determines Eligibility for Special Education Services?

A child who is suspected of having a disability that is interfering with his ability to learn can be identified by either the child's teacher or the child's parent. Under IDEA 2004 (Sec. 614), the school district shall conduct a full and individual initial evaluation to determine whether a child meets eligibility criteria for special education and related services. IDEA 2004 notes that requests for an initial evaluation can be made by either a parent of a child, a state department of education or other state agency, or the school district.

*If a parent suspects a disability,* he or she should contact the school (either the classroom teacher, guidance counselor, or principal) in person or in writing to request a meeting to discuss the child's problem. The parents will be invited to a meeting to discuss ways in which to address the problems. If at some point an evaluation is requested by either the parent or the school, it will be conducted at no cost to the parent.

*If school personnel suspect a disability* and feel that an evaluation is necessary, the child's parents will be advised that the school is recommending an evaluation to help determine whether the child is eligible for special education and related services. Parents must be informed about the nature of the evaluation proposed and must provide written consent for the initial evaluation.

## Is Consent Needed for Evaluation and/or Services?

If a parent refuses to provide consent for an initial evaluation, the school district may choose to engage in due process or mediation. Mediation and due process hearings are discussed further in Chapter 10 and in Appendix D under Procedural Safeguards. Under IDEA 2004, if a parent refuses special education services for a child with a disability, the school district will not be considered in violation of the law by not providing a FAPE, nor will the district be responsible for developing an IEP for the child.

The evaluation process, under IDEA 2004, requires that a comprehensive assessment be conducted. This evaluation, often referred to as an *initial referral for evaluation,* may include the administration of specialized assessment measures, review of existing and previous school history, parent, teacher and student interviews, completing of behavior rating scales and other forms, as well as classroom observations.

IDEA 2004 recognizes the increasing numbers of children in schools who have limited English proficiency and places increased emphasis on the need to provide assessments for these children in a *language and form* that is most likely to yield the most accurate picture of the child's knowledge and understanding.

IDEA 2004 also cautions placing too many minority children in special education programs relative to their Caucasian peers.

Once sufficient information is obtained to make an informed decision regarding whether the child has a disability and the extent to which that disability impairs the child's academic performance, a meeting is held to discuss the evaluation results. Parents are invited to attend this educational meeting where results of the evaluation are discussed and eligibility for special education services are determined. We'll talk more about meetings in Chapter 11.

**Did you know?** Once a child has been referred for initial evaluation, under IDEA 2004, the school district has sixty days from the time of parent consent for evaluation (or as set out in state regulations) in which to complete the evaluation and convene an educational meeting to discuss the results of that evaluation.

Under IDEA 2004, eligibility determination must rule out that learning was negatively influenced by:

- Lack of appropriate instruction in reading (as set out in NCLB)
- Lack of appropriate instruction in mathematics
- Limited English proficiency

## Determination of a Student Having Learning Disabilities Under IDEA 2004

Under IDEA 2004, a school district is no longer required to demonstrate a significant discrepancy between achievement and intelligence in order to determine that a child has a specific learning disability in areas of oral expression, listening comprehension, written expression, basic reading skill, reading comprehension, mathematical calculation, or mathematical reasoning. Instead, a district may chose to determine eligibility under the category of *specific learning disabilities* if the evaluation reveals that the child has failed to respond adequately to a scientific, research-based intervention program aimed at increasing skills in the deficit area. Specific learning disabilities and the controversy regarding the achievement/intelligence discrepancy are discussed in greater detail in Chapters 6 and 7.

## How to Advocate on Behalf of Your Child—The Fine Art of Negotiation, Mediation, and Legislation; Knowing Your Rights

Under IDEA 2004, there are provisions that serve as procedural safeguards for students with disabilities. Copies of the *procedural safeguards* are provided to parents:

- When there is an initial referral for evaluation
- Upon notification of subsequent educational meeting on the student
- At the time of the individual educational plan team meeting (once, yearly)
- Upon the filing of a complaint
- When requested by the parent

These safeguards are designed to help parents understand how federal and state laws have been developed to protect their rights regarding such areas as prior written notice of meetings, consent, independent educational evaluation, records, mediation, hearings, due process hearings, and appeals. We will discuss parent rights in more detail in Chapter 10 and Appendix D.

## Delivery of Special Education Services

The term *special education* refers to educational instruction that is specifically designed to meet the needs of a child with a disability. This instruction may differ from regular education in content, delivery, or the location in which the instruction takes place. Instruction may occur in the regular education classroom or one of two special educational classroom settings: a resource room, where children can receive specialized help for brief parts of the day (generally one or two academic areas), or a self-contained room, where they remain for the majority of their day. Special education instruction can also be provided in the home, hospitals, or alternative settings. School districts are responsible for providing a continuum of special education placements that adhere to a policy of offering the *least restrictive environment* ranging from minimal services (such as twenty minutes weekly) to full-time placement in an alternative setting.

**Did you know?** Under IDEA 2004, children must be educated in their home school (local school), unless alternative placement is recommended by the child's IEP because services cannot be provided adequately in the home school.

Specialized instruction is developed and documented in an Individualized Education Program. You can learn more about the requirements for an IEP and the new IEP regulations in Chapter 9.

### How Can I Obtain a Copy of IDEA?

Parents wanting to learn more about IDEA 2004 can obtain a copy of the final federal regulations by writing to the Superintendent of Documents, U.S. Government Printing Office, P.O. Box 371954, Pittsburgh, PA 15250-7954. Please request "H.R. 1350: The Individuals with Disabilities Education Act Amendments of 2004." The final federal regulations also may be obtained by requesting a copy of the latest IDEA regulations: Code of Federal Regulations: Title 341 Education; Part 300–399. Documents can also be accessed on line at www.ed.gov/offices/OSERS/IDEA/index.html, or you can call in your order to 202-512-1800.

### How Can I Get a Copy of My State's Special Education Law?

To find out more about your state's special education laws, visit the National Dissemination Center for Children with Disabilities Web site at: www.nichcy.org, and log on to the State Resources Web page.

## Highlights of the Individuals with Disabilities Education Improvement Act of 2004

Many parts of IDEA 2004 are different from the 1997 version. An outline of some of the major changes that are of interest to parents is presented in the following list. (A more detailed summary of many of these changes can be found in Appendix A.)

### State and School District Accountability

- Federal funds for special educational programs can be withheld if states do not meet federal standards as dictated by IDEA 2004.
- Accountability for meeting standards of educational achievement.
- Emphasis on empirically based interventions.
- Requirement for state policies and procedures to prevent overidentification or disproportionate representation by race and ethnicity of children with disabilities, including identification of children with a particular impairment.

### Educational Accountability

- Includes provisions relating to children with disabilities meeting adequate yearly progress.
- Eliminates requirements for short-term objectives in IEPs.
- Requires that IEPs include a child's current levels of academic achievement and functional performance.
- Requires progress updates to provide parents with specific, meaningful, and understandable information on the progress their child is making.

### Evaluation Requirements

- Requires that tests and evaluations used to determine eligibility be in the language and form most likely to yield accurate information about what the child knows academically, developmentally, and functionally.

- Allows some children with disabilities to obtain certain necessary accommodations or even an alternate assessment.
- Revises exit evaluation requirement in certain circumstances.

### Efficiency (Paperwork, Meetings, etc.)

- Allows fifteen states to participate in a pilot program to reduce the amount of paperwork they produce.
- Encourages school districts to combine IEP meetings and reevaluation meetings.
- Allows a member of the IEP team to be excused from an IEP meeting under certain circumstances.
- Provides for a resolution session to give parents and school districts an opportunity to resolve their complaints before going to a due process hearing.
- Includes a two-year limit for requesting a hearing on claims for reimbursed or ongoing compensatory education services, such as private school, unless there is a state timeline.

### Student Conduct

- Requires IEP teams to provide positive behavioral interventions and supports for children with disabilities whose behavior impedes their learning or the learning of others.
- Allows schools to consider any unique circumstances on a case-by-case basis when determining whether to order a change in placement for a child with a disability who violates a code of student conduct.
- Schools now have the right to make decisions about educational placement changes when behavior is not a result of the child's disability, although parents can appeal the decision.
- Students can now be placed in an alternative educational setting for forty-five school days rather than forty-five calendar days.

### Early Intervention

- *Early Intervention: Preschool.* Previously, funds were allocated for early intervention programs at two separate levels: infants and toddlers (under 3 years of age) could receive funds for *early intervention services,* which would be implemented in an IFSP, or children 3 to 21 years of age could receive *special education or related services* that could be developed and implemented according to the IEP. Currently, the possibility exists for states to develop a "seamless system of service" that could serve children from birth through 5 years of age.

• *Early Intervention: School Age.* Allows district to use up to 15 percent of the funding for students in regular education who are at risk of needing special education services in the future for academic and behavioral problems. The funds can be used for direct service or teacher training.

CHAPTER 2

Not All Roads Lead to Special Education
Placement: The 411 on 504 Plans

In Chapter 1, we talked about IDEA 2004 as it relates to special education services. Yet children identified with a disability do not necessarily require these services. Some may have a disability but are not eligible for special education services
under IDEA 2004. This chapter will briefly address Section 504 of the Rehabilitation Act of 1973 and how modifications can be implemented in the *regular education setting* through the use of a 504 Plan.

## Section 504 of the Rehabilitation Act of 1973

Section 504 of the Rehabilitation Act of 1973, which will be referred to as 504
from this point on, is a civil rights law. It protects individuals with disabilities from
discrimination, and it ensures that children with disabilities have equal access to
education. Special accommodations to a child's program are required if there is a
substantial mental or physical impairment that limits, to a considerable or large
degree, one or more of the child's major life activities, such as caring for one's
self, performing manual tasks, walking, seeing, hearing, speaking, breathing,
learning, or working. A physical or mental impairment can include a facial disfig-
urement, blindness or visual impairment, cancer, diabetes, mental illness, specific
learning disability, mental retardation, heart disease, AIDS, cancer, deafness or
hearing impairment, diabetes, heart disease, and attention-deficit/hyperactivity
disorder (ADHD).

A child may also qualify if he has a physical or mental impairment that substantially limits major life activities due to the attitudes of others toward such an impairment (peers' reaction to burn scars, for example); has a physical or mental
impairment that does not substantially limit major life activities but is treated by
others as having a limitation; or has none of the mental of physical impairments
mentioned previously but is treated as having such an impairment. Therefore, even

if a child's disability does not directly impair functioning, the act covers impaired functioning resulting from discrimination based on other people's attitudes or responses to the disability. These last two options offer some flexibility. If your child is treated as having substantial limitations or impairments, he may qualify under 504.

> **Did you know?** The nondiscrimination requirements of the law apply to organizations that receive financial assistance from any federal department or agency. This includes school districts.

## Determining Eligibility

Determining eligibility under 504 is a team decision. Team members may include regular education teachers, a school administrator, school psychologist, school counselor, speech-language pathologist, school social worker, school nurse, and occupational and physical therapists, the parents, and the child. The 504 team will review all the information presented to its members and determine whether a child qualifies for assistance. Possessing a physical or mental impairment does not necessarily mean your child will automatically qualify. A medical report from your child's doctor or a psychological evaluation by the school psychologist or a psychologist in private practice may also be required. The nature and severity of the disability plus its expected duration will also be considered.

Under 504, unlike IDEA 2004, a child does not need to possess a specific psychological or medical condition. Section 504 requires only that the physical or mental impairment affects one of the body systems (neurological; musculoskeletal; special sense organs; respiratory, including speech organs; cardiovascular; reproductive; digestive; genitourinary; hemic and lymphatic; skin; and endocrine) or that the disability be considered a mental or psychological disorder.

Figure 2-1 illustrates the differences. The largest circle includes *all* children in a school district. Among all children, some will qualify under 504 (middle circle). And of those children, some meet the more rigid IDEA 2004 eligibility standards (smallest circle).

## A 504 Plan

A 504 Plan is a legal document designed to create a program of instructional services for children with special needs to assist them in the regular education setting. The team writes the plan after receiving all necessary feedback. A 504 Plan includes reasonable instructional accommodations and modifications based on the child's individual needs. After it has been developed and everyone agrees with its

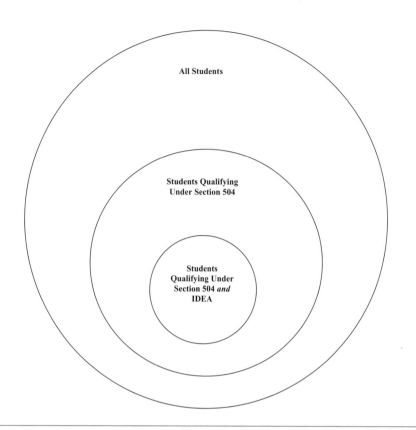

*Figure 2-1.     Students qualifying under IDEA vs. 504.*

contents, the general education team is responsible for the plan's implementation. Sample 504 Plans are included in Appendix B.

**Did you know?** Unlike IDEA 2004, Section 504 does not grant federal financial support to school districts for providing additional services to children. Therefore, districts may appear unwilling to provide these services and may instead push for finding your child eligible under IDEA 2004. If you do not wish your child to receive special education services and would prefer accommodations are made in the regular education classroom, stand your ground and insist on a 504 Plan. In cases where the district continues to refuse, you may wish to consult with a parent advocate or an attorney.

## 504 Plan Accommodations

Accommodations provided to a child in the classroom are decided by the 504 team and will depend on his needs. Two children with the same disability may require very different accommodations. In our experience, the following classroom accommodations can be helpful to many children, although there are many more that are equally as effective. We will outline some accommodations for the classroom and include suggestions that can also improve your child's performance at home.

*Behavioral Strategies*

**Your child's teacher may:**

- Post rules and consequences for classroom behavior.
- Use a journal to report your child's daily behavior.
- Encourage self-monitoring and self-recording for your child's behaviors using a journal or a sheet to tally his behaviors.
- Use a behavioral contract to provide your child with structure and self-management skills.
- Use positive verbal and/or nonverbal cues and reinforcements.

**At home you can:**

- Post house rules and responsibilities in a conspicuous place (like on the refrigerator).
- Check your child's daily agenda to monitor his assignments and read the teacher's comments.
- Encourage self-monitoring and self-recording of behaviors. Praise your child for bringing the agenda home and for following through on assignments.
- Develop a behavioral contract with clear expectations and rewards or consequences for specific behaviors or task completion goals.

*Organizational Strategies*

**Your child's teacher may:**

- Use an organizational system such as folders for different assignments or classes. Each folder should be labeled with the name of each subject; a different colored folder for each subject works best.
- Provide your child with a homework journal for recording assignments. The teacher(s) should check it before your child leaves class.
- Set a time limit on assignments. For example, a child with obsessive-compulsive disorder may benefit from the use of an egg timer so that he knows when to stop working on one assignment and move on to another.

**At home you can:**

- Make sure your child's work space is uncluttered.

- Provide your child with the supplies necessary to complete his work.

- Use a timer if your child has difficulty completing his work in a timely manner. It can be set for a certain amount of time (thirty minutes, for example), after which your child can take a short break.

*Environmental Strategies*

**Your child's teacher may:**

- Provide a structured learning environment. It is helpful if a schedule is posted daily and indicates when each subject will be discussed. It should also include break times, and art, music, computer lab, or physical education classes. Some children require this type of structure to be successful.

- Provide preferential seating. For example, a child with ADHD may need to sit next to the teacher's desk so that his behavior can be monitored more closely, while a child with a visual impairment, even one that may be corrected, may need to sit close to the board.

- Use a study carrel to minimize distractions. This is especially helpful when a child completes class work or tests.

- Change the location of classroom supplies for easier access or to minimize distraction. A child using crutches should not have to navigate a maze of desks to get to a pencil sharpener. In addition, a child with ADHD should not sit next to a high-traffic area, such as a pencil sharpener, since it increases the distractions and the opportunity to talk to others.

**At home you can:**

- Provide your child with a quiet place in which to work, without the distractions from TV, radio, games, toys, or conversations.

- Keep your child visible in case he needs any assistance and to monitor progress.

- Review your child's work once it is finished to make sure that he has completed all the work.

*Presentation Strategies*

**Your child's teacher may:**

- Provide a lesson outline for each day's lesson so your child knows what to expect that day.

- Post the lesson plan outline in the same location each day, such as in the upper right corner of the blackboard, and direct children to review the outline prior to beginning the lesson.
- Provide a study guide for tests.
- Use alternative textbooks and workbooks or books on tape.
- Highlight the main ideas of a passage in the textbook/workbook.
- Tape-record lessons so they can be reviewed at a later time.

**At home you can:**

- Sit down with your child and provide an overview of the work that must be completed that night.
- Have your child circle the signs on math worksheets so he does not do the wrong operation.

*Evaluation Methods*

**Your child's teacher may:**

- Provide a practice test.
- Provide for oral testing for children who have difficulty with written expression or manual dexterity.
- Limit the amount of material presented on a single page.
- Allow extra time to complete work.
- Require the completion of fewer test items.

**At home you can:**

- Use math drills.
- Allow your child to practice writing his spelling words repeatedly.
- Have your child read aloud, keeping track of the words that cause difficulty. Keep a word bank of those words, and put those words on flash cards for later practice.

**Did you know?** If your child is not responding well to the accommodations in a 504 Plan, you can request a meeting to create a new one. A new 504 Plan will be written and include those accommodations that are working, as well as new ones to be implemented and monitored. It should be revised as often as needed to make sure the interventions are working for your child.

## Accommodations for Specific Disabilities

The accommodations required for a child vary based on the child's needs as well as strengths and weaknesses. In general, there is a common set of accommodations for children who have a particular disability. We will address some disabilities and include accommodations that may be helpful.

### Asthma

**Major Life Activity Affected: Learning**

- Provide rest periods.
- Share with school personnel the child's medical needs.
- Train appropriate school personnel to properly dispense medication and monitor for side effects (as needed).
- Develop health care and emergency plans (such as what to do when a child does not respond to medical intervention).
- Assist with inhalant therapy.
- Adjust schedule for administration of medications.
- Allow time to make up work when absent for medical reasons.
- Provide the child with peers who can carry books and other supplies as needed.
- Adapt activity level for recess, physical education, and other times as needed.
- Minimize allergens (such as perfume, cologne, lotions, paint) in the child's vicinity.

**Did you know?** About 5 million children in the United States have asthma.

### Attention-Deficit/Hyperactivity Disorder

**Major Life Activity Affected: Learning, and Possibly Social Skills**

- Provide appropriate staff training about ADHD.
- Place seat in close proximity to teacher; seat away from distractions.
- Provide the child with a peer helper for classwork and projects.
- School personnel should understand the child's potential need for excessive movement; giving the child an opportunity to stand and/or move while working.

- School personnel should understand the child's tendency to be inattentive; establish nonverbal cues between teacher and child to get his attention and increase on-task behavior.
- Post classroom rules and review on a regular basis.
- Reinforce the child when he displays appropriate behavior.
- Give a five-minute warning for a change in activity, so the child can begin to disengage from the task.
- Provide supervision during transition times (switching from one activity to another; moving from one class to another).
- Ask the child to restate directions.
- Assist the child with organizational strategies.
- Allow tests to be completed in several short testing sessions.
- Provide extended time to complete assignments and tests.
- Train appropriate school personnel to properly dispense medication and monitor for side effects (as needed).

**Did you know?** ADHD affects approximately 2 to 3 million children in the United States. Every classroom from kindergarten through twelfth grade on average has one or two children with ADHD.

## *Bipolar Disorder*

### Major Life Activity Affected: Learning

- Provide appropriate training to staff on bipolar disorder.
- Implement a crisis intervention plan in case child is uncontrollable, impulsive, or dangerous.
- Immediately report any suicidal comments to the school psychologist, the school counselor, and the child's parents.
- Give the child advanced notice of transitions.
- Create strategies for handling unpredictable mood swings.
- Allow the child to complete difficult classwork at times when he is more alert.
- Provide extended time to complete assignments and tests.
- Monitor the child's understanding of directions.
- Break down assignments into manageable parts.
- Train appropriate school personnel to properly dispense medication and monitor for side effects (as needed).

**Did you know?** Some researchers suspect that a significant number of children in the United States diagnosed with ADHD have early onset bipolar disorder instead of, or occurring along with, ADHD. This is one of the many ADHD look-alikes. For a list of others, go to http://www.umm.edu/patiented/articles/other disorders associ ated with attention-deficit disorder 000030 5.htm.

## Emotionally Disturbed

### Major Life Activity Affected: Learning

- Provide appropriate training to staff on emotional disturbance.
- Post classroom rules and review on a regular basis.
- Create effective behavior modification plans.
- The child's parents and teachers should work together to ensure that the behavioral interventions used at home and at school are monitored closely.
- Teachers must be consistent in setting behavioral expectations and following through on reinforcements/consequences.
- Create a behavior contract for the child.
- Ask the child to keep a daily journal to self-record behavior.
- Allow the child to participate in group counseling sessions with the school counselor or school psychologist.
- Train appropriate school personnel to properly dispense medication and monitor for side effects (as needed).

**Did you know?** According to the National Dissemination Center for Children with Disabilities, about half a million children and adolescents with an emotional disturbance receive special education and related services in the schools.

## Epilepsy

### Major Life Activity Affected: Learning

- Provide appropriate training to staff on epilepsy.
- Train both staff and children on what to do in the event the child has a seizure.
- Observe for consistent triggers of seizures.
- Should seizures occur, document the characteristics of each seizure.
- Seat the child in an area where he will not be injured if a seizure occurs.
- Prepare an emergency plan should a seizure occur. For example: (1) protect the child from injury by clearing space around him; (2) ask other

children to keep the area clear; (3) loosen tight clothing and protect the child's head from injury; (4) do not insert an object into the child's mouth; (5) if he is unconscious, place the child on his side to keep him from choking on vomit; and (6) stay with the child until he fully recovers.

- Do not allow him to be unsupervised, especially during physical education or field trips.

- Give the child time to make up any work he missed because of absence due to seizures.

- Train appropriate school personnel to properly dispense medication and monitor for side effects (as needed).

**Did you know?** The brain of a child is more prone to seizures than the brain of an adult. Causes of childhood epilepsy include genetics, brain tumors, head injury, and infections of the brain, among others. In the majority of cases, the exact cause cannot be determined.

CHAPTER 3

A Comparison of IDEA 2004 and Section 504, and a Brief Look at No Child Left Behind

When considering placement options, both IDEA 2004 and Section 504 require school districts to adhere to the following guidelines in the interpretation of data and in making placement decisions:

- Draw upon information from a variety of sources
- Ensure that all information is current, documented, and considered
- Ensure that eligibility decisions are made by a group of individuals who are knowledgeable about the student and can interpret the available data appropriately to make informed decisions regarding placement options
- Ensure that the student will be educated with nondisabled students to the maximum extent possible (least restrictive environment)

## IDEA 2004 and Section 504: A Comparison

The following table will help parents better understand the similarities and differences between regulations and procedures under IDEA 2004 and Section 504. These comparisons can assist parents in making more informed decisions about how to advocate for their child, and in determining which laws best meet the needs of their child's unique disability.

| Area Addressed | IDEA 2004 | Section 504 |
|---|---|---|
| 1. Purpose of the law | IDEA is a federally funded statute developed to provide | Section 504 is a civil rights law. The law was designed to protect the rights of individuals |

| Area Addressed | IDEA 2004 | Section 504 |
|---|---|---|
| | states with financial assistance to ensure that students with disabilities receive free appropriate services. | with disabilities who are served in programs that receive federal financial assistance from the U.S. Department of Education. |
| **2. Protection** | Students with disabilities who meet criteria for eligibility in one or more of the thirteen areas of disability designated by IDEA. | All disabled students who meet the following criteria for disabled persons as set out in Section 504:<br>1. A person who has a disability, or<br>2. Has had a physical or mental impairment which substantially limits one or more major life activities*, or<br>3. Is regarded as disabled by others.<br>*Major life activities include: walking, seeing, hearing, speaking, breathing, learning, working, caring for oneself, and performance on manual tasks |
| **3. Provision for a Free Appropriate Public Education** | Requires provision for FAPE for eligible students, including individual instruction. In addition, requires:<br>• Written IEP<br>• IEP meeting | Requires provision for FAPE for eligible students, including individual instruction.<br>In addition requires:<br>• Written plan<br>• Educational meeting |
| **4. Appropriate Education** | A program designed to provide "educational benefit," and related services as required, to allow the student to benefit from specially designed instruction. | A program comparable to education provided for nondisabled students. The program provides for reasonable accommodations to enable the student to learn in a way not encumbered by his disability. |
| **5. Special Education vs.** | Under IDEA, students are deemed el- | A student is eligible for program accommodations if he |

| Area Addressed | IDEA 2004 | Section 504 |
|---|---|---|
| **Regular Education** | igible for special education services if the multidisciplinary team determines that the student has met the designated criteria for a disability as detailed in IDEA and that the disability adversely impacts the student's ability to learn. | meets the definition of a "disabled person" as described in # 2 above. It is not a requirement of Section 504 that the disability adversely affect the educational performance of the student, or that the student requires special education services in order to be protected under the act. |
| **6. Funding** | School districts receive funding for all students who are deemed eligible for special education services under IDEA | No additional funds are provided for students under Section 504. The act provides protection from discrimination, not access to special education services. |
| **7. Accessibility** | IDEA mandates that modifications to the program must be made if these are necessary for the student to profit from FAPE. | Under Section 504, accommodations for disabled students include equal access to buildings (physical accommodations), communication systems (FM systems), modifications to the program (increased time for test taking) and so on. |
| **8. Procedural Safeguards** | Parents must be given notice for the identification, evaluation, and/or placement. | Parents must be given notice for of the identification, evaluation, and/or placement. |
| **9. Identification** | Requires a written notice. | Districts may require a written notice. |
| **10. Evaluations** | A full comprehensive evaluation may be required to assess all areas related to the suspected disability. Evaluation is completed by a multidis- | Evaluation is conducted by a group of people knowledgeable about the student and depending on the area of disability and district regulations, may include anecdotal information, medical and school records, ob- |

| Area Addressed | IDEA 2004 | Section 504 |
|---|---|---|
| | ciplinary team or group. | servations, rating scales, and social history. |
| | Requires informed consent. | If limited to an existing document review, may not require consent, only notice. |
| | Requires informed consent prior to initial evaluation. | Does not require consent, only notice. |
| | Reevaluations are required every three years. | Requires periodic reassessments. |
| | Provisions for independent evaluation, at district expense, if parent disagrees with evaluation and hearing officer concurs. | No provisions for independent evaluations at district expense. |
| 11. Grievance Procedure | Does not require a grievance procedure. | Districts with more than fifteen employees must designate an employee to be responsible for overseeing 504 district compliance and to provide a grievance procedure for parents, students, and employees. Grievances are filed as discrimination against disabled persons. |
| 12. Due Process | District must provide impartial hearings for disagreements regarding the identification, evaluation, or placement of students. Specific requirements are set out for due process hearings (See Chapter 10). | District must provide impartial hearings for disagreements regarding the identification, evaluation, or placement of students. Parents may participate in due process hearings and be represented by counsel; however, procedural details are left to the discretion of the local school district. |
| 13. Exhaustion | IDEA requires that the parent or guard- | An administrative hearing is not required prior to OCR involve- |

| Area Addressed | IDEA 2004 | Section 504 |
|---|---|---|
| | ian engage in the hearing process prior to seeking redress in the courts. | ment or court action; compensatory damages are possible. |
| 14. Enforcement | IDEA is a federal law that is enforced by the U.S. Office of Special Education Programs. The State Departments of Education and the Office of Special Education Programs monitor compliance. Complaints are ultimately resolved by the State department of education | Section 504 is enforced by the U.S. Office of Civil Rights. The State Department of Education has no monitoring, complaint resolution, or funding involvement. |

*The authors would like to thank Lake County Schools, Lake County, Florida, and Janice Tobias, chairperson of the 504 Manual Development Committee, for permission to use information from their 504 Manual in developing this comparison table for parents.*

## No Child Left Behind

The No Child Left Behind Act of 2001 was designed to improve student achievement and change America's schools. We will provide an overview of NCLB and address the many ways in which it can benefit both you and your child.

With passage of NCLB, Congress reauthorized the Elementary and Secondary Education Act, the federal law affecting education from kindergarten through twelfth grade. In amending ESEA, the new law represents a dramatic overhaul of the federal government's efforts to support elementary and secondary education. NCLB addresses four main areas: accountability for results, an emphasis on doing what works based on scientific research, expanded parental options, and expanded school district control and flexibility.

There has been much controversy surrounding the goals of NCLB. The legislation has strong supporters and harsh critics, and many have called for changes in the law that some view as unrealistic. However, IDEA 2004 has aligned itself more closely with NCLB and for these reasons, rather than discuss the pros and cons of NCLB, this book will outline its potential benefits, as envisioned by sponsors of the legislation, and discuss how IDEA 2004 has attempted to align itself with sections of NCLB.

### *No Child Left Behind supports learning in the early years, which can prevent many learning problems when the child gets older.*

Students who begin school with language skills and prereading skills (things like understanding that print reads from left to right and top to bottom) are more likely to learn to read well in the early grades and succeed in later years. Researchers have found that most reading problems in adolescence and adulthood are the result of problems that could have been prevented through good instruction in early childhood.

IDEA 2004 recognizes the need for early intervention in two important ways: attempting to create a seamless delivery of service from preschool (infants and toddlers) to school-age programs (3 to 21 years of age); and in allocating a percentage of funds (up to 15 percent of a school district's IDEA 2004 funds) that may be used to develop early intervention educational services for students not receiving special education, but who would likely require educational or behavioral support from special education programs in the future.

### *No Child Left Behind provides parents with more information about their child's progress.*

Under NCLB, each state must assess every public school student's progress in reading and math in each of grades three through eight, and at least once between grades ten and twelve. By school year 2007 to 2008, assessments in science will begin. These assessments, which must be aligned with state academic content and achievement standards, will demonstrate to parents where their child stands academically.

IDEA 2004 now requires IEPs to include a statement of measurable annual goals that relates to academic and functional goals. In order that children with disabilities may participate in statewide assessments, IDEA 2004 has revised the requirements for accommodations and alternate assessments.

### *No Child Left Behind gives parents important information about the performance of their child's school.*

NCLB requires that states and school districts give parents understandable, detailed report cards on schools and districts. These report cards indicate student achievement data by race, ethnicity, gender, English language proficiency, migrant status, disability status, and low-income status. Information about the professional qualifications of teachers will also be included.

### *No Child Left Behind provides you and your child with educational support and options.*

Under NCLB, low-performing schools must use their federal funds to make needed improvements. If a school continues to do poorly, parents have the option to transfer to higher-performing schools nearby or allow their child to receive tutoring, after-school programs, or remedial classes.

## *No Child Left Behind improves teaching and learning by providing better information to teachers and principals.*

Annual testing to measure students' progress provides teachers with data on each student's strengths and weaknesses. Teachers can use this information in the development of their lessons to create opportunities for students to meet or exceed the standards.

IDEA 2004 revises standards of academic achievement and functional performance of children with disabilities to conform to accountability systems established by NCLB and ensures that the annual yearly progress (AYP) of children with disabilities is evaluated as an appropriate subgroup.

## *No Child Left Behind ensures that teacher quality is a high priority.*

NCLB defines the qualifications needed by teachers and paraprofessionals (such as teacher assistants) who instruct students. It requires states to develop plans to achieve the goal that all teachers of the core academic subjects (English, reading or language arts, math, science, foreign languages, civics and government, economics, arts, history, and geography) be highly qualified. This can help teachers by ensuring that districts provide them with the necessary training and professional development support to meet this goal.

IDEA 2004 requires states to ensure that teachers of special education programs are highly qualified in keeping with standards set by NCLB, and removes the waiver, in cases of emergency or provisional basis, for personnel who have not met certification or licensure requirements.

## *No Child Left Behind gives more resources to schools.*

NCLB initially provided $23.7 billion worth of federal funding, most of which was used during the 2003 to 2004 school year. A large portion of the money went toward grants for states and school districts. These grants were awarded to help them improve the education of disadvantaged students, turn around low-performing schools, improve teacher quality, and increase choices for parents.

IDEA 2004 allocates 15 percent of federal funds reserved for special education and related services to be allocated to direct service for high-risk students and teacher training and professional development programs to train teachers to work with children who are likely to require special education services in the future.

## *No Child Left Behind allows more flexibility.*

NCLB gives states and school districts more flexibility in how they can use their federal education funding. This gives school district administrators the freedom to implement innovative programs, based on the needs of their district and feedback from parents.

IDEA 2004 authorizes more flexible use of up to 15 percent of IDEA 2004 funds, which may be used for direct student intervention for at risk students or teacher training, as previously outlined, to ensure professional development for teachers providing educational and behavioral evaluations and supports, or scientifically based literacy instruction.

## *No Child Left Behind focuses on what works.*

Focus is placed on well-designed research studies that demonstrate which educational programs and practices are considered effective. These programs will receive federal funding.

IDEA 2004 has allocated funds for professional development for teachers to deliver scientifically based academic and behavioral interventions. IDEA 2004 has also altered the criteria for determining eligibility for special education services for students with learning disabilities to include an inability to benefit from a scientific, research-based intervention, and excluded eligibility for students who have not had the benefit of adequate instruction.

## Summary

On paper, NCLB has lofty goals for improving our schools and our children's education. Time is needed to demonstrate whether all of these goals are achieved. We understand that changes will be made in future years in response to feedback from states, parents, and the performance of students and school districts. However, many believe that the four areas of focus—accountability for results, an emphasis on doing what works based on scientific research, expanded parental options, and expanded school district control and flexibility—will most likely remain the same as they serve to support the legislation's core values.

This information was prepared with assistance from *No Child Left Behind: A Parents Guide*, published in 2003 by the U.S. Department of Education, Office of the Secretary, Office of Public Affairs in Washington, D.C. To order your copy of this free thirty-seven-page document, write to ED Pubs, Education Publications Center, U.S. Department of Education, P.O. Box 1398, Jessup, MD 20794-1398. You may also request it by phone (877-433-7827), fax (301-470-1244), e-mail (edpubs@inet.ed.gov), or Internet (http://www.ed.gov/pubs/edpubs.html).

# STEP TWO:

Understanding the

Psychological Assessment

and Your Child's Disability

CHAPTER 4

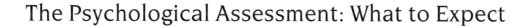

# The Psychological Assessment: What to Expect

When most people think about a *psychological assessment,* the first thing that comes to mind is testing. However, although psychologists often administer a number of different tests, assessment is better understood as part of the overall *process of evaluation.* The evaluation process can be viewed in three progressive stages. As an overview, we will look at three stages in the evaluation process that are outlined in Table 4-1.

Prior to discussing the stages involved in the evaluation process, we would like to briefly discuss the nature of the evaluation process itself.

## Understanding the Evaluation Process

When a child experiences a medical problem, parents usually take the child to see the family physician or pediatrician. The physician begins his evaluation by asking

*Table 4-1.    Stages in the student evaluation process.*

**Stage 1:** Initially, a number of school-based interventions are attempted to assist children who are experiencing school difficulties. Often, these interventions (such as a change in seating or peer tutoring) can be an effective method of increasing academic performance.

**Stage 2:** Further school-based evaluations and informal assessments, such as educational tests or classroom observations, may be undertaken to obtain more information about a child's performance.

**Stage 3:** If a child continues to experience school problems despite interventions, and more specific information is required to determine why the child is having problems, then a referral for psychological assessment may be initiated.

a series of questions about specific symptoms (fever, chills, or pain) to assist in determining the nature and severity of the problem. Often, the physician performs some routine tests (taking the child's temperature; listening to the heart and lungs) to find out how the child's bodily system is currently functioning compared with how a normal, healthy child should be functioning. For example, we know that the average body temperature should be about 98.6°F. The physician compares the child's temperature with this normal standard to determine whether the child has a fever. If the child had a fever, the physician would attempt to *diagnose* what was causing the high temperature (a virus, an infection, or some other medical cause). At this point, the physician might be able to diagnose the problem and provide the appropriate treatment (prescription for medication). However, if the doctor is unsure of the cause of the problem based on the information he has, he may order more tests (X rays, blood work-up, and so forth) to rule out some possible explanations and confirm others; a process called *hypothesis testing* or *differential diagnosis*.

A psychological evaluation involves many of the same steps that were just outlined in the previous medical evaluation. A psychologist's goal is to determine the nature of a child's learning problem or social/emotional problems in much the same way that a physician seeks to find the cause of medical problems. Through the use of interviews, tests, and observations, the psychologist attempts to pinpoint or diagnose the nature of the child's learning or social/emotional problems. Results from various tests are compared with so-called normal or *standard scores*, similar to the way that the physician compares test results with what would be expected for a normally developing and healthy child. In this way, the psychologist can determine *the nature of the problem* (learning problem, emotional problem, behavioral problem, and so forth) and *the severity of the problem* (the degree to which the child's scores differ from what is expected, given the child's age and grade level).

## Psychologists

Psychologists differ based on the nature of their education and training. Most psychologists working primarily with children and adolescents engage children in therapy and/or assessment activities and are trained in clinical or counseling psychology, school psychology, or pediatric psychology. Licensing requirements vary from state to state and country to country.

In the majority of states, a psychologist licensed in clinical and/or counseling psychology must have a Ph.D. or Psy.D. in clinical or counseling psychology, satisfy pre- and post-degree internships and pass a series of professional exams. Licensed mental health counselors may practice with a master's degree after satisfying a period of post-degree supervision requirements. Clinical psychologists and pediatric psychologists often practice in private practice, clinics, hospitals, and mental health centers. Licensing requirements can vary from state to state, and when psychologists move from one state to another, they must qualify to practice in that state under the state's standards. A psychologist is not permitted to practice in any state without a state-recognized license or certification.

**Did you know?** If you have questions about whether a psychologist is registered or certified to practice in your state, you can contact the Association of State and Provincial Psychology Boards (ASPPB) at http://www.asppb.org. The ASPPB is the association of psychology licensing boards in the United States and Canada and can provide access information for contacting your state psychology board.

Because our book primarily concerns children with disabilities and special education and related services, we will talk primarily about the role of school psychologists in the schools. However, we feel that it is important that parents understand the different types of psychologists who may be available, if they choose to have an independent evaluation conducted.

**Did you know?** Parents can have an independent evaluation of their child conducted, at their own expense, by contacting an independent psychologist. Family physicians are often good sources to contact regarding information on how to locate a psychologist in the community who works primarily with children.

Under certain circumstances, which will be discussed further in Chapter 10, a school district may pay for the cost of an independent evaluation, when a parent requests an alternative assessment to the one conducted by the district's school psychologist. The majority of psychological evaluations of children and adolescents take place within the school system.

**Did you know?** Most school psychologists are employed by the public school system and provide assessments to children free of charge to parents. Under the law, the public school system is also responsible for providing assessments free of charge to students enrolled in private schools.

Although school psychologists may also practice in clinics, private practice, mental health facilities, and hospitals, most practice within the public education system. Although the degree of post-graduate training varies from state to state, school psychologists have at least a master's or specialist degree, which they receive after their bachelor's degree, while some hold a doctorate (Ph.D., Ed.D., or

Psy.D.). Most school psychologists function as part of the child's professional school team that is composed of professionals from multiple disciplines (teachers, family physician, speech pathologist, occupational therapist, physiotherapist, school social worker) and results of the psychological assessment often complement information obtained from other diagnostic services. The resulting comprehensive assessment package provides an overall picture of the "total child" A school psychologist may also be licensed for private practice.

Some particular areas of concern that school psychologists are likely to investigate in the schools and the types of instruments that can be used in their evaluations are presented in Table 4-2.

> **Did you know?** Parents may request an evaluation of their child from the school or the school may recommend, and ask permission for, an evaluation. According to IDEA 2004, a parent, state agency, including a State Educational Agency (SEA: a state department of education), or Local Education Agency (LEA: a school district), have a right to request an initial evaluation to determine whether a child qualifies for special education and related services under IDEA 2004.

## How will I know when a psychological assessment is necessary?

### Stages in the Student Evaluation Process

There are typically three steps involved in the student evaluation process.

**Stage One**   Before the school recommends a psychological evaluation for a child, difficulties have often been evident and monitored for some time. In this way, the psychological assessment should be thought of as part of the overall process of problem solving, whose goal is to better understand the nature and extent of a child's difficulties. In the initial stages of monitoring a child's school difficulties, schools often conduct regular in-school meetings to discuss various child problems and generate informal interventions in an attempt to address initial concerns. Most children will benefit from these initial interventions and no further assistance may be required. Examples of early and informal types of school-based interventions may include a change in seating arrangements (seating the child closer to the teacher); teaming the child with a student who has stronger academic performance; or including the child in small group instruction.

In the initial stages, progress review meetings may be informal, such as a discussion between a teacher and guidance counselor. If concerns continue to exist, despite several interventions, more formal meetings may take place, involving a variety of professionals, including the teacher, guidance counselor, special education teacher or resource, curriculum specialist, speech pathologist, school psychologist, school social worker, and or/school administrator. Parents are encouraged to

*Table 4-2.*    *Types of psychological assessments and evaluations.*

| Area Assessed | Common Assessment Instruments Used | Examples of Information Obtained |
|---|---|---|
| Intelligence | Wechsler Scales:<br>—WISC-IV<br>—WPPSI-III<br>—WAIS-III | Full Scale IQ (Intelligence Quotient)<br>Verbal Reasoning<br>Visual/Perceptual Problem Solving |
| | Stanford Binet 5 | Verbal and Visual Intelligence |
| | Differential Ability Scales (DAS) | Verbal and Visual Intelligence, includes a Special Nonverbal Composite Score |
| | Reynolds Intellectual Assessment Scales (RIAS) | Verbal and Nonverbal Intelligence and Memory |
| | Universal Nonverbal Intelligence Test (UNIT) | Nonverbal Intelligence |
| | Woodcock-Johnson III Tests of Cognitive Ability (WJ III) | Verbal Ability, Thinking Ability and Cognitive Efficiency |
| Academic Performance | Wechsler Individual Achievement Test-Second Edition (WIAT-II)<br>Woodcock-Johnson III Tests of Achievement | Reading (Single Words & Passage Comprehension);<br>Mathematics (Calculation & Problem Solving);<br>Written Expression (Spelling and Sentence/Paragraph Writing) |
| Cognitive Processing and Memory | Wechsler Scales | Working Memory; Processing Speed |
| | WJ III Cognitive Tests | Working Memory, Broad Attention, Cognitive Efficiency, Short-term & Long-term Memory<br>Phonemic Awareness |
| | Children's Memory Scale (CMS) | Short-term and Long-term Visual and Auditory Memory, Attention, |
| | Behavior Rating Inventory of Executive Function (BRIEF) | Behavior Regulation, Planning/Organization and Monitoring, Task Initiation & Working Memory |
| | Continuous Performance Test (CPT) | Attention & Concentration |
| Behavior, Social/Emotional Problems | Parent Rating Scales<br>Teacher Rating Scales<br>Child & Adolescent Self-Report Scales<br>Child and Adolescent Personality Inventories | Internalizing Behaviors:<br>  Anxiety, Depression, Somatic Complaints;<br>Externalizing Behaviors:<br>  Aggression, Rule Breaking, Oppositional-Defiant; Disruptive<br>Social Problems:<br>  Peer relationships |
| Classroom Performance | Classroom Observation | Attention, classroom participation, compliance, independent seat work; |
| Social Interaction Skills | Playground Observation | Peer acceptance/rejection, cooperation, self control, assertive/passive; aggression |

attend these school meetings to share information about their child's progress and
any additional concerns they may have. The names of these school team meetings
will vary depending on the school district and may include student assistance
team, child study team, student support team, or student intervention team; however, the meeting goals are universal and aimed at information gathering to provide for informed decision making.

**Did you know?** According to IDEA 2004, school districts may use up to 15 percent
of their IDEA funds to develop and provide early intervention services for students at
risk of being referred to special education programs and services at some later date.
These programs may address educational or behavioral supports necessary to increase the likelihood of success in the regular program.

**Stage Two**   At this stage, informal assessments like the Brigance tests might be
conducted by the special education teacher to evaluate academic skills, while the
school psychologist might be asked to review the school file or observe the child
in the classroom setting.

**Did you know?** The Brigance tests are administered by special education teachers
to evaluate a child's academic strengths and weaknesses. Results reveal whether
the expected curriculum goals have been mastered for each grade level, based on
expected levels of performance, given a child's age and grade level. For example, a
child in the first grade should be able to add one digit numbers. To determine
whether the child has mastered this curriculum goal, the child would be required to
correctly solve three out of four one-digit math addition questions to prove mastery
at 75 percent for that curriculum goal. The test's author, Albert Brigance, is a former
classroom teacher of both regular and special needs students, and a school psychologist.

    Parent permission is always required before the school psychologist can inten-
tionally observe an individual child, unless he is observing the entire class. Teachers can do classroom observations or administer screening tests like the Brigance
without parent permission. Independent observations of classroom performance
may also be requested to gather information from other teachers who have observed the child (such as guidance counselors, resource teachers, or assistant principals). Some school districts may require several parent interviews, interventions,
and observations be completed prior to initiating a request for formal psychological assessment. Ultimately, results of these information assessments /observations

are shared with parents during an educational meeting held to discuss whether a more formal psychological assessment may be required.

**Did you know?** If a child is experiencing academic problems, one of the first things that a parent can do is have vision and hearing evaluated to rule out whether hearing or vision problems are contributing to the child's school difficulties.

**Stage Three** In the final step, a request is made for a formal psychological assessment.

When the school team requires more specific information about a child's learning or emotional problems, or a parent requests an initial evaluation, a referral for psychological assessment may be generated. As noted previously, parent permission is required before the school psychologist can become involved. When information is available from the evaluations conducted by the diagnostic team (special education teachers, curriculum specialist, guidance counselor, school psychologist, speech pathologist), a team meeting is convened to discuss recommendations concerning interventions, and/or special class placement based on the evaluation results.

The various professionals meet with the parents to share the results of their individual evaluations (this can be done individually or as a group). Ultimately, the *diagnostic team*—professionals who have conducted assessments of the child's performance in several areas—present the evaluation results and recommendations to the staffing specialist who presides over the staffing team committee meeting whose joint role is to decide whether special education services are warranted. Under IDEA 2004, parents must be notified of this meeting (often called the *staffing meeting* or *eligibility meeting*) two weeks prior to the meeting date.

## The Psychological Assessment

The psychological assessment process may involve a number of steps. An overview of the psychological assessment process is provided in Table 4-3.

### How to Prepare Your Child for the Assessment

If you are taking your child for an assessment to a psychologist in a clinic or private practice, you should discuss the assessment prior to your arrival. Your actual explanation will depend on the age of your child, but it should begin with sharing your concern and feelings about your child's frustrations at school and wanting to help make things better for him. The psychologist should be described as a person who has studied how children think, learn, and feel. The psychologist will be working with your child to find out how he solves problems and feels about

Table 4-3.       *Possible steps in the psychological assessment.*

**Steps that may be involved in the school evaluation process:**

1. Child is referred for psychological assessment.
2. Parent gives consent for assessment.
3. Screenings are conducted to determine that vision, hearing, and speech/language functions are normal.
4. If limited English proficiency is suspected, language dominance testing is conducted to determine the appropriate language for assessment that would yield the most accurate picture of a child's knowledge and understanding.
5. The referral is directed to the special services department of the school district.
6. The referral is assigned to the school psychologist for the school, or to the bilingual school psychologist, whichever is most appropriate.
7. The school psychologist reviews the child's cumulative file (school records) to gather information concerning academic progress, interventions, absenteeism, grade retentions, previous assessments, standardized testing, and so on.
8. The school psychologist meets with the child's teacher(s) to obtain current information.
9. The school psychologist begins the formal assessment process, which *may* include:
   Observation of the child in the classroom or on the playground
   Administration of a variety of standardized assessment instruments
   Parent interview
10. Results of the assessment are documented in a written report.
11. The report is discussed in the educational meeting and parents receive a copy of the evaluation report.

things. After working with a child for one or two sessions, the psychologist can help parents and teachers understand why the child is experiencing difficulties learning and can suggest ways to present information that will make it easier for the child to be successful in school.

If the child is being seen by the school psychologist, there may be a time lag between giving permission for an assessment and having the actual assessment take place. As you saw in Table 4-3, several steps in the assessment process must occur before the school psychologist actually makes contact with the child. Therefore, parents should inform the child that help is on the way. You should state that at some time in the future, the school psychologist will be working with him to help you and his teacher understand why he is having problems at school and how to best help him to be more successful.

**Did you know?** Most children do not feel pressured or anxious, but actually enjoy the individual attention afforded by the assessment sessions. In the assessment session, the child is the center of attention and has the undivided attention of the school psychologist who is positive and encouraging of the child's efforts. Most children thrive in this situation. In fact, after the assessment situation, it is not uncommon for children to approach the school psychologist to ask if they will be working together another day.

## What Takes Place in the Assessment Session

Parents are often concerned about how their child will respond to being tested. When the school psychologist begins working with the child, he initially engages the child in a rapport-building task that might involve a discussion of the child's favorite movies, books, or hobbies, or the psychologist may ask the child to draw some pictures, if that is the child's interest. The rapport session is used to help the child relax and become more familiar with the school psychologist. Once rapport is established, the school psychologist usually begins by describing the nature of the tasks to be introduced.

## Types of Psychological Assessments and Evaluations

There are many different types of psychological assessments that can be conducted depending on the nature of the difficulty that the child is experiencing. The assessment may focus on a number of different areas (see Table 4-2 for some examples) or concentrate on a specific area. Based on the nature of the problem, the school psychologist may be interested in evaluating performance in several different areas, including intellectual, academic, processing, and/or social/emotional/behavioral development. In most cases, an intelligence test is conducted to provide a broad estimate of a child's potential and a range of expectations for where the child should be functioning on several levels. The majority of assessments for academic concerns will include, at a minimum, an evaluation of intelligence (ability) and academic skills in order to compare expectations with performance. If a significant discrepancy exists between ability and performance, this signals the need for further assessment to investigate what might be causing the difficulty. Additional evaluation may include an investigation of potential processing problems (attention, memory, visual motor problems, organization, and so forth) and/or social/emotional/behavioral problems.

In addition to academic concerns and processing problems, children may present with behavioral problems that do not meet expectations. A child may be demonstrating disruptive behaviors or acting out in the classroom, so assessment may be requested to determine the nature of the behavior problem(s). A key question is: *What is causing this child to act out?*

**Did you know?** Some children with behavior problems can be acting out because of academic frustration, while other children with behavior problems do not learn effectively, because the behavior interferes with learning. Which came first: *the be-havior problem or the academic problem?* Often the school psychologist attempts to address this difficult question as part of the assessment process.

Other more subtle emotional problems may also be evident, such as a child's withdrawal from social contact due to poor social skills, anxiety, or depression. Although a child's externalizing behaviors (acting out, aggression, or disruptive behavior) are far more obvious and readily observable than possible internalizing problems (anxiety or depression), finding out the reason why a child is experiencing emotional/behavioral difficulties is often a daunting task for the school psychologist. Rarely are the answers obvious, and the psychologist is often required to include several steps in the evaluation process such as meeting with the child, observing the child in the classroom (or on the playground), meeting with the child's teachers (present and past), and talking to the parents. Further discussion of the types of assessment instruments and interviews that might be used to investigate the nature of emotional/behavioral problems are addressed in Chapter 6.

Parents should become familiar with the different types of tests that professionals use and what each of these instruments measures. Increasing your knowledge in this area will not only help you to better understand your child's assessment results but will also provide a better understanding of how your child learns compared with other children. Knowing what to expect will also be helpful in knowing what questions to ask the school psychologist.

Since professionals vary in their choice of psychological assessment instruments, and test instruments are frequently revised and renamed, the majority of comments in the following two chapters will relate to the overall goals of the assessment in each area and restrict the discussion to the most commonly used instruments.

## Goals of the Psychological Assessment

School psychologists rely on *standardized* tests, which means that the tests have specific instructions as to how they are to be administered and have *established norms* (expected ranges of scores) based on previous administrations of the test to a wide range of children across the United States. The use of these tests allows the school psychologist to compare a student's performance with a large number of children of similar ages.

**Did you know?** The newly revised Wechsler Intelligence Scale for Children (WISC-IV, 2003) was administered to 2,200 children age 6 years to 16 years, 11 months across the United States, in addition to many children representing special groups (gifted, mentally retarded, learning disabled, and so forth). Based on these multiple administrations of the WISC-IV, the test authors developed a set of norms that are used to compare a child's test results with what would be expected of the average child his age.

As discussed earlier, school psychologists have several different tests that they can use to look at different types of problems. More than one assessment instrument (referred to as a *battery of psychological tests*) should be administered, and additional information should be obtained from more than one source (such as parents *and* teachers). In this way, the school psychologist can determine whether the problem is evident in more than one area (all or some academic areas, behavior, social/emotional difficulties) and whether the problem exists across situations (home and school), or only occurs in one situation, such as in school but not at home.

In addition to *norm-referenced tests,* school psychologists also obtain information through observation (classroom observation, playground observation, test-taking behaviors), interviews (parents and teachers) and the use of less formal assessment measures (review of child school records or asking the child to bring a classroom reader to the assessment session and read from it).

**Did you know?** The classroom observation is one of the most common methods that school psychologists use to get a firsthand look at how the child is functioning in the classroom setting. The child is unaware that the school psychologist is there to observe him, and it can provide the school psychologist with excellent insight into the amount of time a child spends in on-task versus off-task behavior, and how well a child responds to classroom instruction compared with other classmates.

### Should I Meet with the School Psychologist Before the Assessment?

If you have any concerns about the nature of the assessment or the types of assessment instruments that will be used, you should contact the school and make an appointment to visit with the school psychologist prior to your child's assessment. In that way, you can make an informed decision regarding the nature of the assessment process and feel more comfortable about the evaluation. Certainly, if you have any information that you feel might influence the assessment which the school is not aware of (family difficulties, such as a recent separation or pending divorce; previous history of abuse or violence, and so forth), you should share this information with the school psychologist prior to the assessment. This information could have a significant impact on how the assessment results are interpreted, or the nature and direction of the evaluation itself.

*Why Can't I Sit in on the Assessment with My Child?*

Occasionally, parents—especially parents of younger children—become upset when they are told that they cannot sit in on the psychological assessment. It is understandable that these parents feel that their request is reasonable, especially since they accompany their young child to the medical examinations conducted by the family physician. However, this situation is very different in several ways. Parents usually want to sit in on the assessment to be more supportive of their child, rather than based on a curiosity about the testing situation. If curiosity is the main objective, however, we would highly recommend seeking out a school psychologist who has access to a two-way mirror (shaded on one side) system. In this way, the parent can observe the assessment without distracting the child from his performance. In reality, there are virtually no schools and few clinics that have access to a two-way mirror, which is more likely to be found in a clinical training facility.

*What Is Wrong with Parents Sitting in on the Assessment?*

There are several arguments for prohibiting parents from sitting in on the assessment, including:

- Increased level of distraction for the child
- Increased tendencies for the child to be inhibited in his verbal responses
- Less opportunity for the school psychologist to establish rapport
- Increased sense of anxiety for the child
- Violation of test instrument confidentiality
- Increased risk of invalidating results, as will be discussed next

**Did you know?** Psychologists cannot release item content of the test items to parents because this would be in violation of the test's privacy and confidentiality. The psychologist will discuss the results of your child's assessment in a psychological report. We have provided some examples of the more technical parts of these reports to help you better understand what these results mean. You can find examples of sample report content in Chapters 5, 6, and 7.

There are several reasons why it is not advisable to have a parent sit in during an assessment. Many of the instruments have timed portions of the test. If a parent is sitting in the room, the addition of another person creates a natural distraction, which can reduce the child's performance and overall score. In addition, having a family member in the room (mother, father, or sibling) can make a child more apprehensive in responding. From a very young age, children look to their caregiver (mother, sibling) for nonverbal cues regarding whether they are on the right track or wrong track. This phenomenon is called *social referencing*. The process is instinctive and although words are rarely shared, children learn to read their parent's signals for a "yes" or "no" based on subtle visual cues such as an eye blink, raised eyebrow, shift in seating position, and so forth. If a parent were allowed to sit in during the assessment, children would instinctively look for these visual cues to monitor and gauge their performance. This could also result in changing their responses, if they were incorrect.

**A Slice of Life: A True Story.** A parent arrived early to pick up her seven-year-old daughter who was seeing a psychologist in private practice. The psychologist had only a few items left to administer on one of the tests, and asked the parent to please wait quietly in the adjoining room. Since the psychologist never closed the door when conducting an assessment with a child for her own comfort's sake, the door was left slightly ajar. For the next few minutes, when the child gave an incorrect response or one that was slightly off, her mother softly grunted or shifted in her chair (unfortunately, the chair had a squeak). The little girl received these faint and subtle sounds coming from her mother, as if they were coming in loud and clear, and the little girl quickly changed her responses, on each occasion. Although the mother was not intentionally signaling the child, she was nevertheless doing so. This story provides one real-life example of why it is not advisable to sit in on your child's assessment.

Finally, test construction and copyright laws prohibit the sharing of test item content with those who are not licensed to use the products. Sharing the test questions with a parent who is sitting in on an assessment is a violation of test copyright. The reason for this is that significant amounts of time, money, and effort go into standardizing the instruments and constructing tables that have test results based on age expectations (remember that more than two thousand children were involved in obtaining norming standards for the WISC-IV, for example). If item content were to be distributed outside of professional circles, the test would no longer have value because results can be tampered with.

# CHAPTER 5

# The Assessment of Intelligence

In this chapter, we will discuss how intelligence is defined and how it is measured. We will also talk about why intelligence tests were developed and some of the important ways that intelligence test scores can be helpful in better understanding a child's particular strengths and weaknesses.

## What Is Intelligence?

Intelligence is a measure of how well you can solve problems compared with other people your own age. We can define intelligence in many ways. Some of the most common ways of describing intelligence include the ability to learn, the ability to adapt to one's environment, and the ability to solve problems that have never been encountered. Although most of the emphasis to date has been on intelligence scores as a predictor of academic success, recently some researchers feel that success is more than so-called academic smarts and also requires people skills or what they call emotional intelligence. People often refer to intelligence as IQ for short. Actually, IQ really stands for "intelligence quotient," or the actual score obtained on an intelligence test.

When a psychologist assesses intelligence in a school setting, he is most interested in determining how well a child can be expected to perform on tasks of school-related learning. In this way, intelligence is more closely thought of as "learning ability." When talking about intelligence, psychologists will often use the term *cognition* or refer to *cognitive factors* that are involved in intelligence. Cognition refers to *knowledge* or *knowing* and is related to intelligence when we try to evaluate the extent to which a child has acquired knowledge, compared with peers of a similar age, and how well the child applies this information to new tasks.

In school, children are taught a number of key academic skills. The child's ability to learn these skills is based on several factors: previous exposure to information; problem-solving ability; memory; and the ability to draw on previous experiences to help find solutions to new problems. Children with higher IQ scores are more likely to draw on past experiences and use that information to help them solve new problems. Psychologists and educators refer to this process as being able to transfer information from one context (or situation) to another. Children with lower IQ scores may acquire enough knowledge to solve a specific problem; however, they do not understand how this information might relate to solving a different, but similar problem. In other words, they have more difficulty transferring information from one context to another.

**Slice of Life:** A teacher was working with a kindergarten child who was having significant problems learning the letters of the alphabet. The teacher even made a personal set of letters for John out of green construction paper (John's favorite color). After much practice, John was finally able to identify the entire alphabet, letter by letter, as it was presented to him. The teacher was so excited about John's progress that she marched John into the adjoining classroom so that John could demonstrate his alphabet skills to the other kindergarten teacher. In that classroom, the letters of the alphabet were written in bright red letters on the white board in the front of the classroom. To the teacher's dismay, John could not recognize one letter of the alphabet. Returning to her classroom, John immediately recited the alphabet pointing to each letter. Ultimately, the teacher realized that John had learned the alphabet in green, and he did not recognize that the letters remained the same even though their color had changed to red. As unbelievable as this may seem, *this is a true story.*

Fortunately for John, the story has a happy ending. When the teacher realized what had happened, she asked the parent if the school psychologist could observe John in the classroom. The school psychologist also noted that John had problems transferring information from task to task, but that he would watch the child next to him, for clues on what to do next. Building on this strength, the school psychologist suggested that John buddy up with the stronger student, which helped John considerably. Another suggestion that increased John's ability to transfer information between situations was using multicolored letters, and letters in different textures (wood, plastic, and felt) to help John understand that the letters remained the same, despite the different colors or textures.

The previous case study is a classic example of how difficulties in transferring information from one situation to the next can have a profound influence on a child's ability to apply what has been learned in one situation to another situation.

## Where Does Intelligence Come From?

Children's intelligence can be influenced at birth by heredity (genes), prenatal toxins (alcohol, drugs), chromosomal anomalies (Down's syndrome), or birth trauma (lack of oxygen). A child's environment can also have a powerful influence on intelligence. Some children have many opportunities to learn because they are exposed to a wide variety of learning experiences. Other children may have less exposure to new situations and consequently may experience less opportunity for learning. Unfortunately, intelligence can also be lowered by exposure to brain injury (accident) or environmental toxins, such as a child's exposure to lead-based paint or drugs, such as inhalants.

Although IQ scores can predict academic and later occupational success, merely having a high IQ does not ensure success. An IQ test does not measure motivation, or other more subtle learning problems, such as difficulties with memory, that might interfere with success.

> **Remember that** IQ scores are considered more stable with increasing age, and IQ scores obtained for preschool children should be regarded cautiously because they are not as reliable. Some young children may score low due to a lack of experience or fewer opportunities, while others may score higher because of an environment rich in experiences.

### Why Were Intelligence Tests Developed?

Before we talk about how IQ is measured, let's first discuss why IQ tests were developed in order to better understand what the IQ score represents.

In the early 1900s, educators were faced with a dilemma. Prior to that time, many children were working and not attending school. However, with the passing of child labor laws, school attendance became mandatory, which meant that all children, regardless of past learning experiences, would be thrust upon the education system and expected to learn at the same rate in the same classes. The situation started in Europe but quickly spread to the United States.

Alfred Binet was commissioned by the French government to develop a test to determine which children might need special assistance and which children would be able to learn in the regular classroom without additional services. Binet developed a test to measure the extent to which a child could answer a set of questions and solve a series of problems compared with other children of his/her own age. At its most basic level, Binet developed a measure of IQ that evaluated how a child measured up to his own age-based peers. Based on this measure, Binet developed a formula to determine a child's IQ score based on the child's mental age (test score) relative to his chronological age (birth age).

> **Did you know?** Psychologists use the term *mental age* to refer to a child's test score, which represents his problem-solving age, and *chronological age* to refer to a

child's age in birth years. For example, a child who is 5 years old (chronological age) may have the thinking capacity of a much younger or older child (mental age).

The formula took mental age and divided it by chronological age. The resulting score was then multiplied by 100. Using this formula, Binet determined that a child with a chronological age (CA) of 10 years who scored at a mental age (MA) of 10 years would obtain a score of MA/CA $\times$ 100 = IQ of 100. The IQ of 100 was considered to be the average IQ score.

**Sample Example:** Ward is 10 years old and takes an IQ test. On this test, his score is more typical of an 8-year-old than a 10-year-old. If we take the mental age (8 years) and divide it by the chronological age (10 years) and multiply by 100, we end up with 8/10 $\times$ 100 = IQ of 80. Now, Ward's younger brother Ted takes the same IQ test. Ted is very bright. Although Ted is 8 years old chronologically (birth time), his score on the IQ test is more typical of a child 10 years old (mental age). When we do the mental age/ chronological age $\times$ 100 calculation, we get 10/8 $\times$ 100 = 125. Ted has an IQ of 125.

Using this formula, a child with a mental age of 7 who was chronologically 10 years old would score an IQ of 7/10 $\times$ 100, or an IQ of 70. The actual math is more complicated but this explanation should provide a general idea of how an IQ score is determined.

**Sample Example:** Here are several examples of how the mental age/ chronological age can be explained. Let's use 10 years of age, as an example. The following children are all 10 years old. Each child takes the same IQ test. We take their mental age (test score)/divided by their chronological age (birth date) and multiply by 100. Based on their responses, we might have the following distribution of scores that represent each child's mental age relative to the others:

Abby scores like a 13 year old: Her IQ is 13/10 $\times$ 100 = 150 (Very Superior)

Wes scores like a 12 year old. His IQ is 12/10 $\times$ 100 = 120 (Superior)

Juan scores like a 10 year old. His IQ is 10/10 $\times$ 100 = 100 (Average).

Julie scores like an 8 year old. Her IQ is 8/10 $\times$ 100 = 80 (Low Average).

Pat scores like a 7 year old. Her IQ is 7/10 $\times$ 100 = 70 (Borderline).

John scores like a 6 year old. His IQ is 6/10 $\times$ 100 = 60 (Extremely Low).

It is not uncommon for parents to be skeptical and concerned about the use of IQ scores in the educational system and how this information might be misused. For example, a parent might start wondering:

*Question:* If a teacher knows my child's IQ score, does that mean the teacher will have a certain expectation about my child's chances for academic success?

*Answer:* In some cases, yes. However, as we will discuss shortly, some children who have very high IQ scores do not perform as expected and struggle academically, while other children with lower IQ scores achieve well beyond what might be expected. For these reasons, if there is a difference between our expectation for academic success and the evaluation results, in the majority of cases further assessments will be conducted to obtain a clearer picture of what is interfering with academic success.

*Question:* Is it possible that if a teacher knows that my child has a low IQ, she will not expect my child to succeed?

*Answer:* Good question, and a question that has been asked by researchers and child advocates alike. In Chapter 8, we will discuss this question further. For now, let's just say the positive side of knowing an IQ is that it helps us to understand, at a basic level, where a child's problem-solving abilities are in relation to other children at the same age level. Furthermore, although we tend to think of IQ as a single score, the IQ actually is a composite score based on several different areas of the tests (called subtests). When we look at the subtest scores, we often find a pattern of strengths and weaknesses that can assist greatly in developing an IEP. In Chapter 9, we will discuss how the child's initial IEP is developed based on information provided by the initial comprehensive assessment and the results and recommendations of that assessment.

### What Do Intelligence Tests Look Like?

The majority of intelligence tests are developed to measure problem-solving skills in two major areas: verbal ability and visual ability. Tasks that measure verbal ability are usually presented orally and require the child to provide verbal responses. Areas evaluated can include measurements of vocabulary knowledge, verbal reasoning, and practical information. Children who score high on verbal tasks usually have better developed communication skills, good listening skills, and are likely to be avid readers. On the other hand, visually oriented tasks require hands-on performance (completing puzzles, constructing block designs) or visual scanning (selecting one response from several visual alternatives). Visual tasks require minimal verbal expression. Some visual tasks are timed (using a stopwatch), resulting in either bonus marks for speed or no points for solving the problem beyond the given time limit.

### How Reliable Are IQ Tests?

Any test score can fluctuate from assessment to assessment based on many other factors, such as illness, fatigue, lack of sufficient rapport, performance anxiety, and so forth. However, IQ tests have been developed to increase the reliability of the assessment results to within a 5 to 10 percent range of accuracy. In the psychological report, there should be a statement to the effect that "there is a 90 percent or 95 percent chance that the scores reported are a true indicator of the child's ability, and that the child's IQ score falls within the range of _____ to _____." The report should also include the predicted range of the IQ, rather than a single IQ score. Also, the reliability or validity (true nature of the score) can also vary given a child's age at the time of testing.

Since different IQ tests sample different types of abilities, it is possible that a child's IQ on one test can differ from that obtained on another IQ test. In addition, different environmental conditions present at the time of testing can also contribute to variation in IQ scores. However, having said this, research has shown that scores among the major IQ tests are relatively consistent, making them reliable measures of intelligence. Remember that one of the main purposes of assessing intelligence in school-age children is that IQ scores are a strong predictor of a child's ability to learn academic subjects.

*What Do the Test Scores Mean?*

IQ scores can be reported in several ways: standard scores, percentiles, and age equivalents. Each of these scores is obtained by comparing the child's performance with the available range of scores for his or her peer group.

**Don't stop now!** Numbers can be intimidating. When some of us see math, we just want to run the other way. But, if you walk through this, one step at a time, we promise that you will have a better understanding not only about IQ scores but what the whole psychological report has to say about your child.

## Here Come the Numbers: Put on Your Safety Belts—We Are In for a Numbers Ride!

In this section, we will talk about how scores from IQ tests can help us understand a child's potential in terms of strengths and weaknesses, as well as possible expectations for performance. We will start our discussion by explaining how standard scores can be used as the common measurement that allows for comparisons across a number of different types of assessment instruments.

*Standard Scores*

IQ tests report their scores as *standard scores*. Remember when we talked about using a thermometer to measure how a child's temperature compared with the normal standard score, which in temperature numbers is 98.6°F. IQ tests also provide a score that can be compared with a normal standard equivalent. IQ test scores are based on the normal distribution of scores that look like the bell-shaped curve presented in Figure 5-1.

Based on scores obtained from the general population, approximately 50 percent of the population would score between 90 and 109 on an IQ test. These scores are considered to be in the Average Range of intelligence. The exact mean or average IQ score is located at the 50th percentile and is an IQ of 100. As we move farther away from the average score, we move out of the Average Range. An IQ score between 80 and 89 falls within the Low Average Range. Approximately 16 percent of the population will score within this range. An IQ score between 110 and 119 falls within the High Average Range. Once again, approximately 16 percent of the population will score within this range. The Standard Deviation (SD) is a unit of measurement that has been determined to locate a level of significant deviation from the Average Range. The IQ test uses standard scores with an average of 100 and a standard deviation of 15. It would be expected that 68 percent of the population will score within one standard deviation of the average (100). Therefore, 68 percent of the population will obtain an IQ score between 85 (100 − 15) and 115 (100 + 15). In Figure 5-1 which depicts the bell-shaped curve, we can see that an IQ of 70 is two standard deviations below the mean

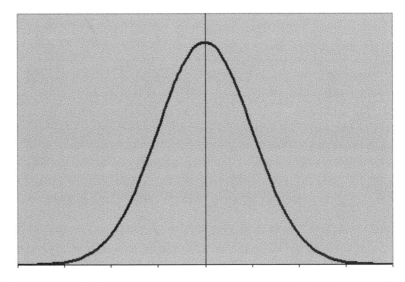

| IQ Ranges | | | | | 110–119 | 120–129 | 130+ |
|---|---|---|---|---|---|---|---|
| | −69 | 70–79 | 80–89 | 90–109 | | | |
| Range | | | | Average Range | | | |
| Percent of Population | 2 | 6 | 16 | 50 | 16 | 6 | 2 |
| Standard Deviation | −3 | −2 | −1 | 0 | +1 | +2 | +3 |
| Percentile Rank | .1 | 2 | 16 | 50 | 84 | 97 | 99 |

*Figure 5-1.*     *The bell-shaped curve and distribution of IQ scores.*

(100 − 30 = 70), while an IQ of 130 represents an IQ score that is two standard deviations above the mean (100 + 30 = 130). Because the scores are equally distributed on either side of the bell, only 2 percent of the population would be expected to score below an IQ of 70, and only 2 percent of the population would be expected to score above an IQ of 130.

> **Did you know?** Two out of three people who take an IQ test will obtain an IQ score somewhere between 85 and 115.

The standard scores presented in Table 5-1 reveal the entire range of possible IQ scores and how these scores can provide expectations for performance. The percentiles that accompany the standard score ranges represent the percentages of the population who are expected to score within these levels.

> **Remember:** The shape of the range of IQ scores resembles a bell (called the *bell curve*) with approximately 2 percent of the population scoring at the lowest extreme, or *Extremely Low Range* (at or below the 2nd percentile), and 2 percent of the population scoring at the *Very Superior or Gifted Range* (at or above the 98th percentile). The midpoint or mean IQ is 100 and 50 percent of the population would score above and 50 percent below this level.

## A Word About Percentiles

> **Did you know?** When we talk about percentiles as cumulative percentages, we start at the bottom and work up. For example, if I scored at the 2nd percentile on a test, that would mean I was at the bottom of the test scores and that only 2 percent of the population would have my score or lower and 98 percent of the population would score above me. If, however, I scored at the 98th percentile, that would mean I was at the top of the test scores, since only 2 percent of the population would score above me.

**Extremely Low Range**   Children who score in this range are in the bottom 2 percent of the population. Children who are within this range would be expected to find academic skills very challenging and would most likely require special education services to master basic academic concepts. When a child scores within this range, the school psychologist (or social worker) will require additional information about *adaptive functioning levels* (daily living skills). Obtaining information

*Table 5-1.*      *Interpreting IQ Standard and Scale Scores.*

| Standard Score Ranges | Standard Score Range | Percentile Ranges | Description |
|---|---|---|---|
| **Extremely Low Range** | 45 to 69 | .02 to 2nd %ile | Children in this range will find academic tasks very challenging and will likely require special education services. |
| **Borderline Range** | 70 to 79 | 2 to 8th %ile | Children in this range will experience increasing academic difficulties, especially in the upper grades. |
| **Average Ranges:** Low Average Range | 80 to 89 | 16 to 23rd %ile | 68 percent of the population score within the average ranges. The majority |
| Average Range | 90 to 109 | 25 to 73rd %ile | of children at the lower end will likely experience |
| High Average Range | 110 to 119 | 75 to 90th %ile | more academic challenges. The majority of children at the upper end will likely solve tasks with relative ease. |
| **Superior Range** | 120 to 129 | 91 to 97th %ile | Children in this range will likely need additional challenges and enriched programming. |
| **Very Superior (Gifted)** | 130 to 160 | 98th %ile + | Children in this range often qualify for gifted programs to augment their advanced learning needs. |

about adaptive behavior can take place in an interview where parents are asked a number of questions about the child's developmental history (when the child started walking, talking, and so forth) and medical history. Another way of obtaining adaptive information is through the use of rating scales, such as the Vineland Adaptive Behavior Scales or Adaptive Behavior Assessment System. These scales assess daily adaptive functioning or living skills in areas such as self-care, independence, communication skills, social skills, leisure activities, and so forth. In addition to obtaining information about where the child is functioning currently, questions may also be asked about the child's development in the past. An example of some of the questions that may be asked about past development can be seen in Table 5-2 in the section entitled Developmental History.

Scores for adaptive functioning can also be reported as standard scores and comparisons can be made with IQ level and adaptive levels in several areas. Informed decision making for children within this IQ range requires consideration of several factors, including intellectual level, academic performance, and adaptive functioning (strengths and weaknesses in adaptive skills). Interventions would be expected to target skill development in the adaptive as well as academic areas.

**Borderline Range**   Children who obtain scores in this range are midway between the average ranges and the extremely low range: They are on the borderline, hence the term *Borderline Range* is used. These children pose the most difficult challenges for decision-making teams because they may or may not qualify for special education assistance, depending on specific criteria that vary from state to state.

Children within this range often experience significant difficulty transferring information from situation to situation. For example, what they learn one day might not be transferred to the next day's lesson. What they learn in reading may not generalize to their written work. Therefore, rather than building a cumulative learning curve, based on an increasing body of knowledge, their learning may be based on individual pieces of information that do not connect into the bigger picture. As a result, these children may have less benefit from their prior learning experiences. However, some children in the Borderline Range may do relatively well, especially in the earlier grades, if they have strengths in long-term memory. If this is the case, they may amass a good sight vocabulary and spell or decode words with relative ease. As work becomes more complex, these children may struggle with reading comprehension and the more challenging aspects of written expression. Comprehension difficulties may also be evident in understanding how to solve wordy math problems, especially problems that required a decision regarding which numbers are required to solve the problem and which numbers are to be ignored. Children in this range perform best in situations of high structure, clear directions, and consistent limit setting. Frequent repetition may be required to consolidate learning.

**Average Ranges**   Children in the average ranges should not experience significant academic difficulties unless they have other contributing problems like a specific learning disability, attention problems, emotional/behavioral problems, or motivational problems. As would be expected, children who fall within the *Lower Average Range* would be expected to have more academic difficulties than children in the other two average ranges. Depending on the particular pattern of strengths and weaknesses, children in the *Low Average Range* may struggle with comprehension problems, or they may require more time and more repetitions of a concept before they can consolidate the information.

Children at the lower levels of this range may experience similar problems to

*Table 5-2.        Questions about a child's developmental history.*

### A. Information That Parents Can Bring to an Educational Meeting

As a parent, you can bring valuable information to the school team meeting. The following questions might be helpful in better preparing you for a school meeting:

- How long is your child spending on homework each evening? Ask the teacher what is a reasonable amount of time.
- Does your child play well with children in the neighborhood? Ask whether your child has friends at school.
- Is there anyone your child is frightened of at school? Ask if your child is fearful of any of his classmates.
- What subject does your child like best? Ask which subject(s) your child is doing best in, and in which subject(s) he is having problems.
- Are you getting everything that the teacher sends home for you to read? Ask if there are any parent groups or parent meetings that you can attend.
- Does your child have an agenda (a school planner)? Ask whether the teacher writes assignments in the planner or checks if the assignments are written down by the student.

### B. Questions the School Psychologist or Social Worker Might Ask

#### Developmental History:

- At what age did your child first, sit, stand, walk, say a first word, or talk in sentences?
- Was your child easy or difficult to manage as a baby?
- Did your child have any major illnesses or injuries as an infant, toddler, or child?
- Was your child overactive as a toddler?
- Is your child a good sleeper? How about your child's appetite?

#### Family History & Family Context:

- Is there a family history of mental illness, ADHD, or learning disabilities?
- How many children are in the family and do they all live at home?
- How well does the child get along with his siblings?
- Is this a single-parent or two-parent family? If a single parent, who has custody of the child and what are the visitation arrangements?
- What chores is your child responsible for at home?
- What is the main method of discipline? Who is the disciplinarian?
- How does your child respond to being disciplined?

#### Child's Current Health and Mental Status:

- How is your child's health? Is he frequently ill or relatively healthy?
- Does your child complain of aches and pains often?
- Is your child currently taking any medications?

- Does your child look forward to going to school, or would he prefer to stay home?
- Does your child have friends in the neighborhood? Is he invited to other children's homes?
- Does your child bring work home for you to see, or does he lose it or hide it?
- Does your child belong to any groups or clubs outside of school?
- What does your child like to do best when he is at home?

---

children in the Borderline Range described previously. Homework may be challenging, especially if the child does not have an adequate grasp of what knowledge is required to complete the work successfully. Children in this range may seem to be one step behind the pace of the majority of children in the class and are in danger of falling farther behind if not given time or practice to consolidate foundation skills. Parents will need to be in touch with teachers and monitor progress to ensure academic success.

**Average and High Average Ranges**    Children who score in these ranges demonstrate normal to above-normal capacity to learn and should not be experiencing significant academic difficulties. If significant academic concerns are evident, further assessment will be conducted in different areas (processing, behavior/emotion, and observation) to help pinpoint and clarify the nature of the difficulty.

**Superior and Very Superior (Gifted) Ranges**    Children who score in these ranges are in the top 10 percent of the population intellectually. Often students in these ranges may require more-challenging academic tasks and enhanced learning environments. If academic concerns are evident, there is serious need to investigate why the child is not performing to potential. Children with intelligence scores in the Superior and Very Superior Ranges are not immune from problems such as a learning disability, attention problems, or emotional/behavioral problems that can also contribute to a lack of adequate performance for these children as well.

## Common Instruments That Measure Intelligence

There are many instruments available to assess psychological functioning in all areas of development (IQ, achievement, information processing, and social and emotional development). These measures are continually being updated to reflect more contemporary norms. Ethically, psychologists are required to remain informed about important changes in these instruments.

A discussion about all possible IQ tests is beyond the scope of this book, so we will focus on the three most commonly used measures. The selection of which measure to use will be based on the psychologist's preference and the circumstances surrounding the assessment. If a child has a language deficit, for example, the psychologist may want to use the Differential Ability Scale, since it contains a special nonverbal scale. The Universal Nonverbal Intelligence Test may also be used since this instrument requires only motor responses (point to an answer or construct a design).

> **Did you know?** Some school districts have a list of acceptable psychological instruments, including IQ tests, which may be used as part of the initial assessment. Although the school psychologist will be aware of what the district requires and the range of acceptable instruments, a psychologist in private practice may not be familiar with the district's specific requirements. If parents are seeking an independent assessment outside the public school system, it is important to determine ahead of time what the district will accept prior to seeking out an external practitioner. You can obtain this information from the school psychologist or by contacting the student services department of your local school district.

### Wechsler Scales

Depending on the child's age, one of three scales can be administered: Wechsler Preschool and Primary Scale of Intelligence-Third Edition (*WPPSI-III*: Ages 2 year, 6 months to 7 years, 3 months); Wechsler Intelligence Scale for Children-Fourth Edition (*WISC-IV*: ages 6 years to 16 years, 11 months); and Wechsler Adult Intelligence Scale-Third Edition (*WAIS-III*: ages 16 to 89 years). Since the majority of school-age children would be administered the WISC-IV from among these three alternatives, emphasis in the following discussion will focus on this particular test. A short discussion will provide insight on how the WPPSI-III and WAIS-III differ from the WISC-IV.

**WISC-IV**   The newly revised WISC-IV (2003) provides scores for an overall Full Scale IQ, as well as four index scores: Verbal Comprehension Index, Perceptual Reasoning Index, Working Memory Index, and Processing Speed Index. Full Scale IQ and index scores are reported as standard scores (mean of 100, standard deviation of 15). The four index scores measure abilities in the following areas:

**Verbal Comprehension Index**   The Verbal Comprehension Index is a measure of a child's verbal reasoning, verbal concept formation, word knowledge, and practical/social judgement.

**Perceptual Reasoning Index**   Tasks involving perceptual reasoning require minimal/no verbal response and measure nonverbal concept formation and visual problem-solving ability. Visual motor performance (speed) can earn bonus points in constructing block designs.

**Working Memory Index**   Working memory is a measure of a child's ability to mentally hold information in short-term memory, while manipulating (performing an operation on) the information in some way, like doing mental math problems.

**Processing Speed Index**   Processing speed measures a child's speed of copying and/or scanning visual information.

The following case study of Stuart will help to illustrate how intelligence test scores can assist in better understanding learning difficulties.

> ***Introducing Stuart:*** Stuart has a history of academic difficulties. Stuart repeated the Kindergarten Program to allow for consolidation of core skills. Stuart has been diagnosed with ADHD and takes 15 mg. of Adderall each morning at the beginning of the school day. Despite retention and Title I assistance (a federally funded program to assist children with reading, mathematics, and writing), Stuart continues to struggle academically, especially in reading. Stuart has just turned 8 years old, and the class is more than halfway through the first-grade curriculum; however, Stuart's parents and teacher are concerned that he has not yet mastered prereading skills. Stuart's scores on the WISC-IV are presented in Table 5-3.

Stuart's Full-Scale IQ on the WISC-IV was 87 (Range 82–92) which is at the upper limits of the Low Average Range. Based on Stuart's overall IQ score, his learning potential would not predict serious academic difficulties. However, when looking at the index scores, the picture begins to get somewhat clearer. Stuart's index scores ranged from a high of 102 (Average) for Perceptual Reasoning to a low of 78 (Borderline) for Processing Speed. When we look up this twenty-four point difference between these two index scores in the test manual, we find that this highly significant difference would occur in fewer than one in twenty students.

Although Stuart demonstrates an obvious strength in Visual/Perceptual Reasoning, other scores are less well developed. Stuart is very slow to copy and scan information (Processing Index).

> **Did you know?** The IQ scores of children with ADHD often appear similar to other "normal" children for several reasons: the testing situation is novel and therefore helps sustain interest/attention; the IQ test is organized by the administrator; and the testing situation is usually relatively distraction-free. The two areas most likely to show weaker performance in children with ADHD are Processing Speed and Working Memory.

The individual subtests that make up the four index scores (see lower portion of Table 5-3) are presented as scaled scores with a mean (average) score of 10 and standard deviation (unit of comparison) of 3. Therefore, average scale scores range from 8 to 12. Any scores below 8 (weakness) or above 12 (strength) deserve extra consideration. Stuart has significant problems seeing how verbal concepts

*Table 5-3.      Stuart's scores on the WISC-IV.*

**WISC-IV Full Scale and Index Scores for Stuart L.**

| Scale | Standard Scores | Range | Percentile | Description of Range |
|---|---|---|---|---|
| Verbal Comprehension Index (VCI) | 85 | 79 to 93 | 16 | Low Average |
| Perceptual Reasoning Index (PRI) | 102 | 94 to 109 | 55 | Average |
| Working Memory Index (WMI) | 88 | 81 to 97 | 21 | Low Average |
| Processing Speed Index (PSI) | 78 | 72 to 90 | 7 | Borderline |
| Full Scale IQ | 87 | 82 to 92 | 19 | Low Average |

**WISC-IV IQ Subtest Scores**

The following scores represent Stuart's performance on the WISC-IV subtests.

| Verbal Comprehension Index | Scale Scores |
|---|---|
| **Similarities:** *verbal reasoning & concept formation* | 5* Weakness |
| **Vocabulary:** *word knowledge & verbal concept formation* | 9 |
| **Comprehension:** *conventional standards, social judgment, maturity, & common sense* | 9 |

| Perceptual Reasoning Index | |
|---|---|
| **Block Design:** *ability to analyze & synthesize abstract visual stimuli* | 12* Strength |
| **Picture Concepts:** *abstract visual reasoning ability* | 8 |
| **Matrix Reasoning:** *visual information processing & abstract reasoning skills* | 11* Strength |

| Working Memory Index | |
|---|---|
| **Digit Span:** *auditory short-term memory, sequencing, attention, & concentration* | 8 |
| **Letter-Number Sequence:** *sequencing, mental manipulation, visuo-spatial imaging, short-term memory, & processing speed* | 8 |

| Processing Speed Index | |
|---|---|
| **Coding:** *processing speed, visual-motor coordination, visual scanning , cognitive flexibility* | 6 |
| **Symbol Search:** *visual memory, visual discrimination, concentration, & processing speed* | 6 |

and ideas are related (Similarities) and, to a lesser extent, how several visual pictures might share a common theme (Picture Concepts). Based on these scores, we would anticipate that he would have problems using examples from life's experiences to help make concepts more meaningful to him, unless directed to do so. Another area of weakness would be the actual time it takes Stuart to complete tasks (Processing Speed) compared with other children in the classroom. His strengths in visual/perceptual reasoning suggest that the use of visual symbols is one method that can assist Stuart in better understanding the relationships that exist between concepts.

Based on the results of Stuart's performance on the IQ test, the school psychologist can now assess academic performance to determine how closely these scores match what would be predicted given his Full-Scale IQ.

## Other Wechsler Scales

For children of Stuart's age (most school-age children), the WISC-IV is the appropriate intelligence test. However, versions of this instrument are also available for preschool children and youth older than 18 years of age.

**WPPSI-III**   The Wechsler Preschool and Primary Scale of Intelligence, Third Edition (2002) is the appropriate instrument to use for children within the age range of 4 years, 0 months to 7 years, 3 months. A younger modified version (2 years, 6 months to 3 years, 11 months) also exists. Since the upper age limit (6 years, 0 months to 7 years, 3 months) overlaps with the WISC-IV, the psychologist can use either instrument for children in this age range. The WPPSI-III is similar to the WISC-IV described previously.

**WAIS-III**   The Wechsler Adult Intelligence Scale, Third Edition (1997) is the Wechsler version that is given to adolescents 16 years of age through adults age 89 years.

## Stanford-Binet Intelligence Scales, Fifth Edition (SB5)

Another instrument commonly used to assess intelligence in children is the SB5 (2003). Unlike the multi-instrument format of the Wechsler Scales, the SB5 uses a single instrument for all age levels (2 years, 0 months to adults age 80 years and over). In addition to the Full-Scale IQ, the Binet provides standard scores for Verbal and Nonverbal IQ, based on composite scores obtained for five verbal and nonverbal scales. The five scales on the SB5 include Fluid Reasoning (*problem solving in novel situations*), Knowledge (*acquired information*), Quantitative Reasoning (*reasoning with numbers*), Visual/Spatial Processing (*spatial analysis*), and Working Memory (*mental manipulation*).

## The Differential Ability Scale

The Differential Ability Scale provides a General Conceptual Ability Score (GCA) for very young children (2 years, 6 months to 3 years, 5 months). For young children between 3 years, 6 months and 5 years, 11 months, two cluster scores are also available (Verbal Ability and Nonverbal Ability). Children over 6 years of age have the added cluster of Spatial Ability, in addition to their CGA Score and Verbal/Nonverbal Ability scores. The DAS also has a Special Nonverbal Composite Score that can substitute for the CGA. The Special Nonverbal Composite score is used if the examiner believes that administration of the verbal tasks is not appropriate due to a child's language problems, speech problems, or hearing impairment.

### Other Measures of Intelligence and Cognitive Ability

There are several other measures of intelligence, including the Reynolds Intellectual Assessment Scales, Universal Nonverbal Intelligence Test, Kaufman Assessment Battery for Children, Second Edition (KABC-II), and the Woodcock Johnson III Tests of Cognitive Abilities. The WJ III will be discussed further in Chapter 6, when we discuss the use of this instrument to probe potential processing difficulties.

### Preview

Chapter 6 will look at how intelligence test scores are used to predict academic achievement and how potential processing difficulties may interfere with learning.

CHAPTER 6

## Other Psychological Assessments: Achievement Testing, Process Testing, and Emotional/Behavioral Assessments

As we mentioned previously, the assessment of intelligence is usually only one component of the assessment process. Psychologists often administer several other tests to investigate the extent and nature of a child's learning problems, and to investigate factors that might be contributing to a child's lack of school success.

## Achievement Testing

Once a psychologist obtains scores from the intellectual assessment, the next step might involve an assessment of academic achievement.

### How Do Psychologists Measure Achievement?

*Re-introducing Stuart:* Remember Stuart, the 8-year-old boy who was struggling with the first-grade program that we talked about in Chapter 5? His teacher knows that Stuart is not mastering classroom tasks, especially in language arts. Last week, Stuart got only three words right on his spelling list of ten words. Stuart can only recognize about half of the sight words compared with other children in his class, and even then, he is inconsistent in his attempts. On the other hand, Stuart has no problem in math. But how far behind is Stuart, actually?

**Standardized Achievement Tests**   When the psychologist investigated Stuart's learning potential, he administered an intelligence test. Based on a comparison of

Stuart's responses with responses available for other children Stuart's age (norms), the psychologist was able to determine that Stuart's IQ was roughly within the Average Range (Upper Low Average). Although weaknesses in abstract verbal reasoning and his slow speed of copying could contribute to academic concerns, all things being equal, results of the intelligence test (average ability to learn) ruled out IQ as the sole contributing factor for Stuart's academic difficulties.

The next step in the process would likely be to compare Stuart's academic performance with academic scores of other children of similar ages to determine where Stuart's academic abilities fall and to look at his functioning levels in three core areas of academic performance: reading, written expression, and mathematics. The psychologist would be interested in obtaining answers to the following questions:

- Given Stuart's age, where should he be functioning academically?
- Given Stuart's IQ, is he functioning at the predicted academic levels?
- Is Stuart's academic performance consistent across the three major academic areas of reading, written expression, and mathematics?

In order to answer these questions, the psychologist administers a *norm-referenced* achievement test, which allows him to compare Stuart's performance with the academic skills expected of other children Stuart's age, and additionally, to compare academic levels to levels expected, given his IQ level.

### How Can the Psychologist Compare Stuart's Academic Scores with "Normal" Scores Expected at His Age Level or IQ Scores?

Remember that IQ scores were reported as *standard scores* with a mean (average) of 100 and a standard deviation (unit of comparison) of 15. A number of individual achievement tests such as the Wechsler Individual Achievement Test and the Woodcock-Johnson Tests of Achievement also report results of achievement test scores as standard scores that allow for a more direct comparison between expectations (IQ scores) and academic performance.

Stuart's scores on the WJ III Achievement Test are presented in Table 6-1 and indicate that both reading and written expression are in the *Extremely Low Range* based on age expectations.

**Comparison of Academic Scores Based on Age Expectations (Age Norms)**
When Stuart's academic responses on the WJ III Achievement Test are compared with the expected responses based on norms available for 8-year-old boys, Stuart performs well below the expected levels for reading and written expression. In fact, Stuart's responses are more typical of an average child between 6 years, 1 month of age (written expression) and 6 years, 4 months of age (reading).

*Table 6-1.*      *Stuart's scores on the WJ III Tests of Achievement: age, grade*
                  *equivalents, percentiles, and standard scores.*

| Academic Cluster | Age Equivalent years/months | Grade Equivalent | Percentile | Standard Score | Description |
|---|---|---|---|---|---|
| Broad Reading | 6/4 | 1.1 | 1 | 65 | Extremely Low |
| Broad Math | 7/1 | 1.7 | 23 | 89 | Low Average |
| Broad Written Expression | 6/1 | K.8 | 1 | 63 | Extremely Low |

In considering grade equivalents, while the majority of the class has passed the midway point of the first-grade program, Stuart is at a late-kindergarten (written expression) to beginning first-grade (reading) level in language arts. However, because Stuart is already one year behind his classmates (remember, he repeated kindergarten), these lags are even more pronounced than they appear on the surface. In reporting test scores, it is more important to base comparisons on age rather than grade-based comparisons for this and other reasons that are beyond the scope of this book.

**Comparison of Achievement Scores Based on Intellectual Expectations**   Remember that IQ scores are presented as standard scores with a mean of 100 and standard deviation of 15 (unit of comparison). A child's standard score for achievement should be within one standard deviation (15 points) of his IQ score.

> ***Given that*** Stuart has an IQ score of 87, we would expect his academic standard scores to range between a low of (87 − 15) 72 and a high of (87 + 15) 102. Scores within the range of 72 to 102 would be within one standard deviation above and one standard deviation below the score predicted by his IQ of 87.

A comparison of Stuart's achievement scores and IQ scores are presented in Table 6-2.

When we compare Stuart's standard scores for reading (65) and written expression (63) to his expected level of performance suggested by his IQ (87) we find that Stuart is well in excess (22 to 24 point differences) of this 15-point discrepancy in both areas. However, when we compare his mathematics score (89) to his predicted level (87), we find that the difference between these two scores is very small. Stuart is just about where we would predict he would be in

*Table 6-2.    WJ III Tests of Achievement standard scores and expected performance based on IQ.*

| Academic Cluster | Age Equivalent years/months | Percentile | Standard Score | WISC-IV IQ | Discrepancy |
|---|---|---|---|---|---|
| Broad Reading | 6/4 | 1 | 65 | 87 | − 22 |
| Broad Math | 7/1 | 23 | 89 | 87 | + 2 |
| Broad Written Expression | 6/1 | 1 | 63 | 87 | − 24 |

math. The relationship between standard scores obtained for academic perform-ance relative to Stuart's Full-Scale IQ score is shown in Figure 6-1.

### Do All School Districts Use a Discrepancy Formula and Is It the Same for All Districts?

Comparing standard score differences between ability and achievement is referred to as a discrepancy model. This model has met with great controversy. Some people feel that this method penalizes children at the lower extreme. For example, if a child has an IQ of 85, he would need to score below 70 to demonstrate a significant discrepancy between ability and achievement. However, if a child has an IQ of 115, he could score 100 academically, which is in the Average Range, and still be considered to have a significant discrepancy between ability and achievement.

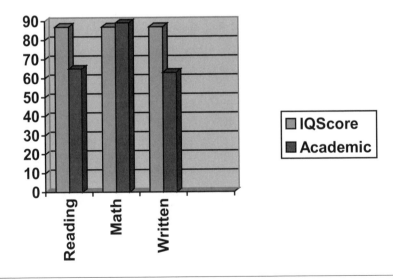

*Figure 6-1.    A comparison of standard scores for IQ and academics.*

Some districts consider a 15-point discrepancy between ability and achievement significant for younger children (under 11 years of age), but then require a 22-point difference (one and a half standard deviations) for children above eleven years of age. Other school districts may require as much as a two standard deviation difference, which would mean a 30-point difference between achievement and IQ. The rationale is that it is more difficult to have a large gap in achievement/ ability at younger age levels. Despite the inherent flaws in the discrepancy model noted previously, many districts will continue to use this model, while others may follow a response-to-intervention (RTI) approach, as allowed by IDEA 2004. This three-tiered model includes the following phases:

1. Determining whether effective instruction is in place for groups of students

2. Providing effective instruction to target students and measuring its effect on their performance

3. Referring students for an assessment whose response-to-intervention warrants additional interventions

**Did you know?** IDEA 2004 changed the wording about eligibility for children with a learning disability. Schools are *no longer required* to demonstrate a severe discrepancy between achievement and intellectual ability to find a child eligible for special education services under the category of specific learning disability. Instead, the school district *may use* an evaluation of the child's failure to respond to scientific, research-based interventions to document a specific learning disability.

### What Are the Academic Skills That Achievement Tests Measure?

As outlined in the previous example, most standardized achievement tests provide a composite score for reading based on a number of subtests, which may include tasks of single-word decoding, reading fluency, and comprehension. A composite mathematics score would likely involve tasks of calculation, fluency, and problem solving. Written expression is often measured through spelling tests and tasks designed to measure sentence/paragraph construction. It is important that whatever instrument is used to measure these core academic areas that a measures include more than just decoding, spelling, and math calculation skills, but also include assessment of a child's reading comprehension, math problem solving, and written expression (beyond spelling).

## Assessment of Processing Skills

In our case study, the psychologist has found that Stuart has a significant discrepancy between what is predicted by his intelligence score and his actual academic performance in the areas of reading and written expression. The next step in the assessment process might be to administer additional tests to determine if learning difficulties result from problems that Stuart might have in processing auditory or verbal information.

### What Is a Processing Assessment?

A significant discrepancy between ability and achievement suggests that there is some factor other than learning ability that is undermining a child's academic success. There are several possible reasons why a child may encounter academic difficulties, including a lack of motivation, lack of interest, frequent absenteeism, emotional/behavioral difficulties, family/adjustment difficulties, and processing problems. Children whose academic success is compromised by processing difficulties often can be diagnosed with a specific learning disability that describes the nature of their specific processing problem.

### What Kinds of Processing Problems Exist?

Children with specific learning disabilities likely have no physical vision or hearing problems and the majority of these children have average to above average intelligence. However, their ability to be successful academically, and sometimes socially, can be compromised by unique deficits in how information is processed. Further discussion of the various types of specific learning disabilities can be found in Chapter 7. At this point, the focus will be on the role of assessment in determining the nature of processing difficulties.

Information processing can break down as information is received at the *input stage* (auditory, visual, or motor recognition problems), at the *integration stage* (interpretation, short- and long-term memory, or organization of information), and/or the *output stage* (oral, written communication, or motor responses). Children who have problems with attention and concentration often experience difficulty receiving information and sustaining attention long enough to allow for sufficient interpretation. Impulsive children may jump to the expression stage and virtually bypass the interpretive process.

Weaknesses in processing information can occur at several different levels and can result in specific learning problems as a result. Some of the more common types of processing skills/deficits are listed in Table 6-3. Possessing difficulties in any of these areas can result in poor academic performance despite good intellectual ability and motivation. Children with these types of processing problems are often very frustrated, painfully aware of their poor academic progress, and may suffer from low self-esteem.

### How Are Processing Deficits Assessed?

The psychologist may use one or more of the several available instruments for measuring processing skills/deficits. Some of the more common instruments used include:

Woodcock-Johnson III Tests of Cognitive Abilities (WJ III)

Children's Memory Scale (CMS)

Wechsler Memory Scale-Third Edition (WMS-III)

Test of Memory and Learning (TOMAL)

Wide Range Assessment of Memory and Learning, Second Edition (WRAML2)

As might be expected, these instruments also present results as standard scores, and they allow for a direct comparison of how processing skills align with intellectual ability. As a case in point, let's look at how our 8-year-old, first-grade student Stuart scored on his processing assessment. The psychologist administered the WJ III Tests of Cognitive Abilities battery and a summary of Stuart's processing scores are presented in Table 6-4.

By now, the standard scores should begin to take on a more meaningful role, as we look at a third set of scores. Although Stuart's scores suggest a significant strength, there are also several areas of processing deficits. On the extreme posi-

*Table 6-3.*     *Information processing: types of processing and impact on learning.*

| Information Processing | Description |
|---|---|
| Attention and Concentration | Ability to attend to auditory and/or visual information; Ability to selectively attend to important versus extraneous information; Ability to sustain attention over time; Ease of distractibility. |
| Memory | Auditory and visual memory; Short-term memory (use within a few seconds, e.g., use for task instructions); Working memory (ability to hold information in a state of mental awareness, while mentally manipulating information or performing some operation on the information); Longer term storage and retrieval of information. |
| Executive Functions | Planning and organization |
| Cognitive Fluency | Ease of ability to retrieve information from storage and apply that information to current problem solving tasks; decision-making speed. |
| Processing Speed | Ability to perform simple cognitive and motor tasks that are automatic, repetitive, and require sustained attention over the course of time. |

*Table 6-4.*    *WJ III COG standard scores and expected performance based on IQ.*

**Stuart's responses to subtests of the Woodcock-Johnson III Tests of Cognitive Abilities Assessment.**

*Woodcock-Johnson III Tests of Cognitive Abilities (WJ III COG)*

| Processing Area | Age Equivalent | Percentile | Standard Score | Description |
|---|---|---|---|---|
| Visual-Spatial Thinking | 10-3 | 77 | 111 | High Average |
| Short-Term Memory | 7-4 | 22 | 89 | Low Average |
| Long-Term Memory/Retrieval | 4-8 | 0.1 | 54 | Extremely Low |
| Working Memory | 6-0 | 9 | 80 | Low Average |
| Cognitive Fluency | 5-9 | 4 | 72 | Borderline |
| Processing Speed | 6-4 | 5 | 76 | Borderline |
| Auditory Processing | 6-0 | 16 | 85 | Low Average |
| Phonemic Awareness | 5-8 | 12 | 82 | Low Average |

tive end, Stuart has an obvious strength in Visual Spatial Thinking. This result is consistent with previous scores obtained on his IQ test. Strengths noted on Block Design and Matrix Reasoning of the WISC-IV also measure visual spatial reasoning. Remember that these were two of Stuart's strongest subscale scores on the IQ test. Children with strengths in these areas often do well with mathematics.

However, at the other end of the spectrum, Stuart is slow to get information down onto paper (processing speed), which would likely result in having problems finishing written work or paper-and-pencil tasks. Stuart's ability to retrieve information from long-term memory is very poor (Extremely Low Range), and may result in the frustration of information being "here today and gone tomorrow." In addition, Stuart is not an efficient thinker (which may result from poor organizational skills or be influenced by his poor ability to retrieve information). Basically, it takes Stuart longer to solve problems because he does not use the most-efficient ways to sort, retrieve, and respond to information.

**Did you know?** Retrieving information from long-term storage is similar to trying to locate a file in a filing cabinet or trying to locate a file on your computer. If you can't remember how the information was stored (file name, etc.), you can experience significant problems trying to access that information.

As you might anticipate, it is now time to compare these processing scores to expected levels that would be predicted given Stuart's IQ or ability levels. A quick glance at scores presented in Table 6-5 tells the story. When we compare standard scores obtained on the processing assessment with Stuart's IQ score, it becomes evident that Long-Term Memory/Retrieval is well in excess of the 15-point difference (standard deviation) needed to suggest a significant difference between ability and processing skill in this area. Cognitive fluency is also significantly below what would be anticipated (-15), while processing speed also approaches significance (-11).

Although the majority of an assessment of processing skills/deficits would involve the psychologist working directly with the child, it is also possible to obtain information concerning processing skills through other techniques, such as classroom observation, teacher/parent interviews, and parent/teacher completion of standardized questionnaires.

In Stuart's case, there are no complicating emotional/behavioral or social problems, so the assessment ends at this point, since assessment of IQ, academic ability, and processing all present a consistent picture. Stuart has a specific learning disability that is impeding his progress in reading and written expression. Stuart's learning disability is manifested in significant difficulties retrieving information stored in long-term memory. Stuart is also slow to generate solutions to problems. This sluggish tempo has an impact on his learning to the extent that Stuart will often be "one step behind" his fellow classmates. The danger in this type of processing deficit is the cumulative impact of always playing catch-up in an academic world that is most likely full speed ahead. By the time Stuart has come up with the correct solution, or retrieved the information from his memory bank, the class has most likely moved to another topic. As a result of the assess-

Table 6-5.    A comparison of standard scores and expected performance based on IQ.

| Processing Area | Standard Score | WISC-IV IQ Score | Discrepancy |
|---|---|---|---|
| Visual-Spatial Thinking | 111 | 87 | +24 |
| Short-Term Memory | 89 | 87 | +2 |
| Long-Term Memory/Retrieval | 54 | 87 | -33 |
| Working Memory | 80 | 87 | -7 |
| Cognitive Fluency | 72 | 87 | -15 |
| Processing Speed | 76 | 87 | -11 |
| Auditory Processing | 85 | 87 | -2 |
| Phonemic Awareness | 82 | 87 | -5 |

ment information, Stuart's educational team can now begin working on an intervention plan to help Stuart develop more efficient memory strategies and to increase his fluency in thinking, reading, and writing.

## Assessment of Behavioral/Emotional or Social Problems

Stuart did not exhibit any behavioral/emotional or social problems. If he had, the psychologist would have included instruments in the assessment battery to assist in identifying the nature of these problems.

> **Did you know?** According to a Surgeon General's report issued in 1999, 20 percent of all children (one in five children) have a diagnosable mental disorder.

As we discussed in brief earlier, children who act out or whose behavior is disruptive are often readily observable. These are the first types of children that the school psychologist usually hears about. However, there are many reasons why children behave poorly. Sometimes, there are things going on in the child's life, at home, or at school that the child does not understand. Children can act out when they are frustrated, either emotionally, mentally, or academically. Children who act out (disruptive behaviors, aggression) are said to demonstrate *externalizing behaviors*.

However, not all children respond to stress and frustration by acting out. Some children may withdraw, become sad or anxious, or have a wide variety of physical (somatic) complaints. Children who respond to stressful events by bringing the problem inside them are said to have *internalizing behaviors*. Unfortunately, internalizing behaviors, such as depression, anxiety, or physical complaints, are often difficult to detect and may go unnoticed for some time. Once these internalizing problems are detected, it can be difficult to determine why the child has these feelings. One reason the assessment is so difficult is that children often do not fully understand their emotions. Unlike adults, children are often not able to verbalize what is causing them to be unhappy, sad, or worried.

Another difficulty in determining the nature of a child's emotional or behavioral problems is that children often have problems in more than one area at the same time, a condition that is called *comorbidity*, which basically acts as a *double whammy*. Some of the common problem areas that often go together are children who may have ADHD and another set of behavioral problems called oppositional defiant disorder (ODD). Children who have ODD can be very negative and refuse to comply with requests or chose to ignore requests to comply. The previous example of ADHD and ODD occurring together is an example of two externalizing behaviors. However, it is also common for children to have more than one internalizing disorder at the same time. In this instance, a child may have symptoms of both depression and anxiety, or express feelings of anxiety through many physical (somatic) complaints.

## What Are the Tools for Evaluating Emotional and Behavioral Concerns?

There are several types of instruments available to assist in evaluating the degree to which children may be suffering from emotional or behavioral difficulties. In addition to observing children either in the classroom or on the playground, the psychologist may also want to interview teachers and parents to determine if concerns are consistent across situations. Interviews can be either informal or very structured. Often psychologists will ask teachers and parents to complete behavior-rating scales. Some of the more common behavior rating scales are listed below:

> Child Behavior Checklist (CBCL)
>
> Teacher's Report Form (TRF)
>
> Behavior Assessment System for Children, Second Edition (BASC-2) (parent and teacher forms)
>
> Conners's Rating Scales-Revised (CRS-R) (parent and teacher forms)
>
> Devereux Behavior Rating Scale-School Form (parent and teacher forms)

Parents may be surprised at the number and range of questions sampled by these rating scales. The CBCL, TRF, and the BASC-2, for example, include more than one hundred questions. The reason there are so many questions is that the scales evaluate behaviors across several different domains (depression, anxiety, attention, acting out, and so on) and several questions are required to provide an adequate picture of whether the child is experiencing significant problems in any given area. However, completing the questionnaire can be quick, since respondents are only required to indicate the degree to which a behavior occurs (never, sometimes, or often).

## Do Parents and Teachers Agree or Disagree in Their Ratings?

As might be expected, differences between raters are common. Not only do parents and teachers often differ in their ratings of a child, differences also exist between teachers (different classes) and between parents (mother and father). However, it is important to collect as much information as possible to obtain a better understanding of where the behaviors are taking place to develop the most appropriate plan for assisting the child. A child may have few problems in a math class because he excels in this area but exhibits more inappropriate behaviors in an intensive reading class because he is a poor reader and is lost in the program. Or a child may have few problems in the morning classes, but get progressively worse as the day wears on and the child's frustration mounts. A child may not experience any problems at home because the focus is less structured and the child can relax. The child may also experience many problems at home because he is able to vent his frustration in this setting and not at school.

**Individual Assessment of Emotional and Behavioral Difficulties**    In addition to asking parents and teachers to complete rating scales, the psychologist will likely want to talk with the child and have the child complete a number of different tasks to help evaluate the child's emotional and behavioral responses, relative to similar-age peers. There are many types of instruments and techniques available, ranging from unstructured requests for the child to draw pictures, to having the child complete personality inventories, or having them rate their own emotional responses on rating scales similar to those given to parents and teachers.

If a psychologist is concerned that a child may be depressed or anxious, he may ask the child to complete one of many available depression or anxiety scales that ask children to rate whether they feel sad or anxious (a lot, a little, or not at all) in different situations. The psychologist can then compare the child's pattern of responses with responses of other "normal" children and "depressed or anxious" children of similar ages to determine whether the child is more depressed or anxious than would be expected. Of course, evaluations of emotional and behavioral responses are more difficult with younger children because they often do not understand the nature of their own feelings and have limited expressive vocabulary. For younger children, observations of behavior and obtaining parent and teacher information are likely to yield the most accurate picture of problems.

As children grow older, there are more assessment instruments available to assist the psychologist in evaluating the nature and extent of a child's emotional or behavioral problems. However, the value of these instruments is only as valid as the child's honesty in providing the responses. Some children, despite significant behavioral or emotional difficulties, will respond as if they are having no problems whatsoever. Other children may exaggerate their difficulties in an attempt to obtain increased attention. Regardless, psychologists are trained to "read between the lines" and evaluate a child's emotional and behavioral status based on the how the "total picture" evolves from information obtained from a variety of methods and sources (observations and/or interviews with the child and rating scales completed by the child, as well as information obtained from parents and teachers).

# CHAPTER 7

# Understanding Your Child's Disability

Understanding your child's disability begins with the recognition that disabilities are classified in various ways by different sources.

## The Different Ways That Disabilities Are Classified

As was discussed in Chapter 1, federal disability law classifies disabilities according to different laws and acts: the Americans with Disabilities Act of 1990 (ADA); Individuals with Disabilities Education Improvement Act of 2004 (IDEA 2004); and Section 504 of the Rehabilitation Act of 1973.

The ADA is a civil rights law that was developed to protect individuals with disabilities by prohibiting discrimination in employment or public services and may include such areas as education, housing, transportation, and employment. According to ADA, an individual is considered *"disabled" if they have either a physical or mental impairment that severely limits major life activities*. Accommodations under ADA may include, but are not limited to, alterations such as redesigning equipment or structural areas to ensure reasonable access to facilities (wheelchair ramps) or information (Telecommunication Devices for the Deaf: TDY).

Similarly, under Section 504 of the Rehabilitation Act, a handicapping condition exists if there is a physical or mental impairment that significantly limits major life activities.

*Major life activities* include walking, seeing, performing manual tasks, speaking, breathing, learning, and working. Section 504 includes adults in the workforce or school-age youth under 22 years of age. Under Section 504, an attention-deficit/hyperactivity disorder could be considered a handicapping condition.

Unlike ADA, IDEA 2004 specifically defines disabilities as they refer to *educationally handicapping conditions*. Children and youth between 3 years and 21 years of age who have had an individualized evaluation can be deemed eligible for special education and related services by a multidisciplinary team, *if they qualify for services in one or more of thirteen designated categories*. In addition, children age 3 years through 9 years who evidence developmental delays may also qualify for services.

Under IDEA 2004, *special education* refers to instruction that is specifically designed to meet the educational needs based on the child's unique disability. *Related services*, such as speech-language, physical, and occupational therapy can also be provided, at no cost to parents, if it is determined that these related services are required to assist the child to benefit from special education services.

Infants and toddlers with disabilities (birth through 2 years of age) and their families receive support services through an *early intervention system*. IDEA 2004 supports early intervention for infants and toddlers with disabilities due to developmental delays (cognitive, physical, communication, social/emotional, adaptive areas) or those having a diagnosed physical or mental handicapping condition.

### Developmental Delays

IDEA 2004 allows each state and local educational agency—a school district—to classify children between the ages of 3 and 9 years as developmentally delayed without having to specify one of the thirteen disability categories.

**Did you know?** The developmental delay classification is an option that may or may not be utilized by every state. In some districts in Florida, for example, the developmental delayed classification must be removed prior to the child's sixth birthday, while in other districts in the state, the time is extended to the seventh birthday. Under IDEA 2004, the classification of developmental delay can be retained until the child's ninth birthday; however, this is at the discretion of the State Educational Authority.

## The Thirteen Categories of Disability Designated Under IDEA 2004

IDEA 2004 provides definitions for each of the thirteen categories of disability that have been developed to serve as federal guidelines. The thirteen categories of disability listed in IDEA 2004 are shown in Table 7-1.

*Table 7-1.       The thirteen categories of disabilities listed in IDEA 2004.*

1. Autism*

2. Deaf-blindness

3. Deafness

4. Emotional disturbance*

5. Hearing impairment

6. Mental retardation*

7. Multiple disabilities

8. Orthopedic impairment

9. Other health impairment (ADD/ADHD)*

10. Specific learning disability*

11. Speech or language impairment

12. Traumatic brain injury

13. Visual impairment including blindness

*Categories discussed at greater length in this chapter.

Although the categories are consistent across states, each state may have slightly different ways of determining who may be eligible for classification under each of these categories. For example, while all states require evidence of subaverage IQ and impaired adaptive functioning as part of the eligibility criteria for educable mentally handicapped (EMH), educable mental retardation (EMR), or mental retardation (MR), the actual scores used to determine if a child qualifies for the program may vary from state to state. In addition, even though a child may qualify for EMH/EMR/MR status based on IQ and adaptive functioning, if the child's academic skills do not fall within this specified range, he still may not qualify for services.

**Did you know?** In some states, an IQ below 70 is required for an EMH/EMR/MR designation, while in other states, a child with an IQ of 75 or even 80 may qualify in this area.

Furthermore, educational definitions of disabilities focus on how the disability will have an impact on a child's ability to learn, with the goal of developing an IEP to address specific learning needs. However, mental health practitioners define disabilities by criteria outlined in the Diagnostic and Statistical Manual of Mental

Disorders-Fourth Edition (DSM-IV-TR), and are more concerned with diagnosis as a means of identifying appropriate treatment planning regarding mental health issues.

A general discussion of all thirteen categories can be found in Chapter 8. This chapter will focus on five categories of exceptionality that represent the most challenging and complex areas of concerns for educators and parents: autism, emotional disturbance, mental retardation, attention-deficit/hyperactivity disorder, and specific learning disability. Our intent in this chapter is to provide additional information for these complex categories concerning mental health issues, prevalence rates, and associated features for these disorders.

## Autism

Autism is a neurological disorder listed in the DSM-IV under the main category of Pervasive Developmental Disorders (PDD).

### Defining Criteria

IDEA 2004 recognizes the three primary features of autism that result in severe and pervasive difficulties in the following areas:

1. Restricted range of social interaction
2. Impaired communication skills
3. Persistent pattern of stereotypical behaviors, interests, and activities

Onset of autism is usually evident in one of these three areas prior to 3 years of age.

### Prevalence and Cause

Autism is not very common (2 to 5 cases per 10,000 children). Like many other disorders, it is far more prevalent in males than females (four males to every female).

The majority of children (approximately 75 percent) with autism have some degree of mental retardation. Significant controversy exists regarding how children can develop autism, and no single gene or genetic link has been established.

### Associated Features

The following features are typically evident in a child with autism.

**Language and Communication Skills**   There is likely to be delayed language development and minimal use of nonverbal communication (pointing, gesturing, eye gaze) to compensate for poor verbal skills. If language does develop, it is rarely used to initiate, engage, or sustain communication with others. Speech patterns often exhibit an odd monotone (flat) or echolalic (repeating what was someone else has said) pattern. Children with higher functioning autism, or Asperger's disorder, may "talk at" others, producing lengthy speeches on topics of high interest to themselves while paying no attention to their audience.

**Play, Imitation, and Social Interaction**   Children with autism often seem to be in a world of their own. They do not spontaneously participate in social interaction. Normally, toddlers often engage in symbolic play or make-believe play. However, youngsters with autism do not develop age-appropriate peer relationships and are more intent on playing with parts of objects (spinning a wheel on a car), rather than using objects as a means of sharing interests with others. Rather than form attachments to people, these children may form strong attachments to inanimate objects, such as a plastic spoon or button.

**Stereotypical and Repetitive Behavior Patterns**   Children with autism are preoccupied with repeating behavior patterns in a way that can severely restrict their development because they are so resistant to change. Often, it is difficult to disengage these children from their intense focus on repetitive motor movements (hand flapping, twirling), often called self-stimulation, which serve to prevent these children from engaging in their social world. There is often a rigid adherence to routines and rituals that have little function in the real world, such as spending considerable time lining up objects (cars in a row, for example). These children are often highly resistant to any changes to their schedules and routines, regardless of how minor. While some professionals believe that these children hold on to the predictable because they are overwhelmed by external stimuli, others believe that these behavior patterns result from children being under-responsive to their environment.

**Learning and Development**   Approximately 75 percent of children with autism also suffer from mental retardation. However, skill development can be uneven and some children with autism can demonstrate higher functioning skills in specific areas, such as hyperlexia (reading at an advanced rate), or possess unusual ability to perform mathematical calculations. Despite these elevated skill levels, comprehension is often lacking.

Learning is often compromised by behavioral problems that can include hyperactivity, attention problems, aggressiveness, self-injurious behaviors, and temper tantrums, especially, in younger children.

*Controversy Among Professionals Regarding Autism and Asperger's Disorder*

Asperger's disorder is a condition that shares deficits in two of the three areas noted for autism: impaired social reciprocity, and stereotypical and repetitive movements. However, unlike children with autism, those with Asperger's disorder do not have clinical delays in communication skills. Although Asperger's disorder is listed as a separate disorder under PDD of the DSM-IV, the disorder is not mentioned by IDEA 2004. Because language skills are not impaired and due to their higher level of functioning, Asperger's disorder is often diagnosed much later than autism.

Children with Asperger's disorder often score well above children with autism on IQ tests, and some children can even have above average or superior IQ. Because the difference between autism and Asperger's is primarily one of functioning ability and communication skills, many clinicians prefer to think of these two disorders as the Autistic Spectrum Disorders to reflect the higher and lower levels of functioning on a similar continuum.

## Educational Planning

Educational programs for children with autism emphasize early intervention and focus on increasing skills in communication, social, behavioral, and adaptive functioning. Often, it may be necessary to first address behavioral issues before an educational plan can be put into place. A *functional behavioral assessment* is often developed to determine which behaviors should be targeted for change. Once the behaviors are selected, and the situations that trigger these behaviors are identified, then a *behavioral intervention plan* can be developed to alter behavior patterns into more appropriate ways of responding. An example of a functional behavioral assessment and behavioral intervention plan are presented in Table 7-2.

## Meeting the Needs of Children with Autism

Children with autistic-like features can represent a wide range of functioning. Therefore, there is no single program or educational plan that will meet the needs of all children with autism. However, all programs should emphasize the importance of reinforcing common goals consistently in the home and school environments.

Educational planning should include:

- Consistency and predictability:
  *Children with autism will likely overreact to any changes in their program, even minor changes.*
- High degree of structure:
  *Structure will increase predictability, reduce anxiety resistance, and optimize the learning environment.*
- Maximum use of visual supports to illustrate verbal comments:
  *Because language is often impaired, children with autism tend to perform better on tasks that use manipulatives (blocks, shapes) or rely on their stronger visual skills.*
- Breaking down complex tasks into small steps:
  *Children with autism have difficulty with abstract concepts, or those that require sequential processing.*

Table 7-2.    A sample Functional Behavioral Assessment and Behavior
                 Intervention Plan.

George is not successful academically because he does not complete his schoolwork.
Based on observation and interviews, the resulting FBA and BIP were developed by
the school psychologist to help George increase his productivity in the classroom.

| | |
|---|---|
| Problem Behaviors Identified | High number of off-task behaviors (looking around the room, staring into space, playing with his pencil, talking to his peers). |
| Conditions occurring before the behavior occurs | Teacher is working with another student; Teacher is writing on the blackboard. |
| Conditions occurring after the behavior occurs | Teacher reprimands George for not having his class work finished; Teacher sends unfinished work home. |
| Function of the behavior | George does not have to finish his work in class (escape/avoidance); George's mother helps him with his homework (attention/avoidance). |

Based on the previous FBA, the following BIP was developed:

| | |
|---|---|
| Specific Goals | 1. Increase on-task behavior. 2. George will complete his seatwork assignments with 80 percent accuracy. 3. George will do his homework independently, with 80 percent accuracy. |
| Interventions | 1. George will receive one "star" for each completed in-class assignment. 2. George will remain after school to complete missing in-class assignments. 3. George will receive one "star" for each completed homework assignment. 4. Parent will sign completed homework sheet. 5. Stars can be traded in for free time or to purchase items at the school store. |

- Reinforce tasks completed at school with similar tasks at home:
  *This will increase the opportunity to generalize information across situations, rather isolate learning into specific situations.*

## What the Research Says About Treatment

Based on several studies in the field, the consensus is that, at a minimum, successful early intervention should include individualized and systematic instruction, intense programming effort, and parent involvement in the educational process. Although controversy exists regarding which is ultimately the best program, two programs have documented research support of their positive impact on learning potential: the UCLA ABA Program by Lovaas and the Treatment and Education of Autistic and related Communication handicapped CHildren (TEACCH) Program.

O. Ivar Lovaas developed the UCLA ABA Program at the University of California at Los Angeles (UCLA). This program involves intensive programming (forty hours per week over a three-year period) in the clinic and home environments.

---

**ABA Program Three-Year Goals:**

- **Year One:** Increase compliance, decrease inappropriate behavior

- **Year Two:** Increase social play and language

- **Year Three:** Emotion expression and pre-academic skills: refining skills for integration into school system

---

Lovaas and his team of graduate students used a variety of behavioral techniques to reward increasingly more appropriate behaviors over this intense period of training. The time was extensive but the follow-up outcomes were very positive, with almost half the children in the program receiving promotions to the second grade requiring little or no special education support.

The TEACCH Program was developed in the early 1970s by Eric Schopler. The TEACCH program is motivated by the belief that children will learn to communicate in order to reach their goals. For example, if a child is thirsty, and the only way he is going to get a drink is to say "juice," then the child will learn to communicate. Rather than teach language as an academic subject, the focus in this program is developing the child's awareness of the practical use of language to satisfy everyday needs. The program also includes visual charts and displays to assist children with autism to better understand more abstract concepts, such as time and space.

**Want to learn more about these programs?** Readers can find contact information to obtain more information about these two programs and more at http://www.teacch.com and http://www.lovaas.com.

## Emotional Disturbance

The IDEA 2004 definition of emotional disturbance focuses on emotional or behavioral problems that *interfere with educational performance* in one of five areas:

1. An inability to learn that is not explained by intellectual, sensory, or health factors
2. An inability to develop or maintain interpersonal relationships with peers or teachers
3. Age-inappropriate behaviors
4. Pervasive mood of unhappiness or depression
5. Tendency to exhibit physical symptoms or fears associated with school or personal problems

IDEA 2004's definition of emotional disturbance also includes the category of *schizophrenia,* a severe emotional disorder, although this disorder is rarely diagnosed in children. According to the Surgeon General's report on *Children and Mental Health,* published in 2000, almost 21 percent of children—or approximately 1 in 5—in the United States between 9 and 17 years of age have a diagnosable mental disorder. In the 2000 to 2001 academic year, the U.S. Department of Education reported in its Twenty-Fourth Annual Report to Congress that approximately 472,000 children and youth were receiving special education and related services for emotional disturbance.

### Associated Features

All children can demonstrate fears, anxieties, and aggressive behaviors from time to time in response to specific events, such as worries related to school success or peer pressure. However, children with emotional disturbance demonstrate disturbed emotional responses as a dominant or pervasive reaction to the majority of environmental circumstances. Some children demonstrate characteristics of *externalizing behaviors* (acting out, aggression, or behavioral problems), while other children respond primarily by *internalizing their feelings* (depression or anxiety), or transferring these reactions into feelings of physical discomfort (somatic complaints). Some children demonstrate a mix of both externalizing (aggression) and internalizing (anxiety/depression) responses, a condition called *comorbidity.*

Children with emotional disturbance experience difficulties coping with environmental stressors and often display immaturity in emotional development, evident in poor coping skills, poor ability to regulate their emotions, and in increased tendencies to respond with inflated emotional reactions.

## Externalizing Behaviors

Children who act out often come to the attention of teachers and parents long before their internalizing peers. Aggressive children often experience social problems and can be rejected by their peers due to their disruptive behaviors. Some of these children may also become school bullies who terrorize and intimidate their more vulnerable peers. Impulsive in their responses, they may get into trouble because they act before they think about the consequences of their actions.

Researchers suggest that many aggressive children interpret ambivalent cues as intentionally aggressive and respond with an aggressively defensive response. These researchers also have found that social skills training to interpret social cues more accurately can be of benefit to these children.

> **Did you know?** Although it was once thought that girls were less aggressive than boys, researchers are now finding that girls often display aggression toward peers but in ways that are different from boys' physical threats. Rather than fight physically, girls will often engage in "relational aggression" by circulating damaging rumors to peers about a victim who is often unaware of why others are turning against her.

## Internalizing Behaviors

Children who are anxious may often withdraw or avoid situations about which they feel anxious or unsure. These children may complain of many physical problems and discomfort (headaches, stomachaches) resulting in visits to the school nurse or family doctor, however, there is often no physical reason that can be linked to these aches and pains. For some children, anxiety may increase around particularly stressful times, due to performance anxiety related to exams or standardized testing. Although fears are common in children, some children may experience debilitating fears and phobias and arrange their lives around rituals (repeated counting, checking, or hand washing) they develop in order to avoid fears related to issues of safety or contamination. Other anxious responses might be evident in *school refusals (a child refusing to attend school)*, after a lengthy illness, or anxieties about separating from a parent, especially after an accident or fear of loss.

Childhood depression is often difficult to detect because young children do not have the ability to understand or express the nature of these complex feelings. Often, young children who are depressed appear more irritable than sad, and can act out their depressed feelings aggressively. Some children demonstrate rapid mood swings that escalate between heightened emotional reactivity (hyper responsiveness) and irritability: a condition called bipolar disorder.

## Severe Emotional Disturbance

Some children may experience emotional disturbance that is significantly more severe than their peers who have mild to moderate emotional problems. If the severity of the emotional disturbance results in fears of safety for either the child (self-destructive behaviors) or the peer environment (threats to others), an alternative educational placement may be required, either on a temporary (such as a forty-five-day program) or more intensive (residential placement) basis.

**Did you know?** IDEA 2004 has changed the time of an alternative placement from forty-five calendar days to forty-five school days. Although the educational placement may be changed, the burden is now on the parent to appeal the decision.

## Educational Planning

As noted initially, IDEA 2004 is most concerned with how the child's disability, in this case emotional disturbance, impacts on *educational performance*. Therefore, educational planning for children with emotional disturbance will need to incorporate emotional and behavioral support systems into the IEP. A Functional Behavioral Assessment (FBA) and a Behavior Intervention Plan (BIP), such as the one presented in Table 7-2, may be necessary before it is possible to address specific learning goals. Positive behavioral interventions may be written into the IEP to assist the child in the regular or special class program. Related services such as individual or group counseling, self-esteem and anger management programs, or social skills programs might also be recommended to assist in the development of more positive and appropriate behavioral patterns. Programs may be accessed through the school or in the community. Often, a multiagency support system can be developed to provide comprehensive services support for families in need.

**Remember that** educational performance can be adversely affected by an inability to learn or establish positive interpersonal relationships, and medical management may be necessary to stabilize mood swings or aggressive impulses.

Parents who have children with emotional disturbance can find helpful information to additional resources in Appendix F and Wilens's book on medications cited in the References.

## Mental Retardation

As we mentioned previously, although IDEA 2004 provides federal guidelines, each state may have slightly different ways of determining who may be eligible for classification under certain categories of disability. The category of mental retardation is a good example of this. For example, while all states require evidence of subaverage IQ and impaired adaptive functioning as part of the eligibility criteria for educable mentally handicapped, educable mentally retarded, or mental retardation, the actual scores used to determine if a child qualifies for the program vary from state to state. Parents are often frustrated to learn that even though a child may qualify for EMH/EMR/MR status based on IQ and adaptive functioning, they may not qualify for services under this category, if their academic skills do not also fall within this specified range. This may also be frustrating because their child may qualify in one state, but not in another where the eligibility requirements are different.

Chapter 5 discussed how learning potential or intelligence is calculated based on ability scores relative to age expectations. With these criteria in mind, the majority of classification systems consider an IQ below 70 to be within the realm of the mental retardation range. Remember that approximately 2 percent of the population would score below an IQ of 70. Given that IQ scores are about 95 percent accurate, we can also add a + or − 5 to produce a range that takes this error factor into consideration. This would establish a potential IQ cutoff range for mental retardation between 65 and 75 (IQ of 70 + or − 5).

**Remember that** in order to establish functioning within the range of mental retardation requires not only an IQ below the Average Range but also evidence of adaptive functioning deficits in at least two areas.

## The Range of Mental Retardation

When we talk about cutoff scores, we are basically referring to the upper threshold that marks a territory. For example, mental retardation can range from an IQ of 75 (at the top) to below an IQ of 20. Given the extent of this range, there is great variability in characteristics of children whose scores fall within this wide range. Although the range is large, the vast majority (85 percent) of children with mental retardation are within the mild range (IQ range from 55 to 75). Children at the lower ranges (IQ less than 40) often have multiple disabilities.

Generally, mental retardation refers to limitations in mental ability that may influence daily living and adaptation to the environment in several areas of functioning, including daily living skills, communication skills, academic skills, social skills, self-help skills, health and safety, community use, and vocational potential.

## Associated Characteristics

Children with mental retardation often encounter problems learning at the same rate and depth of understanding compared with their nondisabled peers. They may require many repetitions to acquire a concept and may be unable to grasp concepts that are too abstract. Developmental milestones (talking, crawling, sitting, walking, or toilet training) may be delayed. Some children with mental retardation have a specific syndrome, such as Down's syndrome (caused by a chromosomal defect), or fetal alcohol syndrome (caused by maternal alcohol consumption during pregnancy). Children with mental retardation due to specific syndromes often have associated physical characteristics (poor muscle tone and slant eyes associated with Down's syndrome, or flattened nose and widely spaced eyes associated with fetal alcohol syndrome).

### Educational Planning

Due to the wide range of abilities possible within this category, a comprehensive psychological assessment is recommended to provide adequate insight into a child's strengths and weaknesses, prior to determining special education eligibility and, if necessary, developing an IEP. Some children may require minimal accommodations to their educational program, while others may require educational programs that address significant concerns in the behavioral, social, emotional, and adaptive areas.

Often it will be important to segment goals into smaller steps to ensure understanding and allow increased time for repetition and consolidation of skills. Parents and teachers can increase a child's opportunities for success by working together to provide a consistent home and school program that allows for generalizing skills across the different environments.

Parents who have children with mental retardation can find helpful links to additional resources in Appendix F.

## Specific Learning Disabilities

Students with specific learning disabilities (SLD) differ from students with mental retardation, because children with SLD have average to above average intelligence, while children with MR have below average intelligence. Although students with mental retardation often experience academic difficulties, these difficulties are often the result of weaknesses in general problem-solving ability. However, children with SLD have a neurological disorder that has an impact on how they process information in a number of possible areas, such as *receiving information, classifying or sorting information, storing information, retrieving information from storage, and expressing information*. These children show a significant gap between their learning potential (intelligence) and their actual academic performance. Children with specific learning disabilities are not a homogenous group because difficulties can exist in one area or a unique combination of two or more of the areas listed previously. The nature of how problems in information processing can interfere with learning for children with SLDs is illustrated in Table 7-3. Problems in processing information can occur at the beginning of the learning process (input

*Table 7-3.     How information-processing problems can interfere with learning.*

| Area of Learning Interference | Associated Processing Difficulties |
|---|---|
| **Input of Information:** Recognition of information; receptive skills | **Recognition of Information:** Sensory input (vision, hearing, touch, smell)<br>***Requires the ability to*** selectively attend to information and discriminate sights (letter orientation, spatial cues) and sounds (auditory discrimination; phonetic awareness). |
| **Integration of Information:** Coding, storage, integration, and retrieval of information | **Interpretation of Information:** Making sense of the information received; Organizing information (sorting, sequencing, linking to previous learning); Storing information (having a mental filing cabinet); Retrieving information (being able to remember how the information was stored, e.g., file names)<br>***Requires the ability to*** concentrate; organize, and sequence information; perform mental manipulations (working memory), and retrieve information from long-term memory; understand cause-and-effect relationships; and associate visual with auditory and motor information (linking sounds to symbols and recalling how to graphically execute a letter). |
| **Output of Information: Responding to Information** Executing appropriate responses to information based on the input and integration of information | **Expression:** Communicating through oral, written, or motor responses<br>***Requires the ability to*** inhibit inappropriate responses while initiating more appropriate responses ("stop and think"); recognition of appropriate *tempo* (too slow or too quick to respond); *spatial* (too close/too far: personal space); and *intensity* (inflated reactions or minimal reaction). |

or receipt of information), in the integration and retrieval stages, or in the final output stage.

> **Three Stages of Information Processing:**
>
> **INPUT ⇒ INTEGRATION ⇒ OUTPUT**

Some children may experience difficulties in all stages of learning. As can be anticipated, given the wide range of potential problem areas that can be influenced by processing problems, children with SLD can encounter mild to severe academic difficulties.

## Prevalence and Types of Learning Disabilities

According to the U.S. Department of Education, approximately 5 percent of children enrolled in public schools have some form of SLD. Although it was once thought that males were more likely to demonstrate SLD than females, more recent studies suggest that this is not the case. Learning disabilities can be inherited, result from problems during pregnancy or birth (lack of oxygen or prematurity), or result from environmental accidents (brain injury) or toxins (exposure to lead-based paint). The following chart presents a list of the more common types of specific learning disabilities and the areas that these disabilities affect:

| Type of SLD | Problem Area | Problems with | Problem Example |
|---|---|---|---|
| **Dyscalculia** | Math | Recall of math facts; Math word problems; Math concepts; Time and money | Unable to count by 2s, 3s; Not knowing what information is irrelevant in word problems |
| **Dysgraphia** | Written expression | Illegible handwriting & poor letter spacing; Spelling; Organizing written information | Poor letter and number formations & spacing between letters; Written output is poorly organized & difficulty beginning written tasks |
| **Dyslexia** | Reading, Spelling | Sequencing letters, sounds, words; Confusion in direc- | Letter: reversals (b and d); inversions (p and d); |

| Type of SLD | Problem Area | Problems with | Problem Example |
|---|---|---|---|
|  |  | tions and spatial orientation (left and right) | transpositions (gril/girl); Word reversals: (saw/was) |
| **Dyspraxia** | Fine motor skills | Manual dexterity; Coordination. | Fine motor tasks: drawing, cutting with scissors, tying shoes. |
| **Nonverbal Learning Disorder** | Visual-spatial organization; motor coordination; math skills | Strength in the verbal areas; Poor sense of spatial awareness; Poor social skills | Poor number sense; Poor social skills due to lack of awareness of subtle visual/spatial social cues: facial expressions and personal space |

*Educational Planning*

Although some of the more severe learning disabilities can be detected at an early age, it is often unlikely that SLD will be evident in school-age children prior to the second or third grade. One reason for the later recognition of SLD is that many children experience processing problems due to immaturity rather than neurological deficits. For example, letter confusions and reversals are quite common prior to 8 years of age, and these tendencies often self-correct with increasing maturity. Another reason is that it is difficult to obtain evidence of being significantly behind academically (rule of thumb is usually two years behind) until a child is in the third grade. However, it is still important to monitor your child's progress if your child demonstrates a number of the problem areas outlined in Table 7-3.

If you or your child's teacher suspects that your child has a specific learning disability, a psychological assessment can provide valuable information to verify whether the problem is due to a specific learning disability. The assessment information can also provide guidelines for better understanding how to develop an IEP that addresses your child's specific areas of concern with accommodations that are suited to your child's special needs. Because many children with SLD encounter academic problems, they may feel inadequate, resulting in lowered self-esteem, or may act out their frustrations, causing behavioral problems. It is important to discuss with your child's support team how to help your child develop a more positive self-image or more appropriate ways of relieving frustration, both at home and at school. Children with SLD often experience difficulties in their social relationships for many of the same reasons that they have academic difficulties. They may fail to recognize social cues or may have a poor sense of timing in social circles. Social skills training programs can be an effective way of helping your child to understand and respond to social cues in a more appropriate way.

Children with SLD may also have difficulties transferring information from situation to situation, so it will be especially important to work toward increased home and school communication.

Parents who have children with specific learning disabilities can find helpful links to additional resources in Appendix F.

## Attention Deficit/Hyperactivity Disorder

Although ADHD is one of the most commonly diagnosed disorders afflicting approximately 3 percent to 7 percent of school-age children, its causes are not yet clearly understood. However, recent research has uncovered less brain activity in areas of the brain devoted to planning, sustained attention, and impulse control in children with ADHD, as well as certain brain chemicals that are not performing properly (the neurotransmitters dopamine and norepinephrine). As a result, children with ADHD will demonstrate a combination of brain-based behaviors noted in symptoms of *inattention, impulsivity, and hyperactivity.*

### Different Types of ADHD

Although many people are aware of the hyperactive-impulsive type of ADHD, few people realize that there are actually three different forms of ADHD based on how the inattentive, impulsive, and hyperactive symptoms are expressed.

**ADHD: Predominantly Hyperactive-Impulsive Type**   A diagnosis of *ADHD hyperactive-impulsive type* is made if the child demonstrates six out of nine possible hyperactive and impulsive symptoms. Hyperactive symptoms are described as:

- Fidgets
- Leaves seat when required to sit
- Runs, climbs excessively, or restless (teen)
- Problems playing quietly
- Always on the go
- Excessive talking

Impulsive symptoms include:

- Answers before question is finished
- Problems with turn taking
- Interrupts other people's conversations or activities

Children who meet the criteria for the hyperactive-impulsive type of ADHD often encounter academic difficulties due to tendencies to sacrifice accuracy for speed and social problems due to their impulsive, impatient, and invasive behaviors (tend to infringe on others' territories). These children also tend to be more disruptive to classroom routines because of their impulsive, loud, and hyperactive nature.

According to Russell Barkley, a researcher who has studied ADHD for many years, children with ADHD impulsive-hyperactive type often have comorbid (occurring at the same time) oppositional and defiant behaviors (oppositional defiant disorder, or, ODD) that begin in the home and eventually spill over into the school environment. Barkley also suggests that a major problem of children with this form of ADHD is that they cannot inhibit unwanted behaviors to allow for the necessary time required to think through the problem and use other resources to help in the problem-solving process. As a result, unwanted behaviors (more attractive and less academically goal-oriented behaviors) often serve as roadblocks to achieving more success-oriented goals. Often, these children will act without thinking (impulsively) and unintentionally find themselves in problem situations.

**ADHD: Predominantly Inattentive Type**   Less is known about the *Inattentive Type of ADHD*. There are several reasons for the lack of information on this type of the disorder compared with those with impulsive and hyperactive behaviors. Children who meet the criteria for the inattentive type present with a host of more subtle and less-obvious behaviors. These children are often undiagnosed and can appear lazy or unmotivated to the untrained eye. Children with the predominantly inattentive type of ADHD, sometimes referred to as ADD, must meet six out of nine possible symptoms. These symptoms are:

1. Poor attention to details (misses key parts of information)
2. Problems sustaining attention in boring/repetitive tasks
3. High level of distractibility; distractions interfere with task completion
4. Insufficient attention to details and organizational framework
5. Doesn't "seem" to listen
6. Problems organizing information
7. Avoids and dislikes tasks requiring sustained mental effort
8. Forgetfulness
9. Loss of tools required to accomplish tasks (misplaces notes, pens, pencils, books, and so on)

**Did you know?** Many adults who seek counseling for depression are later diagnosed with ADHD. Their depression is a result of years of feeling that they have not accomplished their goals, despite being at or well above the intellectual level of their peers.

Children who have the predominantly inattentive type of ADHD are often underdiagnosed and misunderstood compared with their more hyperactive and impulsive peers. It was once thought that this type of ADHD was more closely aligned with females compared to males; however, recent research suggests that this form of ADHD is evident to a comparable extent in boys and girls. Children with this form of ADHD tend to be the most misunderstood types of children and tend to be labeled as *underachievers, unmotivated, or lazy.* The inability to *tune in* to the environmental demands of the moment has caused significant frustration for these children, their teachers, and their parents.

**ADHD: Combined Type**    Children who match the criteria for both the hyperactive-impulsive type and the inattentive type are designated as the *combined type* of ADHD. As might be anticipated, children who fall within this classification experience the most significant difficulties academically and in their peer relationships. Similar to their peers with the hyperactive impulsive type of ADHD, these children will experience significant difficulties due to deficits in areas of the brain responsible for *executive functioning.*

> ***Executive functioning*** is similar to the executive director of a major organization. The brain's executive functions are responsible for ensuring that tasks are executed in ways that involve planning, organization, goal orientation, and monitoring of results.

Children who experience many impulsive and hyperactive behaviors may demonstrate executive functioning deficits in the major areas needed to perform tasks in an organized and goal-directed manner. These children have difficulty inhibiting or controlling their behavior, which results in an inability to block unwanted behaviors that can seriously interfere with reaching one's goal. Problems in regulating emotional control often results in these children exhibiting inflated responses to both negative and positive situations, quickly escalating out of control.

*Educational Planning*

There is no single test that can be used to diagnose ADHD. However, diagnosis of ADHD should involve more than just a visit to the family physician. There is a need to consider whether the behaviors are pervasive across situations because ADHD is not exclusive to the school situation. If a child has ADHD, the symptoms will be evident (to a lesser or greater extent) across all situations, including the home and school environments. The other difficulty in diagnosing ADHD is that many of the symptoms of ADHD share similar features of other diagnoses, such as anxiety, child abuse, depression, bipolar disorder, or posttraumatic stress disorder. Children with ADHD often also have comorbid learning disabilities. For these reasons, it is vital that a comprehensive assessment be conducted by a licensed professional to rule out other reasons for the symptoms or additional contributing factors. At a minimum, teachers and parents should complete behavior-rating scales; school personnel should conduct a classroom observation; and parents should be asked to provide a developmental and family history to help provide information related to the symptoms displayed at home. If medication is prescribed by the physician, rating scales can provide an excellent way of monitoring the effectiveness of the medication.

### 504 Plans and IDEA 2004 Category of Other Health Impairment

Under Section 504, children with ADHD can qualify for accommodations to their program to assist them to be more successful academically. Some possible accommodations might include extended time to complete assignments, reducing the length of assignments, and/or extended time for test taking.

Under IDEA 2004, children with ADHD may qualify for special education and related services under the category of *Other Health Impairment (OHI),* due to an impairment in "vitality or alertness, including heightened alertness to environmental stimuli, that results in limited alertness with respect to the educational environment" (IDEA: Code of Federal Regulations). For children who are evaluated by the school system to establish eligibility for special education services, parents will find that eligibility criteria will differ depending on the specific policies of the state.

**Did you know?** States differ on how eligibility for special education services are determined for children with ADHD under OHI. For example, in Florida, children can qualify for special education and related services under OHI only after an exhaustive assessment has ruled out all other potential contributing factors, including mental retardation, emotional disturbance, and specific learning disability. Furthermore, children must have had a 504 Plan for at least six months that was not successful in meeting their needs. A medical statement of their ADHD condition is also required.

According to an extensive multisite research project (MTA Cooperative Group) sponsored by the National Institute of Mental Health (NIMH) and the U.S. Department of Education (Office of Special Education) four core features were highlighted as interventions for ADHD:

1. Educating parents and teachers about ADHD and the types of accommodations required
2. Medical management of the disorder due to the neuro-biochemical nature of ADHD

3.  Behavior intervention and strategies to manage problems in areas of compliance, impulse control, delay of gratification, and task completion

4.  Educational interventions to target weak academic progress due to difficulties in areas of:

    •   Task initiation (getting started)

    •   Task completion

    •   Increased on-task behavior

    •   Successful transitions between classes or programs

    •   Increased organizational skills (use of an agenda)

    •   Improved interactions with others

    •   Improved home and school communication

    •   Improved skill levels in note taking, study skills, time management, and prioritizing demands

Parents who have children with ADHD can find helpful links to additional resources in Appendix F.

# STEP THREE:

## Understanding the

## Special Education Process

# CHAPTER 8

# Labels: The Good, the Bad, and the Ugly

As we discussed in Chapter 1, IDEA 2004 outlines the various categories of problems leading to special education services. These labels are used to categorize behavior and are the gateway to providing your child with specific services that may be required for success (see Table 8-1).

## Reasons for Naming the Problem

One of the goals in education is to include children with special needs in the regular education classroom as much as possible. Therefore, children with special needs will most likely have contact with regular education teachers on an ongoing basis, and these teachers may not have experience in working with children having a particular disorder.

Usually, a psychologist or school psychologist conducts an assessment and diagnoses a child to determine into which diagnostic category the child's problems may fall. The child may have an emotional problem, a learning disability, mental retardation, or some other disabling condition recognized by IDEA 2004. But just what do these terms mean? Let's take a child with an emotional disorder, for example. The term *emotionally disturbed* does not really provide a great deal of information about that child. His problem may have been placed in this category for a variety of reasons. Perhaps he has a social phobia, is depressed, feels anxious, or is having difficulty coping with school. So, the term by itself doesn't provide much information about the child's problems, although it *does* tell us about the category in which the child will receive services. That category, which is directly related to a diagnosis such as depression, generalized anxiety disorder, learning disabled, or autistic, helps others to understand some of the child's problems and helps school personnel better understand the child's needs. Every child is different, and children whose diagnosis falls within the same category can be very different from one another.

*Table 8-1.*     *What's in a label?*

Naming a child's problem and giving it a label means access to and assistance from a variety of school personnel. Use this information only as a guide, because some school districts, particularly those that are small, do not employ all these personnel.

| Disability | School Personnel Who May Be Involved |
| --- | --- |
| Autism | Regular Education Teacher, Special Education Teacher, Autism Specialist, School Psychologist, Speech-Language Pathologist, Occupational Therapist, Physical Therapist, Assistive Technology Specialist, Adaptive Physical Education Teacher |
| Deaf-Blindness | Regular Education Teacher, Special Education Teacher, Vision Teacher, School Psychologist, Assistive Technology Specialist |
| Emotional Disturbance | Regular Education Teacher, Special Education Teacher, School Psychologist, School Counselor, Behavioral Specialist |
| Hearing Impairment | Regular Education Teacher, Special Education Teacher, Audiologist, Speech Language Pathologist, Interpreter, School Psychologist |
| Mental Retardation | Regular Education Teacher, Special Education Teacher, School Psychologist, Speech-Language Pathologist, Occupational Therapist, Physical Therapist, Assistive Technology Specialist, Adaptive Physical Education Teacher |
| Multiple Disabilities | Regular Education Teacher, Special Education Teacher, School Psychologist, School Counselor, Speech-Language Pathologist, Occupational Therapist, Physical Therapist, Assistive Technology Specialist, School Nurse, Adaptive Physical Education Teacher |
| Orthopedic Impairment | Regular Education Teacher, Special Education Teacher, Physical Therapist, Occupational Therapist, School Psychologist, Adaptive Physical Education Teacher |
| Other Health Impairment | Regular Education Teacher, Special Education Teacher, School Psychologist, School Nurse |
| Specific Learning Disability | Regular Education Teacher, Special Education Teacher, School Psychologist, Occupational Therapist, Assistive Technology Specialist |

| Speech or Language Impairment | Regular Education Teacher, Special Education Teacher, Speech-Language Pathologist, School Psychologist |
|---|---|
| Traumatic Brain Injury | Regular Education Teacher, Special Education Teacher, School Psychologist, School Nurse, Occupational Therapist, Adaptive Physical Education Teacher |
| Visual Impairment (incl. Blindness) | Regular Education Teacher, Special Education Teacher, Vision Teacher, Assistive Technology Specialist, Mobility Instructor, School Psychologist, Adaptive Physical Education Teacher |

**Did you know?** *School psychologists* have the highest entry-level education of any school personnel. To be credentialed in their state, they must possess an advanced graduate degree, obtain supervised experience in the schools, complete a supervised, full-time, one-year internship, and pass a state and/or national examination. Some are also a Nationally Certified School Psychologist (NCSP), board certified by the American Board of Professional Psychology (ABPP), and licensed for private practice.

## Negative Aspects of Categorization

Let's address some of the drawbacks of categorizing a child's problems. Some will argue there are many reasons why we should not place children's academic and behavior problems into specific categories, some of which we will address here.

### Lowered Teacher Expectations

Teacher expectations may be lowered for a child identified with a disability. This can turn into a self-fulfilling prophecy, where teachers with low expectations for performance and growth may discourage children. As a result, children may achieve at a lower level. Children with a learning disability, for example, may be perceived as not being smart, being lazy, difficult to teach, and unable to learn a lot of information. While children with a learning disability will require special teaching techniques, and accommodations such as teacher notes, additional time to complete assignments, or a peer tutor; these changes to their program do not mean these children are necessarily difficult to teach. The truth is that children with a learning disability *can* learn a lot of information, but it may take them longer to learn it since they may process information either differently or more slowly than children without a disability.

You can help your child by making his teacher's expectation remain high. In Chapter 9, we'll talk about the contents of an IEP, which will create yearly goals for your child. If your child does not qualify for special education services, we encourage you to meet with your child's teacher on a regular basis to ensure that the expectations set for your child are appropriate. Chapter 11 will discuss ways to maximize parent-teacher communication.

---

**Did you know?** The book *Pygmalion in the Classroom: Teacher Expectation and Pupils' Intellectual Development,* written by Robert Rosenthal and Lenore Jacobson (2003), states that when teachers expect children to do well and show intellectual growth, they do, but when teachers do not have these expectations, performance and growth are not as encouraged and may actually be discouraged in a number of ways. This is known as the *Pygmalion phenomenon.*

---

## A Label's Long-Lasting Effects

Categorizing a problem and giving it a name, or label, sometimes results in that name lasting a long time, sometimes for life. Even when it no longer applies, the person is still perceived as having the characteristics associated with that problem. While most children who are blind or mentally retarded, for example, will retain these problems into adulthood, a child with a health impairment may not. These children may outgrow their impairment and no longer show signs of their medical condition as an adult. In a similar manner, children with a learning disability may learn to cope with their disorder.

## Insufficient Time to Rule Out Other Problems

Naming a child's problem too quickly may prevent a school psychologist or a physician from investigating other potential problems. For example, many disorders look like ADHD. Problems such as an emotional disorder, a learning disability, or mental retardation can have behavioral characteristics similar to a child with ADHD. While some of these disorders will occur with ADHD, other disorders sometimes mimic ADHD, and a thorough evaluation by a school psychologist is needed to help establish the causes for the child's problems. Once a thorough psychoeducational assessment is conducted, a school psychologist can then determine what is potentially wrong with a child and decide how the school can help the child learn in the best possible way.

You should always ask the school psychologist to rule out the presence of other disorders, which can be done by doing further evaluation of your child or through the use of questionnaires completed by you, your child's teacher, and possibly your child, depending on the problem being ruled out. In addition, a physician should be consulted to rule out medical issues as the cause of the problem.

## Child's Reaction to the Problem

Most children don't like to be different. They don't like to stand out in any way, whether it's their clothing, their hairstyle, or the car the parent uses to drive them to school. So, a child's knowledge that he has a disability can lead to certain self-perceptions. Parents are often torn between telling their child about the disability and withholding information, for the sake of trying to protect their child. Some parents don't tell a child that a disability is present, thinking that this information can harm the child. Other parents choose to tell their child that he has a problem, or disability, so that he knows that he may need to work a little harder than his peers. The truth is that most children know they are having problems, so protecting them from knowing isn't really the issue.

We feel that it is important to talk to your child about his disability. It's okay to name it; like most people, we feel better leaving a doctor's office with a diagnosis rather than thinking we have a mysterious illness. Explaining the nature of the disability will help your child to understand why he is getting extra help in school when most other children are not. You should first point out that he has not done anything wrong. Each child learns differently, and some children may learn more slowly than others, whether it is because of problems understanding what he learns or because your child's feelings get in the way of her learning. It is kind of like athletic or musical ability; some children have it, while others do not, and even those who have it must work hard to improve. The same is true for learning. Not telling your children he has a disability may lead him to think that he is "stupid" or "bad," and this can often lead to great frustration and lowered self-esteem. As we previously mentioned, he may need to work a bit harder than the other children to keep up with his work. He should know that you and his teachers will provide support both in and out of the classroom. You may want to provide your child with fiction books that include stories about children who have similar problems, which he can read or you can read to him. Regardless of the disability your child may have, you love him the same as you did before you found out about this problem.

### Parental Shame

When a child is found to have a disability, parents sometimes feel ashamed and think they are the cause of the problem. While some disabilities have a genetic basis to them, others occur because of disease or accidents. Regardless of the cause, there is no reason why you should blame yourself for your child's disability.

Many parents feel a variety of emotions once they find out that their child has a disability. Sadness is the emotion we encounter most often because, depending on the disability, parents realize that the vision they had for their child's future has been altered or dramatically changed. So, if you feel this way, we want you to know that you are not alone. And so that you do not feel alone, we suggest you seek out a support group in your area. If there isn't one, you may find one on the Internet. We believe that a support group can provide you with comfort from other parents who are experiencing the same feelings as you. These parents may have been working with teachers and other professionals for many years and probably have a wealth of information that may benefit you. You may learn about interventions that have worked for others, and while it does not guarantee that they'll work for you, it's something worth trying. We will include our own recommendations later in the book. If you are interested in a support group, some are listed in Appendix F. You may also wish to contact one of the many organizations we list, since they often provide referrals to support groups. We hope that you will take advantage of all they have to offer.

## Positive Aspects of Categorization

Categorizing a child's problem helps school personnel to understand and meet the child's needs. Children with a disability may require the services of specific school personnel like an occupational or physical therapist. These personnel, in conjunction with teachers, can work together to provide an atmosphere that is conducive to the best learning situation possible for your child. Let's take a look at the special education categories and discuss some of the accommodations or programs that may be available for each area.

### Autism

Children with autism require a structured, individualized curriculum that places an emphasis on functional skills, language/communication, and behavior management. Speech therapy is often necessary, and occupational therapy (OT) and physical therapy (PT) may be needed if fine and gross motor weaknesses are noted. Your child's case manager should be someone who has experience working with children with autism, as it takes some coordination of the various specialties to provide adequate services to these children.

**Did you know?** The Centers for Disease Control and Prevention (CDC) report that the exact number children in the United States who currently have autism or a related disorder is unknown. Recent figures suggest that nearly 80,000 children and adults 6 through 21 years of age are classified as having autism under IDEA. You can read more about this report at http://www.cdc.gov/ncbddd/dd/aic/about/.

### Deaf-Blindness

Children who are deaf and blind require assistance with orientation and mobility. This special training helps children to learn how to move around safely, efficiently, and independently. An example of training in orientation would be to help a child understand how to navigate around his or her house or classroom. Mobility, on the other hand, actually involves moving. Once a child has become oriented to the home or classroom, getting the child from one place to another becomes the goal. This can be accomplished by crawling, walking, or through the use of a wheelchair.

## Deafness

Children who are deaf may need a sign language interpreter. Many of these children use sign language to receive information and communicate. What goes on in the classroom is conveyed by the interpreter to the deaf children, and what is expressed by the deaf children is conveyed to the teacher and other children. Other accommodations may include lecture notes, visual and written instructions, written exams, visual behavioral cues, and amplification equipment.

## Emotional Disturbance

Children with an emotional disturbance may have a variety of diagnoses. Those with anxiety, depression, schizophrenia, or bipolar disorder would fall under this category. While many children do well in the general education classroom, some of them have severe behavioral difficulties that require a more restrictive setting. They may have frequent outbursts, throw chairs or desks, or be physically or verbally aggressive. In cases of severe behavior, it is best that these children be in a setting that is very structured and includes fewer peers. Some children may require individual or group counseling.

## Hearing Impairment

Children with a hearing impairment who don't meet the definition of deafness still need assistance, such as auditory training, oral and total communication instruction, and hearing aid training. While these children may have fewer communication problems than a child who is deaf, they may still have difficulties because of the hearing loss. Accommodations may include lecture notes, visual and written instructions, written exams, and visual behavioral cues.

## Mental Retardation

Children with mental retardation will have significant weaknesses in both intellectual functioning and adaptive behavior. Children with mental retardation fall in one of four categories: mild, moderate, severe, or profound. Significant modifications to the general curriculum may need to be implemented, depending on the severity of the disorder. Adaptive skills, which are skills needed to live, work, and play in the community, include care of oneself (dressing, toileting, bathing), communicating with others, social skills, and academics. These children may qualify for participation in a work program or vocational training.

**Did you know?** The U.S. National Library of Medicine reports that between 1,600 and 2,000 syndromes of congenital abnormalities (present at birth) are known to be associated with mental retardation. You can read more at http://www.nlm.nih.gov/mesh/jablonski/about_syndrome.html

## Multiple Disabilities

Children with multiple disabilities have special needs depending on the combination of disabilities. Multiple disabilities, or *concomitant impairments*, are a combination that causes severe educational needs that require special education services. Children with multiple disabilities require the coordination of various school personnel and health professionals, often for their entire education.

## Orthopedic Impairment

Children with an orthopedic impairment may have a range of orthopedic needs. An orthopedic impairment may be caused by a *congenital anomaly* (something that is unusual or different at birth), disease, or other causes. A congenital anomaly may include a missing limb or clubfoot. Bone tuberculosis, for example, would be an example of an anomaly causes by disease, while cerebral palsy or an amputation would fall under the "other" category. The services and expertise of a physical therapist are critical in assessing the child's continuing needs and tracking progress, which should occur on a regular basis.

**Did you know?** The American Physical Therapy Association was founded in 1921.

## Other Health Impairment

Children in this category are affected by a chronic or acute health problem. Many disorders fall in this category, including ADHD, asthma, epilepsy, leukemia, sickle cell anemia, and diabetes. It is difficult to suggest typical interventions since the range of disorders is so broad, but accommodations may include completing tests and assignments in a small group, extra time to complete tests or assignments, and the ability to make up work when school is missed for medical appointments.

## Specific Learning Disability

Children with a learning disability have significant weaknesses in one of seven areas: reading, reading comprehension, math calculation, math reasoning (solving problems), writing, listening comprehension (understanding what they hear), or speaking. These children need extra help, support, and encouragement. They often have difficulty learning at the same pace as others. Things like additional time completing assignments, a quiet place to work, abbreviated assignments, or tutoring may be needed. The accommodations implemented will depend on the age of your child and the severity of the disability.

## Speech or Language Impairment

Children with a speech or language impairment are likely be diagnosed with some form of a communication disorder. Problems with stuttering and articulation may be present, and the child may have a noticeable language or voice impairment. In the schools, speech-language pathologists (SLPs), also called speech therapists or speech teachers, work with children who have a variety of speech and language disorders. These disorders may be congenital or acquired, and may include feeding and swallowing disorders in infants and children, language-based learning disabilities, selective mutism, and right hemisphere brain damage. SLPs may help children to obtain normal speech patterns, get rid of their lisp, speak more intelligibly, or learn to retrieve words more easily.

**Did you know?** Speech-language pathologists who hold their "Cs" (Certificate of Clinical Competence) must possess a graduate degree, obtain supervised clinical observation/practice, complete a clinical fellowship, and pass a national examination.

## Traumatic Brain Injury

Children with a traumatic brain injury (TBI) have an acquired brain injury affecting specific parts of the brain. The external physical force, which could be an open or closed head injury, may have resulted in total or partial functional disability. Depending on the part of the brain injured, there will be impairments in things like cognition, language, speech, memory, attention, reasoning, abstract thinking, judgment, motor abilities, psychosocial behavior, and physical functions. The specific personnel needed and accommodations implemented will depend largely on the severity of the head injury.

## Visual Impairment (Including Blindness)

Children with a visual impairment or blindness may have partial sight or be completely blind. While some children are born with an impairment or blindness, others have acquired it through accidents or disease. These children may need books and textbooks on tape, Braille books, computer and typing skills, and assistance in getting around school. Teacher assistants and peer helpers may work with these children, particularly those who are younger or who recently became disabled.

## For More Information

An appropriate diagnosis allows parents to access a wealth of information including recent research and effective interventions. Appendix F contains a list of organizations that you may contact for more information. If you have access to the Internet, visiting each organization's Web site opens up a world of information to you, free of charge. You will find parenting tips, resource guides, treatment suggestions, and other helpful resources to assist you in better understanding your child's diagnosis and particular needs. The Council for Exceptional Children, for example, includes an Information Center on Disabilities and Gifted Education, where you will find fact sheets, information on research-based interventions, links to discussion groups, links to the laws, and more.

**Did you know?** The Council for Exceptional Children (CEC) is the largest international professional organization dedicated to improving educational outcomes for individuals with exceptionalities, children with disabilities, and/or the gifted.

# CHAPTER 9

# You and Me and the IEP

The IEP is perhaps the most important document in your child's education file. It helps to guide the delivery of special education services for children identified as qualifying for these services. It is *individualized* for each child, based on the child's needs, and is based on input from a variety of people. Parents often provide important feedback, and school personnel such as special and regular education teachers, teacher assistants, administrators, school psychologist, school counselor, speech-language pathologist, and occupational and physical therapists may each have important contributions to make regarding your child's needs.

## Preparing for the Meeting

Parents often feel nervous about attending this meeting. However, you shouldn't feel anxious because school personnel truly want to help your child. A little nervous energy is fine, as long as it does not interfere with your ability to fully understand what goes on during the meeting. If necessary, go for a walk or listen to relaxing music before the meeting.

We recommend that you write down all of your questions ahead of time, so feel free to bring a pen and take notes. While you will get a copy of the meeting minutes, it's best to write down some of the comments you'll hear about your child's strengths and weaknesses. You can tape-record a meeting, if necessary, but staff usually will be required to also tape the meeting (or make a copy of your tape). However, people at the meeting may be inhibited and may not speak as freely as they would if they were not being recorded. If you feel you *must* record the meeting, let the school know ahead of time so that staff can have a tape recorder and blank cassettes ready.

## Attending the IEP Meeting

Who will attend the IEP meeting? Most likely the regular education teacher, one or two special education teachers, a school administrator, school psychologist, and others who may have been involved in the evaluation of and ongoing services for your child (like a speech-language pathologist, physical therapist, or occupational therapist). You may bring someone with you to the meeting, and we always recommend that both parents try to attend the meeting if at all possible. An IEP is extremely important and requires input from both parents. Now that you know who is involved in helping to write it, let's turn our attention to the actual IEP.

## Letting the Paper Trail Begin

Although IEP forms vary from district to district, each contains the same basic information. Let's discuss the essential parts of an IEP.

> **Did you know?** An IEP is good for one year and must be revised yearly. Under a pilot program of the Individuals with Disabilities Education Improvement Act of 2004, fifteen states will have the option to pilot multiyear IEPs, which means an IEP can last for as many as three years. Parents still retain the right to request a yearly IEP.

### Present Level of Performance

Teacher input, homework and classwork assignments, tests, and observations all help to answer the question, "How is the child doing?" These sources address your child's current progress in the classroom. Any weaknesses indicating how your child is not meeting the goals of the general curriculum because of his disability will be noted.

### Annual Goals

The annual goal addresses your child's progress during the next twelve months. Goals may address academics, behavioral or physical needs, or socialization. IEP goals should be very clear, and they must be measurable, which means that a goal can be counted or observed. While all goals should be achievable, at any time you or the IEP team can call a meeting to adjust the annual goals. This is likely to occur if a child falls far behind and it is inconceivable that he will meet a particular goal(s) or if he is progressing at a faster-than-expected rate and has already met a goal(s).

Under IDEA 2004, short-term objectives are no longer mandatory unless a child is considered severely disabled, such as a child who has severe cognitive disabilities. Many of these students take alternative assessments, which are created by the IEP team and used in place of a national standardized achievement test like the Iowa Test of Basic Skills or Stanford Achievement Test. The alternative achievement standards created for these children would benefit from short-term objectives, more frequent review, and revision.

> **Did you know?** Under IDEA 2004, parents and the school district can agree not to convene an IEP meeting to make needed changes to the IEP. Instead, a written document can be created to amend or modify the current IEP. This new paperwork is sent to the parents who still have a right to request an IEP meeting so that they can be sure that their requests are incorporated into the revisions.

Another change under IDEA 2004 is to allow fifteen states to participate in a paperwork reduction pilot program. This change will provide an opportunity for states to allow parents and school districts the opportunity for long-term planning by offering the option of developing a comprehensive, multiyear IEP, not to exceed three years, rather than a yearly IEP. Parents still have the right to request a yearly IEP if they prefer that option. Changes to IEPs can be done via video conferences or conference calls if all IEP team members agree with the proposed changes.

> **Did you know?** All special education and related services must be provided at no cost to you.

## Special Education and Related Services/Supplementary Aids and Services

This area addresses the *special education services* a child will receive. Decisions are also made about things like extended school year, physical education, vocational education, and so forth. Physical or occupational therapy, and the frequency and duration of the visits, are considered *related services*. Some children may need help from a teacher assistant, a person to take notes, or access to a time-out room, which are referred to as *supplementary aids and services*. In addition, any program modifications or supports for school personnel, such as computer-assisted devices or a training workshop on autism for the regular education teacher, are included here.

## Participation with Nondisabled Children

In this section, a determination is made regarding the amount of time the child may spend in the regular education classroom. The goal always is to keep a child in the least-restrictive environment to the maximum extent possible. In most cases, this is a regular education classroom. If a child's behavior is so severe that transitioning him back and forth between special and regular education settings is too upsetting, the child's participation in regular education may be minimized for his benefit. Also addressed in this section is whether a child will participate in physical education, computer lab, art/music classes recess, the lunchroom, or extracurricular activities with his or her regular education peers.

**Did you know?** Parents *must* be invited to IEP and placement meetings, which are held at a mutually convenient time, although your presence is not required. However, we recommend that you try and attend *all* IEP meetings, particularly the first one and any meetings where a change of placement is being considered.

### Participation on State and District Testing

This area addresses whether your child will take these tests. Although they are not given to children in every grade, if an IEP is being written in May when your child is in second grade and there are tests that are completed by third-graders each spring, the IEP must address this future testing. Any modifications such as small groups, extended time, or reading the test to the child (at least all sections other than reading comprehension) must be included. These can be changed as needed, based on teacher and parent feedback of what works best for your child, as this sometimes is difficult to do a year in advance. If your child will not participate in these tests, perhaps because of severe mental retardation, the IEP will state why these tests are not appropriate and will discuss a different way in which your child will be assessed.

### Dates and Places

When services start, how long they will last, how often they will be provided, and where they will take place are addressed in this section. Some services may last for one year, but in the case of physical or occupational therapy, services may be provided more frequently for a certain period of time (thirty minutes weekly for the first three months) and then at a decreased frequency (thirty minutes monthly for the remaining nine months) for the duration of the IEP. The actual frequency will depend on your child's needs.

**Did you know?** Schools value your input into the IEP. No one knows your child as well as you. While some teachers prefer to write some of the goals prior to the meeting, this usually is done to save some time. All these goals can be changed or deleted and new ones created.

### Transition Services

Transition services are designed to help a child move from school to post-school activities. These services include postsecondary education (college), vocational training, employment, and independent living. When your child turns 14, the IEP committee must begin to discuss his future. The committee is interested in knowing the child's desires and abilities for education, employment, and independent living. The idea is to identify the child's interests and post-school goals and provide him with the skills needed to best meet these goals. For example, if your child wants to attend college and the committee feels that this is possible based on his present level of functioning, your child should choose a college-track curriculum in high school. Children with lower ability may need a vocational education program, while children with very high ability may need college-level advanced placement (AP) courses.

### Needed Transition Services

When your child is 16, the committee will reaffirm his interests and goals, and assess the services, programs, or supports that may be needed to help achieve these goals. The transition services ensure that your child is prepared for education, employment, and independent living after leaving high school. The IEP must list any needed transition services, and might include the efforts of community agencies to provide your child with training and assistance in finding employment.

### Age of Majority

At least a year before your child turns 18, the IEP must include a statement stating that he has been informed that his rights will transfer to him at age 18.

> **Did you know?** The age of majority is not 18 years in all states. Exceptions include Alabama (19), Indiana (21), Mississippi (21), Nebraska (19), and Pennsylvania (21).

## Measuring Progress

Measuring your child's progress is an important part of his education, and the IEP will discuss the ways in which your child's progress is measured and how you will be notified. This could be a note in a daily journal, a weekly summary, or a monthly report card. We advocate for more frequent progress reports, perhaps weekly or biweekly, in most instances, although we see the benefit of weekly reports, especially after special education services are first initiated.

> **Did you know?** Your child can be a member of the IEP committee. This is especially important when discussing his postsecondary plans. The IEP team will want to hear about your child's plans for the immediate and distant future so that plans can be put in place to work toward these goals.

*After the Meeting*

Once the IEP meeting is over, you will be given a copy of the IEP. Some teachers will give you a copy right away, while others will ask if they can send it home the next day or in a few days. We advocate for a copy of the IEP *immediately after* the meeting. When the meeting is scheduled, we encourage you to tell the school that you want a copy of the IEP before you leave the meeting. Some teachers take the extra time to finish the paperwork, but that increases the chances that pages will get lost or that the teacher will forget and it will delay a copy being sent to you. You must understand the contents of an IEP so that you can advocate for your child. If you don't understand something, *anything*, just ask! You have a right to a clear explanation of everything discussed during the meeting.

*It's Done. Now What?*

Writing an IEP is only half the story. The other half, and the most important part, actually involves its implementation. All persons who will provide services to your child must receive a copy, since they will be responsible for the services everyone agreed that your child needs. The IEP spells out the types of services, frequency, duration, and placement setting, all of which are very important.

> **Did you know?** If you do not think the IEP is adequately addressing your child's needs, you can request a meeting at any time to review and, perhaps, create a new one. Some goals may prove to be too difficult to master, and some goals are mastered quite easily. In these instances, another IEP should be written and include revised goals.

Your feedback to the IEP committee is helpful and appreciated at any time. Committee members need to know whether you see any changes at home. Perhaps your child's behavior is improving and he finds it easier to solve math problems or is socializing better with peers. This kind of information gives the committee members some idea about what is going on in the home, and in conjunction with teacher feedback, they will have a good idea of your child's progress and how the child is meeting his goals.

The IEP committee will meet once each year to review the IEP goals and the progress your child has made. If your child has had a recent psychoeducational evaluation, those results will be presented at the meeting. During this meeting, both you and your child's teacher will talk about how he is progressing toward these goals. The teacher may bring samples of your child's work to show improvement or, perhaps, to demonstrate that goals are not being met. All this information is important because it helps the committee to create new goals for the next twelve months.

A sample set of IEP forms is included in Appendix E. The actual forms used in your school district may vary in style but will be similar in content. These forms, provided by the Paulding County (Georgia) School District, are modeled after ones created by the Georgia Department of Education. It is likely that your district's forms are similar to those created by your state department of education and utilized by other school districts within the state.

# C H A P T E R    1 0

# Beyond Eligibility for Special Education: What's Next?

This chapter will discuss what happens after a student qualifies for special education and related services. Some of the questions that this chapter will answer include:

- How often will my child's IEP be reviewed?
- Will my child be reevaluated again in the future?
- How long will my child be eligible for special education services?
- What if I don't agree with my child's evaluation or special education program?
- Is my child protected under the Individuals with Disabilities Education Improvement Act of 2004 if he breaks a school rule?
- What is transition planning all about, and what is the difference between a standard and special diploma?

## How Often Will My Child's IEP Be Reviewed?

At present, according to IDEA 2004, a child's IEP *must* be reviewed at least once a year; however, IDEA 2004 has made several amendments to the way the IEP may be reviewed and revised, as discussed in Chapter 9. If your child is eligible for special education or related services, the school will contact you to participate in the IEP review. At this meeting, the annual goals for your child's academic program will be reviewed.

**Did you know?** IDEA 2004 encourages schools to streamline the IEP process in several ways to be more convenient for parents. Parents can participate in the development or change of their child's IEP without having to physically be present at the meeting through the use of technology, such as conference calls or video conferencing. IDEA 2004 also suggests that schools make an effort to combine meetings (such as having a single meeting to discuss the IEP and reevaluation, rather than two separate meetings). If this information is relatively new to you, it might be helpful to review these and other important changes to the IEP process that were discussed in Chapter 9.

## Can I Request a More Frequent Review?

Yes. Although the law states that this review and revision of the IEP must take place at least once a year, as a parent, you are entitled to request a review of your child's IEP at any time. As discussed in Chapter 9, it is important to be informed and involved in this critical part of your child's education. There are several ways that you can increase your ability to make informed decisions about your child's ongoing educational progress:

- Schedule frequent meetings with your child's teachers (this topic is discussed in more detail in Chapter 11).
- Ask to visit your child's classroom.
- Request that the teacher send you samples of your child's work, from time to time.
- Ask how you can support your child's educational program and goals, at home.
- Let your child's teachers know that you want to be an active participant in your child's educational program.
- If you find that you are spending too much time helping your child complete homework, contact your child's teacher.
- If you think your child is not completing assignments, ask for an agenda of assignments that need to be completed each week so that you can help your child monitor progress.

## Will My Child Be Reevaluated Again in the Future?

IDEA 2004 continues to support reevaluation for students who are receiving special education services once every three years, unless the school or parent feel that a reevaluation is not necessary. The goal of this reevaluation is to determine if the child continues to meet eligibility requirements for special education services under IDEA 2004. A reevaluation may constitute a wide variety of approaches. Reevaluation may involve a review of educational materials such as standardized group tests that are routinely conducted at the school or grades from the child's academic curriculum. Parent consent is not required if the reevaluation consists of a review of the school records. However, if a formal reevaluation is requested, such as an evaluation conducted by the school psychologist, parental consent is required, just as it was for the initial evaluation. Under IDEA 2004, a school can proceed with a reevaluation without parent consent if the school documents that they have not been able to obtain a response from the parent, despite repeated attempts to do so.

Once the existing educational information is reviewed and the decision is made that no additional data are required, a decision is made regarding continued eligibility for special education services. Parents must be notified of the eligibility decision.

However, a school must conduct a reevaluation to remove a child from special education services, if you or school personnel suspect that:

- Your child no longer has a recognized IDEA disability
- The disability no longer has a negative impact on academic performance

In addition, parents have the right to request an assessment to determine eligibility to continue receiving special education services and also are entitled to request a more frequent reevaluation, if they so desire.

IDEA 2004 states that a child may be dismissed from special education eligibility without an evaluation if:

- Parents are in agreement that an evaluation for termination of eligibility is not required
- A child is graduating from secondary school with a regular education diploma
- The child exceeds the age of eligibility for services (twenty-second birthday)

## How Long Will My Child Be Eligible for Special Education Services?

Under IDEA 2004, children are eligible for special education and related services from age 3 to age 21, or until graduation, whichever is earlier. Students who continue to meet eligibility requirements at the time of their three-year reevaluation will continue to receive special education and related services for the next three years, unless a more frequent reevaluation is requested and results do not support the need for special education services.

## What If I Don't Agree with My Child's Evaluation or Special Education Program?

The following information will be helpful to parents who do not agree with the initial comprehensive assessment.

## Disagreement with Evaluation Results

Parents have the right to request an Independent Educational Evaluation (IEE) by a qualified practitioner not employed by the school, if parents do not agree with the initial evaluation.

> **Remember that** parents have the right to obtain an independent evaluation at their own cost, at any time; however, parents may have the cost paid for at the school district's expense, if they disagree with the results of the initial evaluation, and the district agrees to pay the costs.

The district may ask for a reason why you disagree with the evaluation; however, you are not required to provide an explanation. The district must also respond to your request within a reasonable time and not delay its response to your request. The district may also elect to request a due process hearing to defend the appropriateness of their initial evaluation.

While many districts have no written policy stating the qualifications necessary for a practitioner to conduct the evaluation, your state may have regulations that address this area. Individual school districts may have policies regarding the minimum qualifications needed for their school personnel to complete such evaluations, and those qualifications most likely would be used as the criteria for choosing an independent evaluator. It is also important that the practitioner is familiar with state special education eligibility requirements. Unfortunately, we have seen many parents who pay considerable expense to have a private evaluation, only to learn that the evaluator has not used assessment instruments that are accepted by the district or state, or that the evaluator was not qualified to conduct the evaluation. If you want to learn more about factors to consider in selecting an independent evaluator, you can review the information presented in Chapter 4.

## Disagreement with Educational Program

Since 1997, IDEA has included parents in the decision-making process regarding their child's placement and program, and the emphasis in IDEA 2004 is even more pronounced in this area. To ensure the continued involvement of parents in their child's educational program, IDEA 2004 stipulates that parents must be given sufficient notice of meetings and the opportunity to attend at times that are mutually convenient. As we have already discussed, the current emphasis is on finding ways that parents can participate without actually being physically present at the meeting, via telephone or video conferencing. In addition, schools may participate (fifteen states will be selected) in a pilot project to look at the viability of using a multiyear IEP (for up to three years) to ensure a focus on greater long-range planning.

However, the district can make changes to the IEP in the best interest of the student, and placement decisions without parent involvement if repeated, documented attempts are made to engage parents in the process without success. Furthermore, under IDEA 2004, districts are no longer responsible for providing a FAPE if parents refuse placement or are repeatedly unavailable to give consent for their child's initial participation in the special education program. In the latter case, districts are not required to convene an IEP meeting or develop an IEP. Under IDEA 2004, districts *shall not* provide special education services for a child whose parents refuse to give consent for services, and school districts *may not* use procedures, such as mediation or due process, in order to provide services under IDEA 2004.

If you feel that your child's program or services are inappropriate, or if you feel that your child is not making sufficient progress, you may request an IEP review at any time. You may also call for an IEP review if you have new information that may have an impact on your child's educational services, such as an independent evaluation, a change in your child's medication, or a change in family circumstances that may influence your child's ability to learn. You may also request a conference with your child's teacher or guidance counselor to address any concerns you may have. Parent-teacher communication and meetings are discussed further in Chapter 11.

Serious concerns and lack of resolution may result in more formal procedures. Under IDEA 2004, there are several possible approaches including mediation, hearings, due process hearings, and complaints against the state or school district. These procedures are discussed in greater length later in this chapter, and in the Procedural Safeguard provided in Appendix D.

## Is My Child Protected Under IDEA 2004 If He Breaks a School Rule?

Under IDEA 2004, children with disabilities have some measure of protection from arbitrary suspension or expulsion from school, if their discipline problem is determined to be related to their disability. In this case, it is said that the behavior is a *manifestation of the disability.* If the behavior can be determined "not to be related to the disability"—in other words, is not a manifestation of the disability—the student can be disciplined in a manner similar to children without disabilities.

Schools can be faced with the difficult challenge of weighing a student's rights and the need for safety in the schools. Therefore, more recent amendments to IDEA 2004 have provided additional guidelines regarding the removal of students with disabilities from their school setting. Schools will now be allowed to consider any unique circumstances surrounding disciplinary issues on a *case-by-case basis* when they are determining whether to order a change in placement for a child with a disability who violates a code of student conduct.

### Disciplinary Actions: Shorter-Term Removals

Under IDEA 2004, students with disabilities who violate a school rule or code of conduct may be disciplined in the same manner as students without disabilities for a period of ten consecutive or cumulative school days over the course of one school year. For suspensions of up to ten days, conditions apply to the same extent as they would apply to a nondisabled student, and *without* the need to make a manifestation determination. The school district is not obligated to provide instruction and may authorize a change of placement to an appropriate interim educational setting, another setting, or suspension, for up to ten consecutive school days.

## Disciplinary Actions: Longer-Term Removals and Alternative Placements

A *manifestation determination review* is conducted when long-term removals are being considered or when the removal involves *a change of placement*. Under these conditions, the IEP team must convene within ten days of the disciplinary decision that resulted in the student's removal resulting in a change of placement. The IEP team takes into consideration relevant information, including assessment results, teacher observations of the student, and the student's IEP and placement. A determination is made regarding whether the behavior was significantly related to a child's disability or a result of a school's failure to implement the IEP, by considering whether:

- The IEP and placement are appropriate regarding the behavior of concern
- The disability did or did not impair the student's ability to understand the impact or consequences of the behavior
- The disability did or did not impair the student's ability to control his behavior

If the team finds that the behavior *is* a manifestation of the disability, the IEP team must conduct a functional behavioral assessment and implement a behavioral intervention plan, if the school has not already done so. If there is an existing BIP, the committee must review that plan to determine whether it addresses the behavior in question and whether to modify the plan to address the behavior, as needed, to reduce and/or eliminate the inappropriate behavior. The student will be returned to the placement from which he was removed, unless the IEP team agrees that an alternate placement is the most appropriate placement and the parents agree that a change of placement would be necessary to implement the behavioral intervention plan.

The district may remove a child to an interim alternative educational setting for up to forty-five *school* days, if the student does one of the following:

- Carries a weapon (guns, knife, bomb) to school or school function
- Knowingly possesses, uses, sells, or solicits illegal drugs
- Is a danger to himself or others in the current placement
- Commits a serious bodily injury to another

**Did you know?** A significant change from IDEA 1997 to IDEA 2004 is that the law now stipulates a time frame for alternative placement of forty-five school days rather than forty-five calendar days, which was the previous time frame.

Removal of a student for more than ten days requires that the district provide special educational and related services necessary to work toward the goals of the student's IEP.

An interim alternative educational setting (IAES) is a placement that is selected by the IEP team to ensure the student continues to receive services and modifications in accordance with his IEP goals. The IAES must also address the behavioral concerns that were responsible for the disciplinary action.

If a student commits a weapons violation or knowingly possesses, uses, sells, or solicits drugs at school or a school function, the district may place the student in an IAES for up to forty-five school days, *without parent permission,* and *regardless of whether the behavior was a manifestation of the disability.* Parents who disagree with this decision can request an expedited due process hearing, during which time the student will remain in the forty-five-day program. Similarly, a school district can request that a hearing officer (administrative law judge) place a child in an IAES for up to forty-five school days if the district feels that the student is a danger to himself or others. If the district maintains that the student is still dangerous after the forty-five-day term has ended, the district may seek subsequent forty-five-day placements through an expedited hearing.

## What If the Behavior Is Found to Be "Not a Result of the Disability"?

Under IDEA 2004, if it is determined that the child's behavior was not related to his disability, then although services continue, the district has the right to change the educational placement to an alternative setting. In this case, it is up to the parents to appeal the decision.

## What Disciplinary Measures Will Result If My Child Is "Not Yet Eligible" Under IDEA?

IDEA 2004 states that children can receive protection in matters of disciplinary issues if the school district had prior knowledge that the child might be deemed eligible for services under IDEA 2004, if:

- The child's parents have submitted written documentation to the school district stating their concerns that their child needs special education services

Children *will not* be considered for protection under the law in disciplinary matters if the school district was unaware that a child has a disability, due to:

- Parental refusal for evaluation
- Parental refusal for special education or related services
- Determination that the child was not a child with a disability

### Note of Caution Regarding Disciplinary Measures

IDEA 2004 has changed the wording for several areas of the law pertaining to disciplinary measures. Some of the wording may be subject to a range of interpretations, such as deciding what constitutes *unique circumstances* and how these are to be decided on a *case-by-case basis*. Therefore, it is very important that parents request a copy of their state's Procedural Safeguards to better understand how their state explains specific areas of the law. Further discussion of the procedural safeguards regarding discipline issues can be found in Appendix D.

## What Is Transition Planning All About?

Up to this point we have been discussing the IEP as a yearly review of your child's education. IDEA 2004 has placed more emphasis on long-range planning than the previous versions of the law. As discussed in Chapter 11, IDEA 2004 is attempting to work toward a reduction in paperwork and an increase in long-range planning, such as the proposal to examine the effects of using a multiyear IEP, which we discussed earlier. Another example of long-range planning is evident in the increased emphasis on the development of transition plans.

IDEA 2004 has recognized that the child's IEP should address the four *natural transition points* in developing transition objectives for children with disabilities. The transition periods, which are not to extend beyond a three-year period, include the transitions from:

- Preschool to elementary school
- Elementary grades to middle or junior high
- Middle or junior high to secondary school
- Secondary school to postsecondary school activities

### Preschool to Elementary School Transition

IDEA 2004 requires that schools and agencies develop adequate procedures to ensure that children who participate in early-intervention programs assisted under Part C and those who participate in preschool programs funded under IDEA 2004 experience a smooth and effective transition between these programs and their elementary school placement. Also, the transition plan should ensure that each child with a disability has an IEP developed that will take effect by their third birthday, and that an IFSP has been implemented. Under IDEA 2004, parents have the choice of continuing children in grant-funded preschool programs, or placing their children in preschool programs in their local school. However, schools are not responsible for providing a FAPE for children whose parents place their children in grant-funded preschool programs.

### Transitions from Elementary to Secondary and from Secondary to Postsecondary Activities

In an effort to address the high dropout rates and increased incidents of disciplinary actions noted in the first two years of high school, IDEA 2004 requires that the IEP team address post-school goals prior to the student entering high school at age 14. IDEA 2004 mandates that a transition plan acknowledging *transition service needs* must be in place by age 16 (or younger, if appropriate) and included in the IEP plan for all students receiving special education services.

Students are usually interviewed by their designated IEP team member (formally or informally) to obtain information concerning their future goals and aspirations. For example, students may be asked to consider which career they might like to pursue after school and discuss how their strengths might be further developed to ensure their success. At this time, students are also asked to consider whether they intend to pursue a regular high school diploma or whether their interests are in obtaining a special diploma or vocational completion certificate. The IEP team also considers what transition services the student will require to ensure success in the high school program. It is important that the IEP include special education students in any statewide formal testing that might be later used to determine eligibility for regular versus special diploma options.

According to IDEA 2004, the transition plan must include a wide variety of services that will increase the child's opportunities for future success, including vocational training, cooperative employment opportunities, community participation, and opportunities for continuing adult education. To this end, the IEP should include reasonable transition activities that will help the student to develop skills that can enhance the student's understanding of the roles and responsibilities that will be required in order to be successful in the workplace.

At this stage, the IEP should develop in accordance with the student's future goals and address areas of student need, interests, or preference that are important in establishing future directions in education and the workplace. Where necessary, instruction should be provided in areas of vocational options and adult living arrangements. The IEP should become more coordinated with adult service organizations and help families to identify and become familiar with resources and facilities in the community that will offer continued support when the child leaves high school.

IDEA 2004 states clearly that a student must be involved in the development of the transition plan. Other members of the IEP transition meeting include parents, teachers (special and regular education teachers), the local school representative, and any other individuals who might contribute to the development of the transition plan. Parents must be notified specifically that the meeting will include transition planning, if this is the agenda. The importance of parents attending this transition meeting is that they often have significant information about their child that teachers may not know. For example, parents may share a student's strengths in hobbies that may have a strong influence on directing and maintaining a focus on future vocational choices, such as car repair, crafts, animal care, and so forth. In addition, once the student reaches the age of 14, IDEA 2004 mandates that students must be invited to participate in their IEP meetings, although students can decline the invitation.

**Did you know?** One of the key aspects of transition planning is to link the family to community resources that will be important in sustaining future supports, once the student has graduated from the public school system.

Because IDEA 2004 applies to students until they leave the public system, or until age 22 (whichever is earlier), the protections offered to students with disabilities do not necessarily continue into the community. When students reach the age of majority (which can differ from state to state), the IDEA rights transfer from the parent or guardian directly to the student.

IDEA 2004 mandates that the IEP team must inform families and students at least one year before the student's birthday (age of majority) that rights will transfer to the student. In cases where the student is incapable of making informed decisions, parents should be advised of the need to establish guardianship as an alternative.

## What Happens When Parents Disagree with the School District or State?

In their review of the steps that parents can take to resolve disagreements with decisions regarding their child's education, the National Dissemination Center for Children with Disabilities suggests five different approaches that might be appropriate, given the nature of the conflict. The approaches can be summarized as follows:

1. *Discussions with Your Child's Teacher and School Staff.* When you feel there is a problem, you should talk to your child's teacher, counselor, or principal. It might even be necessary to discuss issues with the Superintendent, Coordinator of Student Services, or Director of Special Education in your school district.

2. *An IEP Review.* If your child is already receiving special education services, you can request an IEP review to discuss any program changes that you feel your child may need. This may also be a good opportunity to address your concerns about your child's academic progress or provide educators with any additional information that you may have about your child, such as the results from an independent evaluation, updating family status issues, or medication changes.

3. *Mediation.* IDEA 2004 mandates that states establish procedures to ensure that a mediation process is available. The state is responsible for funding the costs of the mediator who is usually selected randomly from a list of qualified mediators held by the state. Mediation is a voluntary process for engaging the school district and parents of a child with a disability in discussions about disagreements regarding educational matters. The goal of mediation is to resolve disputes using a qualified and impartial third party (called a mediator). The mediator engages both parties in discussions to negotiate a solution that represents a reasonable compromise. When an agreement is reached, it must be issued in written form. Discussions that are part of the mediation process remain confidential and cannot be used in any future due process hearings or civil proceedings. Confidentiality may be ensured by having both parties sign a confidentiality pledge at the beginning of the mediation process.

Although mediation cannot be used to deny or delay a parent's right to a due process hearing, the state may request that parents meet with a third-party member, such as someone from a community parent resource center, to discuss the benefits of mediation with the parents. Parents are not required to engage in mediation.

> **Did you know?** Under IDEA 2004, mediation may now be used without having to file a hearing. It also encourages the use of a Preliminary Meeting that can be used to discuss issues and perhaps reach a consensus and resolution without having to proceed to a due process hearing.

4. *Due Process Hearing.* If you do not agree with educational decisions regarding your child's identification, evaluation, education placement, or any aspect of your child's educational program that does not conform to a FAPE, you may request a due process hearing. A hearing officer, who is an impartial third party, will listen to evidence presented by you and the school district and will render an impartial decision based on the evidence and the requirements of IDEA 2004. The hearing officer cannot be an employee of the state agency or the district responsible for your child's education. However, the state pays the hearing officer to preside over the meeting.

When you (or your attorney) make a formal request for a due process hearing, you must do so in written form, which includes the following information:

Child's name, address, and school

Nature of the problem

Proposed solution

Upon receipt of the written request for a due process hearing, the school district will respond informing you of your rights to mediation, as an alternative, and also provide you with the names of available free or low-cost legal services in the area. The school district may also request an impartial due process hearing to address parent refusal to consent to an initial evaluation.

5. *Complaint Resolution Procedures.* Complaints alleging that the state or school district has violated an IDEA 2004 requirement may be filed by an individual or organization, as long as the complaint is filed in a signed written document outlining how the agency has violated Part B of IDEA 2004. Complaints may be filed with the district superintendent or the state department of education.

**Did you know?** IDEA 2004 now requires that a complaint be time-limited to a violation that occurred within two years of filing the complaint, dated from the time that the parent or school knew or should have known about the circumstances in question.

Parents may also remove their child from the public school and enroll their child in a private school. If they enroll their child in a private school because the school district did not provide the child with a FAPE, the public school *may* be required to pay for the costs of private schooling.

*Procedural Safeguards*

IDEA 2004 includes an entire section (Subpart E) of the law that outlines how the law serves to protect the rights of parents and students with disabilities. According to IDEA 2004, parents must be given a copy of the procedural safeguards according to the one of the following guidelines:

- Once each year
- Upon initial referral
- Upon a request for reevaluation
- Upon filing a complaint
- Whenever a parent requests a copy

These safeguards, or protective factors, include issues such as confidentiality of information and access to student records and are presented in Appendix D.

# PART II

# HELPFUL HINTS FOR POSITIVE PARENTING

# CHAPTER 11

# A Parent's Guide to Parent-Teacher Communication and School Meetings

Communicating with teachers is an important part of your child's education. Your child's success is, in large part, due to the efforts of his teachers and your efforts to maintain contact with them. Not only do teachers communicate with one another and with school administrators but they also communicate with you. You are an important partner in your child's education, which is one reason why good communication between school and home is essential.

## Create a Positive Relationship with Your Child's Teachers

The first step in enhancing parent-teacher communication is to create a positive relationship with your child's teachers. There are many ways to cultivate a good relationship. Let's review some of them.

### Attend an Open House

It is a good idea to attend each *open house* that the school holds. This is an excellent opportunity for you to meet your child's teachers face-to-face and know who they are. This informal setting allows you to ask general questions about what your child is doing in each class and to meet some of the other parents, too. During an open house, teachers often display children's work as a way of showing off their efforts. Look around the room and see if your child's work is being displayed. A teacher should display at least one piece of good work for each child.

### Volunteer in the Classroom

Another way to be involved in your child's class is to be a *classroom volunteer*. While some principals will not assign parents to their child's room, being a room mother or room father in your child's class is still a possibility in many districts. Volunteering in the classroom not only helps you to see what occurs daily, including classroom management, but it also provides the teacher with an extra set of hands and some necessary help. Teaching is a big responsibility and a lot of work, and your offer to help often is greatly appreciated.

Note, however, that it is not always a good idea to volunteer in your child's classroom, especially if he is very young. Younger children tend to cling to their parents, and they may come to expect to see you there every day. This can lead to problems when the child sees that you are not there. Also, you would not want to volunteer if it embarrasses your child or makes him feel uncomfortable. Be sure to ask your child if it is okay that you act as a classroom volunteer. If your child says no, don't do it.

### Meet with the Teacher Early in the Year

If your child is moving from one grade to the next, it's a good idea to *meet with your child's new teacher* before or when the new school year starts. This gives you an opportunity to discuss with the teacher several concerns, including your child's disability and needs and which classroom interventions have and have not worked. It also allows you to make sure the new teacher has a copy of your child's IEP. That last point is crucial. While schools do a good job of making sure each teacher is aware of every child with a disability, a change in school leadership or teachers may mean that certain things are accidentally overlooked. Parents should make sure each new teacher has a copy of the IEP and access to all the notes in the child's school records.

> **Did you know?** There are more than 23,000 local PTA units in all fifty states, the District of Columbia, the U.S. Virgin Islands, and the Department of Defense schools in the Pacific and Europe. You can learn more about the National PTA at http://www.pta.org.

### Be Open and Available

Try and make yourself *open and available*. If the teacher or school psychologist asks you to attempt a new intervention, try to be receptive and at least attempt it. If you disagree, be sure to vocalize your concerns and ask for more information. Are you available to attend interviews to complete behavior rating scales or adaptive behavior forms? If these forms are sent home, do you return them in a timely manner? Your absence from meetings and unwillingness to implement interventions or complete necessary forms may be interpreted as possessing an uncaring attitude. This can be an unnecessary outcome of simply not being able to free up time in a busy world. If you cannot attend meetings because of your work schedule, for example, be sure to let the school know with a note or a phone call. Teachers will understand, and they'll be happy to hear from you one way or the other. Your contact with the school around these issues will help the school know that you want to be a part of your child's education and increase your opportunity to contribute your thoughts and concerns.

## How Do I Communicate with Thee? Let Me Count the Ways

There are many ways that you can stay in touch with your child's teacher. Some require technology; others are the old-fashioned way of communicating. Regardless of your choice, it is important to maintain a regular, open, and positive channel of communication with your child's teacher.

### Homework Agenda

A *homework agenda,* sometimes called *a student planner,* is a notebook often used to help your child keep track of daily homework assignments. While many teachers write in the agenda the assignments that are due, older children may be required to do this task to increase their independence and responsibility. Teachers may write in the required assignments for children with motor impairments or children who have problems with written expression. In cases where the child is responsible for writing his assignments in the agenda, the teacher sometimes checks the notebook to see if he has completed the task and whether he copied the information accurately. If you want the teacher to check the agenda daily for accuracy, be sure to let the teacher know. You should also make this activity part of your child's IEP.

### Message Notebook

A *message notebook* may be used so that a teacher can communicate what is going on in school and a parent can communicate what is happening at home. Notebook comments from the teacher may include a discussion of your child's progress, behavior, attitude, rate of class work completion, and information about any other area that is important to your child's teacher. This is also your opportunity to ask the teacher questions. The message notebook and the agenda can be excellent methods of two-way communication. Perhaps you want to know the pages your child should be reading over the weekend or you have scheduled a vacation and want your child to keep up with class expectations, or you simply want to give your child an opportunity to get ahead. Maybe you are wondering if the interventions that you are trying at home have helped your child in school. On the other hand, maybe you just want to thank the teacher for all his hard work. The message notebook is a great place in which to do all that.

### Phone Calls and Other Scheduling Nightmares

Phone calls are a nice personal touch, if they are scheduled, expected, and you have the time to ask the questions you want to ask. Whether you call your child's teacher or the teacher calls you, phone conversations can be a good way to communicate because you can ask detailed questions. You don't have to go back and forth with a time lapse, like you would when writing in a message notebook or via e-mail. For complex issues, a phone call may be the better choice. Although we advocate that a face-to-face discussion is usually the best way to communicate, if there are problems with scheduling a personal interview, a phone conversation may be the next best alternative. Understand, though, that scheduling phone conversations may be as difficult as scheduling a personal discussion. Perhaps your employment situation is not suitable for personal conversations (such as an open work area where everyone can hear your call or a busy work atmosphere that does not allow personal calls) and teachers may need to call you at work during one of their breaks. In addition, teachers are often difficult to reach during school hours because of classroom obligations; however, parents may not realize that in the immediate hours after school, teachers are often engaged in meetings, teach in an after-school program, or take classes in the late afternoons or evenings. Also, if you pick up your child from school and you see your child's teacher in the class dismissal line, it's not a good idea to start a long conversation, although you may be able to use this time, very briefly, to schedule a time to talk or ask how to contact the teacher to make an appointment.

**Did you know?** IDEA 2004 has made a greater effort to recognize the need for increased efficiency and effectiveness in streamlining education for children with disabilities by increasing convenience for parents to participate in their child's education and reducing the need for excessive paperwork for teachers.

## Use E-Mail

E-mail has become a convenient way to communicate with other people. If your child's teacher has an e-mail address, you may want to use e-mail to communicate with the teacher if both of you find it more convenient and you agree that this would be a good way to communicate. It can also be used to support other forms of communication, such as a phone call. You can use e-mail to summarize what was discussed during the call. If there was a misunderstanding in communication, this gives either person an opportunity to correct the misinformation. An e-mail also provides you with written documentation that you shared certain information with the teacher. While it does not guarantee that the teacher has received, read, and understood the e-mail, you have proof that you attempted to communicate with the teacher on a particular issue. Certain e-mail programs, like Outlook Express, allow you to request a return receipt. The receipt is sent when the recipient has displayed your message.

**Did you know?** There are free e-mail accounts that also include free, limited dial-up Internet access. Two popular ones are NetZero (http://www.netzero.net) and Juno (http://www.juno.com). They include thousands of local access numbers.

## Homework Hotline

Some districts use a *homework hotline* to allow teachers to communicate homework information to parents. Parents can call a certain number and find out the homework assignments their child has for the day. It will be a recording, often in the teacher's voice, of the work assigned for that night. This may be used in conjunction with other forms of communication. If you don't have access to a phone each day, you may want to rely on the message notebook.

## Web-Based Homework List

Like the homework hotline, the *Web-based homework list* allows parents to log in and find a listing of the reading and homework assignments for the night. It may also include links to Internet resources. The homework list is often used in a program that also allows parents online access to their child's grades. These features, if available, allow parents to continuously monitor their child's grades. This is particularly important if you notice your child's grades slipping because of certain extracurricular activities or because of after-school work. Typically, school districts use this method only if a survey shows that the vast majority of families have a computer and Internet access. If you cannot afford access, be sure to check out NetZero and Juno. Both are reliable and have thousands of local access numbers.

## Request a Meeting

Sometimes it is better to meet face-to-face. Meeting a teacher on a one-to-one basis is more personal and, similar to an open house, gives you access to your child's work, but at a more specific level. Be sure to schedule a meeting ahead of time rather than just dropping by after school when you pick up your child. As we mentioned earlier, teachers may have a meeting, teach in an after-school program, take continuing education classes, or have a child of their own to tend to. If possible, give the teacher multiple dates that are good for you to maximize the chance that one of the dates fits into both schedules. If you write these dates and times down on paper and pass them on, the teacher will have a better opportunity to respond to you about what will work best for both of you. It is also best to meet after school and not during one of the teacher's breaks from class teaching, since these times are often consumed by other teaching duties and would limit the time you have to ask all the questions you may have.

> **Did you know?** Although you can communicate your requests to a teacher, he is not legally required to follow them. If you feel strongly that your child's teacher is not doing something you would like him to do, you need to request an IEP meeting. At that time, you can request that certain tasks—such as a daily agenda or homework notebook—be written into the new IEP. This obligates the school and all its personnel to follow through with any changes.

## How to Prepare for a Meeting with Your Child's Teacher

There are times when it is necessary to meet with your child's teacher. Perhaps you have a question about the curriculum, or are concerned about your child's progress, or want to know how best to help your child at home. Whatever the reason, you should be prepared before you meet with the teacher. Preparation is the key to keeping you focused on your concerns or questions. It also helps to alleviate some of the nervousness that you may be experiencing.

The following list is a six-step process for engaging in an informal meeting with the teacher. These tips will help you to have a successful, productive meeting. Later, more formal meetings such as a parent-teacher conference, an SST meeting, an IEP meeting, or a manifestation meeting (which may also be called disciplinary review meeting, or some other similar title adopted by your state) will be discussed. Each of these meetings requires more detailed preparation, and this chapter will help you to get ready for these meetings as well.

### Step One: List Your Concerns

Many parents feel nervous when meeting with their child's teacher. Being prepared can minimize your anxiety. How many times have you gone to the doctor's office with several concerns, only to realize later on that you forgot to mention one of them? We all do that, and some of us choose to write down our concerns before our appointment. The same applies when meeting with your child's teacher. Don't feel shy about pulling out an index card or a notepad with a listing of your concerns. You can always say something like, "I wrote down some of the things I wanted to talk about to be sure that I covered everything." Your list should not necessarily include all of your concerns in paragraph or even sentence form. A numbered or bulleted list will be fine, unless you have a weak memory, and you can fill in the details during your discussion.

### Step Two: Listen to the Teacher

You had your turn; now it's time to let the teacher talk. Like many of us, once you get on a roll it can be difficult to stop talking. Allowing the teacher time to address your points is important, and how the teacher responds and what is said is key.

Do you feel that the teacher speaks negatively about your child? Does the teacher say that teachers get little support from school administrators and from other teachers? While some teachers feel this way, this is not the proper time or place for the teacher to talk about these issues, nor should you participate in these discussions. Always remember that you are there only to discuss issues related to your child's education.

### Step Three: Ask Questions

Now is the time to ask your questions. It's best to raise one question or concern at a time; a rapid-fire approach can be very confusing. Once the teacher answers your question to your satisfaction, move on to the next point. If the answer is unclear, be sure you understand it before moving farther down your list. This is not the time to pretend you know what was said. If you truly don't understand, let you teacher know that you may need some clarification. If necessary, take some notes. If you feel uncomfortable doing this, you can say something like, "You are doing a great job answering my questions. I am going to write down this information so that I won't forget and so that I can share it with others in my family."

### Step Four: Be Prepared to Brainstorm

The reason you are meeting with the teacher is because your child has problems with his behavior, academics, social skills, or some other issue, and perhaps in more than one of these areas. Brainstorming allows both you and your child's teacher the opportunity to generate creative and imaginative solutions to your child's challenges. There are many obvious solutions to many of these problems, but when those don't work, some creativity may be required. You and the teacher can work together to find solutions that will help your child in the classroom and at home.

**Did you know?** Your school psychologist can be one of your best resources for brainstorming solutions for the problems your child is experiencing. The training and experience of school psychologists prepare them to work with children who appear to be resistant to typical interventions and may be termed by some as being a "difficult case."

### Step Five: Be Open to the Teacher's Suggestions

Brainstorming requires both creativity and patience. You need to allow your teacher to share suggestions with you, even though they may not necessarily make sense at the time. As many teachers and school psychologists will tell you, the best solutions are not always the most obvious ones. Be flexible in your thinking, and open to the teacher's suggestions. The teacher may be suggesting a particular approach because that intervention may have been effective with other children. While every child is unique, many interventions work for most children in a variety of situations. A trial-and-error approach may be necessary.

### Step Six: Remain Positive

Meeting with your child's teacher can be stressful. A good deal of time may be spent discussing your child's problems, misbehavior, lack of class work comprehension, and so forth. Try to remain positive. In order to come up with the best solutions to your child's problems, you and your child's teacher need to discuss the problems in detail. This is the time to think about the interventions to be implemented in the classroom and at home. Most children will improve with the right interventions, even though it may take some time. Stay positive, work closely with your teacher and the school psychologist, and think about how all this time and effort will ultimately benefit your child.

## Types of Formal Meetings

We consider a typical meeting with a teacher, as described earlier, an informal meeting, because there is much less structure when compared with other school meetings.

Formal meetings—including IEP meetings, SST meetings, and manifestation determinations—follow a prescribed format, often involve other school personnel, and typically have a specific outcome. We have already talked about IEP meetings in Chapter 9, so let's turn our attention to the other two formal meeting situations and discuss what you can expect to happen during each one of them.

**Did you know?** School personnel like parents to ask questions at meetings. This gives them an indication of your level of involvement and they know that they can count on you to work with the teacher to help your child. School meetings are not the time to be shy: bring a list of questions, a pen and notepad to take notes and to jot down other questions, and feel free to speak up. Your child's education is at stake.

### Student Support Team Meeting

Perhaps you are reading this book because your child's teacher has indicated that your child is having trouble but has either never been evaluated for special education services or has been found ineligible for these services. If so, your child is most likely being monitored by a student support team (SST), which is sometimes also called a student assistance team (SAT) or child study team (CST). SST meetings are fairly structured. Participants may include you, your child's teachers, the school psychologist, school administrator, and other personnel, as requested by you or your child's teacher(s). Meetings usually last no more than an hour, although this will depend on the number and types of problems discussed. Be sure to get a copy of the meeting minutes before you leave.

A typical meeting will start off with introductions and an explanation of the purpose of the meeting. This will be followed by several possible areas of discussion, including:

- The child's strengths and weaknesses
- Current concerns relating to the child's difficulties
- Review of interventions tried in the classroom and at home
- Brainstorming of ideas
- Summary of what actions will be taken and who is responsible for each task, and the date work is to be completed, or the date of the next review

At this time, it is important for you to share any concerns that you might have regarding your child's education. This information is a valuable resource for SST if team members are to create an adequate plan of action. If you are asked to provide information about your child's study, eating, and sleep habits; illnesses; current medications; temperament; strengths and weaknesses; and interventions you may have tried at home, don't feel that the school team is invading your privacy for no reason. This information is asked because it could help SST to plan for changes within the classroom and provide you with some suggestions for implementing changes within the home. If you feel that something is unclear, or if you disagree with the suggested course of action, it is important to communicate this to SST as soon as possible, so that modifications can be made to the plan.

**Did you know?** Many parents may walk away from school meetings confused and not sure of what has been discussed. This happens despite the best intentions of the school personnel to provide information and the parents' best intentions to be receptive to what is said. Often, this situation results from being overwhelmed due to "information overload." As a parent, if you do not feel comfortable with the information that you have received and need more clarification after the meeting, do not be shy or embarrassed. Your ability to participate in your child's education depends on your ability to understand what is happening. Ask for further clarification on any points about which you are unsure.

## Manifestation Determination

Some children engage in misconduct that results in suspension or expulsion from school. For children receiving special education services, safeguards are in place to prevent schools from treating them unfairly. Chapter 10 discussed student disciplinary issues and the protection under IDEA 2004 for children with disabilities. Also see the procedural safeguards in Appendix D. To review, if a child violates a discipline policy that results in a suspension of more than ten days, or the suspension combined with previous suspensions total more than ten days, a manifestation determination meeting (also known as disciplinary review meeting) must be held because a change in placement (from school to home) would take place. Federal law requires that a school must first determine whether the misconduct was the result, or a *manifestation*, of the child's disability before a change in placement can be made. However, IDEA 2004 has more clearly suggested exceptions where the severity of the violation and expediency of action require otherwise.

**Remember that** under IDEA 2004, if a child commits major bodily harm to others, or is a threat to self or others, or commits a weapon or drug violation on school-related premises, the child can be removed to an alternate placement, without parent permission or manifest determination. Under these conditions, however, the child continues to receive services that allow him to master IEP goals under FAPE.

It is most likely that many people compose the IEP team. Participants may include you, teachers, the school psychologist, school counselor, school administrators, special education director, school resource (police) officer, and other personnel. The IEP team, upon review of all of the child's information, must determine if there is a relationship between the misconduct and the child's disability. This is done to make decisions regarding the consequences the child should face and address his ongoing educational and behavioral needs. This determination must occur no later than ten days after disciplinary action is taken. The team must decide whether the IEP, including the behavior intervention plan, is appropriate; the IEP was implemented correctly; the disability prevented the child from understanding the impact and consequences of his behavior; and if the disability prevented the child from controlling his behavior. If the team determines the misconduct was not a manifestation of the child's disability, the child may be punished with the same disciplinary procedures used for children without a disability, although special education services will continue.

Manifestation meetings are often more stressful on parents because their child has done or been accused of doing something wrong. As a parent, you may feel that an administrator may attempt to convince the team that the behavior is not the result of the child's disability so that the child can be removed from the school and subjected to a long-term suspension or expulsion. Our advice is to remain positive, focus on the information being presented, and ask good questions. If the district does not believe your child's behavior is a manifestation of his disability and you sincerely believe it is, you have the right to request a hearing if you disagree with either the manifestation determination or placement decision. Review the procedural safeguards for your state and see the information on disciplinary matters in Chapter 10 and Appendix D to increase your understanding in this area.

C H A P T E R   1 2

# A Parent's Guide to Stress and Coping

Not all stress is bad. Stress occurs when we have to adapt to change in our environment, whether that change is positive or negative. For example, adaptation to a change in employment circumstances can be a stressful situation, whether that change involves a job loss, relocation, or promotion. The most common factors that can increase stress include lack of predictability, lack of control (or choice), and putting too much pressure on oneself over too long a period of time (burnout). Increased stress and an inability to cope often result in one of two broad responses to frustration: fight (aggression/anger) or flight (depression/withdrawal). Continued stress can take its toll on us physically and actually wear down the immune system, resulting in deterioration in health and making us more vulnerable to illness.

Studies have demonstrated that parenting a child with special needs can result in unique challenges that may increase family stress. Children who experience serious emotional, behavioral, or learning problems can place increased demands on parents who may already be stressed by work and/or financial concerns. However, readers can take a significant step toward reducing stress by increasing their knowledge about the special education process. In turn, this should result in increased feelings of empowerment and help to reduce levels of stress. By knowing what to expect (predictability), parents can gain greater control over their child's educational possibilities by being a proactive member of their child's special education team. Understanding their child's disability and how to effectively manage behavior problems can also be instrumental in reducing potentially stressful situations.

Studies have suggested several common events that can be stressful for adults, such as financial worries, marital conflict, and employment problems. For children, stressful situations can be found in their home (parent and sibling conflict) or school environments (peer relationships or academic difficulties).

## Common Types of Stress

Stress usually occurs when we are prevented from reaching a goal. *Frustration* is often the result. Frustration can occur when we cannot obtain our goal because we lack sufficient preparation, understanding, or ability to achieve that desired goal.

Another common type of stress involves *decision-making conflict,* such as when we have to make a difficult decision between two choices. We can struggle to decide between two positive outcomes (go to the movies or to the dance), two negative outcomes (stay after school to finish class-work, or finish the work at home, instead of going to a baseball game), or a single situation that has positive and negative aspects. An example of this last situation could be wanting to approach a teacher to ask for help, but being afraid of asking because you might think that other children will think you are stupid. Regardless of the outcomes, all three of the previous decision-making situations can create stress for the person who must weigh the alternatives and make a decision.

A third type of stress is the type of response that occurs when we are placed under increased *pressure to perform*. Although a bit of anxiety can be a performance enhancer, such as providing an edge to win a race, too much pressure can cause some people to reduce their performance due to increased anxiety and stress. For example, some children may be able to work well at home in a relatively calm environment, but do very poorly on timed tests at school, since test-taking anxiety develops from increased pressure to achieve under time constraints.

It is important to understand that what is stressful on one day may not be as stressful on another. Some days we may be better able to cope with *conflict, pressure* or *frustration*, while on other days, it may take little in the way of conflict, pressure or frustration to tip the scales between coping and not coping. In addition, stress can increase as our motivation to achieve or our desire to obtain a goal increases. If something is less important to us, we are likely to be less stressed than if we were being challenged in obtaining a more significant goal. Some stresses are predictable, such as a child's feelings of stress when changing schools, while some stresses may not be predictable, such as a surprise test.

### What Are the Symptoms of Stress?

Reactions to stress can be observed physically, emotionally, behaviorally, and mentally. At a physical level, when we are placed under stress our body mobilizes to respond to the stressful threat by *fight or flight*. Our body responds by increasing its heart rate and adrenaline production. While in this state of alert, we are mobilized to combat the stressor. However, this physical response is very taxing on our system and if we remain in this state of alert for too long, we become exhausted. One of the consequences of heightened alert is that ultimately it drains our reserves, resulting in increased susceptibility to illness. Other physical symptoms can include sleep problems and eating problems (overeating or undereating). Our thinking can also be impaired. We can make errors in judgment and make impulsive and rash decisions. Emotionally, we can become irritable, angry, and act out our frustrations toward others.

Children who are stressed may respond with a wide variety of symptoms. Some children may become weepy and break into tears at a moment's notice. Other children may withdraw in an attempt to avoid the stressful situation. Fantasy play may replace a too-stressful reality for some children, while others may respond to stress with physical responses of headaches, stomachaches, and sleep problems (either needing too much sleep or having problems falling asleep or staying asleep). Some children may demonstrate regressive behavior, such as a five-year-old who wants to have a bottle because her new baby sister is getting too much attention. Acting out in an aggressive way is also a common child reaction to stress. Many children will use denial to avoid acknowledging a stressful situation, such as the child who continually forgets to bring his schoolbooks home, because he is at a loss as to how to do the work.

### How Should You Cope with Stress?

The first step in coping with stress is to understand and recognize the symptoms of stress in yourself as a parent and in your child. Parents must recognize that often their feelings of anxiety are a natural reaction to the stresses of parenting a child with special needs. By knowing the early warning signs that could lead to a deterioration in health and well-being, parents can focus on helpful techniques to alleviate stressful symptoms for themselves and their child.

**Stress is inevitable;** it is how you cope with stress that is important.

There are also many common responses that people naturally adopt in an attempt to diffuse the stress or tension. Some of the more common behaviors associated with coping mechanisms for stress include crying, an intense need to "talk it out," using humor to laugh it off, reaching out to others for support, and repetitive dreams that serve to redirect the stressful situation away from the individual.

**A Framework for Understanding and Responding to Stressful Events**   When confronted with a stressful situation or event, it is important to step back and take a look at what is happening. The following framework can help in understanding what is causing the stress and how to approach the situation.

**Sample Example:** A parent is dreading the approach of yet another school meeting to discuss her child's progress—or lack of progress, to be more exact. The last few meetings were stressful and the parent felt on the defensive, feeling like teachers were blaming her for her child's lack of completed assignments. The parent also felt that teachers were not making the accommodations needed for her child, despite the fact that these were clearly articulated in the IEP. The following action plan was developed to help the parent reduce her stress level prior to the meeting.

1. *Take a closer look at the stressful situation.* It is important to pinpoint what is causing the stress. In the previous scenario, the parent is responding to the upcoming meeting in a stressful way because of a past history of meetings that were uncomfortable and stressful for her. If so, the parent needs to address how the current meeting (given her new understanding of special education processes) could be different from previous meetings and why she should feel more confident and less stressed in approaching her child's educators on this occasion.

2. *Develop an action plan.* The parent needs to understand that her newfound knowledge about the special education process can make a significant change in how she presents herself at the meeting and her level of confidence in approaching her child's teachers. One way to reduce stress is to be prepared and proactive. The parent should write down her questions prior to the meeting, based on her increased understanding of the special education process. Questions should address the possible solutions to her child's difficulties completing assignments and how she and the teachers can work together to help her child be successful. The parent should also prepare questions to inquire about the ways teachers are meeting her child's needs for completing assignments based on her child's current IEP.

The parent could also use some of the suggested methods for reducing stressful reactions (meditation or deep breathing exercises, which will both be discussed shortly) prior to attending the meeting, and scheduling the meeting at a time when she is least likely to feel pressured.

3. *Monitor and evaluate the results.* Bringing the written notes to the meeting will help the parent stay on track and will help her to focus on the issues at hand, rather than becoming emotionally defensive or overstressed. After the meeting, the parent should write down her post-meeting impressions while they are still fresh in her mind. She should ask herself questions, such as What could I do differently the next time? What other questions might I have asked? What do I need to do next? Who is responsible for implementing my child's education plan?

**Deep Muscle Relaxation, Breathing Exercises, and Meditation**   When we become stressed or anxious, certain muscles in the body tighten automatically. Deep muscle relaxation involves learning to identify and relax those muscles that are tight and tense. Using this technique, people can learn how to deliberately tighten and then relax certain muscles. Muscle groups can be tightened (face, neck, arms, legs, back, chest, and stomach) and then relaxed. Working from a relaxed position (sitting in a chair with your back touching the chair back, feet flat on the floor, and hands on your lap), tense each muscle group for five seconds and then relax for at least ten seconds, before proceeding to the next muscle group. For example, to tense and relax the arm muscles, put your arm out straight in front of you and tighten your entire arm until you make a fist. Pay attention to each muscle part as it tenses (biceps, forearm, back of arm, elbow, wrist, and fingers). Hold this tense position for five seconds. Gradually release each of the muscle groups in succession, and return your arm to its resting place on your lap. Notice the difference between being tense and being relaxed.

*Breathing exercises* can also be accomplished from the same relaxed position as described earlier. When doing deep breathing, close your eyes and concentrate on relaxing all muscle groups until you are feeling limp. If you notice any muscle group that is still tense, concentrate on muscle relaxation in the way described earlier. Once you are in a relaxed state with your eyes closed, take a deep breath, hold it for about five seconds, and then exhale very slowly. As you exhale, imagine the air moving through your body and taking the tension away as it leaves your body. Starting with your head and proceeding to your toes, relax your body as you exhale. As you are breathing out next time, say the words "B-R-E-A-T-H-E———O-U-T" slowly while exhaling until the final T comes out of your toes. Repeat this exercise five times.

Another exercise that can be helpful in alleviating stress, grounding yourself, or helping you to sleep at night is to focus and meditate on the environment around you. With your eyes closed, ask yourself to listen to your surroundings and identify five different sounds that you hear, or five different physical sensations that you feel in your body, or recall five different sights that you see.

## Children and Stress

Children can also be helped to manage stress in many ways. Knowing how to identify stressful symptoms in your child is the first step toward helping your child develop ways to successfully cope with stressful situations. The following steps can be helpful in teaching children to manage stress more effectively:

- Teach your child how to recognize the symptoms of stress in himself.
- Help your child learn how to relax through deep breathing, stretching, muscle relaxation, and using visual imagery to calm the mind and body.
- Help your child to develop a framework for problem solving that will help to reduce stress and increase opportunities for success.

1. **Stop:** What is the problem?
2. **Think:** What can I do about it?
3. **Try:** A response.

- Encourage your child to use positive methods to solve the problem or to back away and release tensions prior to attempting a solution.
- Normalize stress for your child by talking about how stress can influence everyone, at any age.
- Don't involve your young child in adult discussions about marital conflicts or finances. Children who are given too much information may feel more powerless to help and may feel that they are to blame for difficult times.
- Praise your child's efforts and help your child understand that sometimes not getting what we want can be a powerful lesson to help us learn how to try different approaches in the future.
- Help your child to understand that stress often comes from having to make difficult choices. If your child did not make the best choice, help him to understand how to problem solve in order to make better choices in the future.
- A daily planner can be a great stress buster. Teach your child that a daily planner (student agenda) is his best friend. Knowing what to expect can help your child to be prepared. Being prepared is one of the best ways to fight stress.
- If your child is stressed about a social situation or event, help your child role-play what might happen and what possible responses might be appropriate.

## How to Cope with Stress: Positive and Negative Ways of Coping

Finally, it is important to remember that there are positive ways of coping with stress and there are negative ways. Inappropriate ways of attempting to deal with stress involve withdrawal, avoidance, denial, acting out, and blaming others. Positive ways of coping with stressful experiences result from looking at stressful experiences as learning experiences. Knowing what to expect and preparing for the expected are healthy ways of using stressful experiences to motivate change in a positive way. And don't forget, having a good sense of humor is always a positive way to relieve stress.

CHAPTER 13

A Parent's Guide to Building Your Child's Self-Esteem and Increasing Social Competence

This chapter will focus on how the self-concept changes over time and the importance of social competence in the formation of a healthy self-concept.

The self-concept is a complex system of beliefs about ourselves. We develop our self-concepts based on judgments or evaluations of how we are doing compared with others or to our own so-called ideal self. It is possible to have a good self-concept in one area (like sports) and a poor self-concept in another area (like mathematics).

The self-concept (also known as self-esteem, self-image, or self-worth) is formed from three major sources of information that we obtain from others: words, feelings, and behaviors. "What I think about myself" is often based on others' comments about me; "What I feel about myself often comes from others' emotional reactions"; and "How I behave is often in response to others' responses to me."

Another source of information that helps build or reduce self-concept is the set of internal standards used to judge one's performance. If these standards of ideal performance are too high, a person may feel that he or she does not measure up. Consequently, the person develops feelings that devalue a sense of worth, resulting in a low self-concept or self-image in that area. Children often learn these internal standards from watching how their parents, teachers, and peers judge their performance at school and in the home. (See Table 13-1 for ways to build your child's self-esteem.)

## Changes in Self-Concept at Different Ages and Stages

Very young children (3 to 5 years of age) think in all or nothing terms. Therefore, self-concepts often fluctuate from extremes at this stage, such as happy/sad or

*Table 13-1.* *A parent's guide to building self-esteem: goals and methods.*

**Goal: Provide Emotional Support**

- Reduce negative statements and critical comments; be aware of a sarcastic tone.
- Correct the child's tendency to make negative statements about himself by focusing on the effort, rather than the result.
- Empathize with your child's feelings.
- Listen, acknowledge, and validate your child's feelings. Try to understand the emotions behind the behavior (*anger is a legitimate feeling; how we deal with it is another story*).
- Talk to your child's teacher so that you can better understand how your child is doing academically, socially, and emotionally.
- Let your child know that "It's ok to make mistakes," and that even parents can learn from their mistakes.

**Goal: Increase Social Competency**

- Watch a favorite TV program with your child and talk about the characters' feelings and behaviors.
- Make a favorite meal together and talk about sharing tasks and cooperation.
- Take time to talk to your child about their social day at school.
- Provide increased opportunities for your child to interact with other children and observe how your child is "fitting in."

**Goal: Provide Opportunities for Developing Skills in Mastering Tasks and Challenges**

- Children develop confidence from their increased ability to master tasks.
- Know when to allow your child the opportunity to stumble, and learn how to succeed on future attempts.
- Don't remove extracurricular activities as a punishment for academic difficulties; these activities could have a major impact on increasing self-esteem.
- Provide age-appropriate chores to develop your child's sense of responsibility and independence in completing tasks.
- Break tasks down to ensure success through steps that can be mastered, then build on successes.

**Goal: Provide Opportunities for Developing Skills in Emotion Regulation**

- Help your child learn to step back and cool down when frustrated; teach your child to recognize and label feeling states "frustration, anger" that can lead to a lack of self-control.
- Create an atmosphere of structure, predictability, and natural consequences for misbehavior.
- Include your child in the decision-making process (e.g., selecting a consequence for misbehaving from a range of consequences developed together earlier).

*(continues)*

*Table 13-1.    (Continued).*

**Goal: Celebrate Success**

- Post your child's work in a prominent place (such as refrigerator).
- Reward your child's positive accomplishments with a treat from the "good reward jar."
- Draw attention to at least one positive thing about your child every day.
- Catch your child being good.

good/bad. The child often overgeneralizes and reasons that *If I'm good at coloring, then I'm good at everything. If I'm bad because I spilled the milk, I'm bad. Period!*

By the time a child enters the first grade (approximately 6 years of age), reasoning allows the child to sequence emotions and behaviors. At this stage of development, the child begins to develop a greater understanding that a parent can be happy and then sad, thereby allowing some flexibility and continuity in the emotional repertoire. However, it is not until approximately the third grade (8 years of age) that the child can accept and understand the concept of experiencing two coexisting emotions such as being both happy *and* sad. However, at this stage, the child can only attach the two emotions to two separate people. A child might reason: *Mommy and Daddy may have two separate feelings about me. Daddy may describe me as "good," but Mommy may say I'm "bad."* The child is not yet capable of understanding how both feelings could come from the same person. At this stage, the child is capable of understanding that he can be good at math but poor at spelling.

It is not until approximately 10 years of age that the child begins to understand the concept of ambivalent feelings (one person having conflicting emotions). It is at this point that the child is capable of understanding how a parent can continue to love Johnny or Susie despite being very angry with their behavior. It is also at this stage that the self-concept becomes further influenced by how children evaluate themselves and their achievements compared with their peers. Self-descriptions and comparisons also change in their shift in focus from the more absolute terms used earlier (good/bad; nice/mean) toward descriptors that emphasize the social or more interactive aspects of this developmental period (shy/friendly).

The young adolescent often maintains an idealistic and naive view of "what should be," which has not yet been tempered by experience. The adolescent's awareness that others are capable of thinking about other people results from the self-conscious fear that others are often thinking about and evaluating him or her. It is through comparisons with peers and peer acceptance that the adolescent's fears are alleviated and he or she begins to once again grow in self-confidence.

*The Three Competencies*

In addition to the evolution of the self-concept based on our growing understanding and increased perceptions of ourselves and the world around us, our self-concept is also influenced by our perceptions of self-competence in three specific areas: *cognitive* (academic/school/career), *physical* (athletic/artistic), and *social* (peer groups) domains (see Figure 13-1).

### Self-Esteem Based on Cognitive/Achievement Performance

Children can measure their success relative to their peers in several different areas. For children in special education, learning and achievement can be two areas that cause significant frustration and challenge. These children may work very hard to master tasks, but their efforts may not result in success for many reasons, such as poor memory, processing problems, or difficulties in problem solving. Some children may feel dumb and may begin to avoid academic work because of the frustration and their lack of success. For many children, small group work centers or resource room assistance can provide a safer environment and slower pace to allow them to attempt and acquire new skills.

Children should always be praised for their efforts, and tasks should be presented at levels that are not too challenging or too easy. Challenges that are too steep will serve to frustrate the child and may result in developing feelings of helplessness regarding future efforts to master tasks. Tasks that are too easy can provide a sense of false competence and not prepare the child for taking on greater challenges. Breaking down complex tasks into smaller segments can assist the child to master more difficult tasks in stages that build on earlier successes.

A number of children receiving special education assistance may have a recognizable physical disability (like vision, hearing, or orthopedic problems). These children obtain accommodations for their disability in ways that will enhance their learning (like wearing glasses or a heading aid, or using crutches or a wheelchair). However, children with less obvious disabilities (such as ADHD, learning disabili-

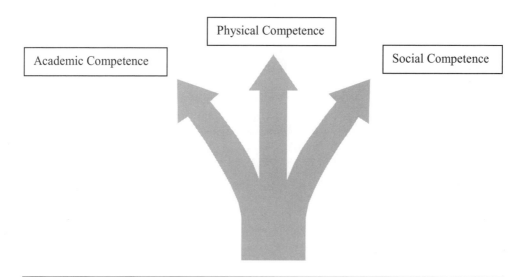

*Figure 13-1.   The three competencies of self-concept.*

ties, or emotional disturbance) may be misunderstood by their teachers, parents, or peers as not achieving adequately because of their lack of effort—the child may be described as lazy or unmotivated or not caring about school. For these children, it is important to praise their efforts and to understand that having a learning problem is a significant burden that they must carry with them throughout their academic years. As a parent, the more you understand exactly where your child's disability lies, the more you can help your child cope academically and develop a healthy self-concept based on success in areas other than academics.

### Self-Esteem Based on Physical Competencies

**Did you know?** When children are having academic difficulties, many parents feel that the first thing to go should be the extracurricular activities. They reason that *since Johnny is failing his spelling tests, he should lose the privilege of playing on the baseball team.* However, for many children, not passing spelling tests may be a legitimate result of their learning disability. For these children, athletics may be the only area in which they are capable of excelling. If these children lose these activities, they also lose the opportunity of feeling successful compared with their peers.

While competence in academic areas might be evaluated by our actual achievement in certain subject areas, our competence in physical pursuits may be a function of our athletic abilities or fine motor (artistic) skills. These different areas of mastery can assist a child in finding an area, other than academics, that they can excel in and increase their self-concept. As was noted in the sidebar example, often parents will remove children from extracurricular activities because of their lack of academic success. However, children who are receiving special education assistance have been determined eligible for special services because of a legitimate learning problem that falls within one of the major categories recognized by IDEA. For these children, developing a healthy self-concept will require stretching outside the academic system to include activities that can increase self-confidence and feelings of success. Parents should look for opportunities in the community for their child to become involved in activities that might contribute to the development of potential competencies and skills in areas such as sports, art, dance, theatre, music, agricultural or horticultural groups, gymnastics, baton, and so on.

Having suggested the need to expand rather than restrict extracurricular activities for children in special education, it *is* important to realize there is a limit to the amount of extracurricular activities that should be scheduled. Recently, there has been an increased recognition that some parents overschedule their children in far too many activities, which can increase stress for many family members. We are not advocating this situation by any means; we simply what to impress upon you that extracurricular activities are an important component in building self-esteem for children in special education.

*Self-Esteem Based on Social Competence and Social Skills*

Although very young children often engage in solitary or parallel play with peers, as they mature, there is an increased emphasis on the need to develop skills that emphasize interactive and cooperative play with others. Therefore, the third competency—social competency—gains increasing importance as an influential factor in the development of self-esteem, as the child matures.

Developing social competence involves four prerequisite skills:

1. The ability to recognize and respond to both nonverbal and verbal information
2. Sensitivity to the needs and feelings of others
3. The ability to engage in interpersonal problem solving
4. Awareness of peer group norms

Children who lack social competence are said to have poor social skills. Children who have special needs, especially those who find it difficult to learn because of a learning disability or attention problems, are likely to experience social difficulties. The reason for the overlap is that social learning requires much the same skills as learning in any other subject in our environment. If children have trouble with problem solving in academic situations, they are also likely to encounter problem-solving difficulties in social situations.

## How We Learn Social Skills

Interpreting social information can often result in difficulties if social cues are misinterpreted, resulting in a social mismatch. At a basic level, social information comes to us in much the same way we learn other information:

> **Did you know?** Interpreting social information follows the same process as interpreting other information in our environment:
>
> *Recognition of Social Cues → Interpretation of Social Cues → Response to Social Cues*

Difficulties with the recognition of social cues may result from poor ability to attend to information that is presented verbally, visually, or motorically (such as touch). A great deal of information can be misinterpreted if we do not pay attention to subtle auditory cues like tone and emphasis. Misinterpretation at this level often results in missing the main message. If we don't pay attention to a person's facial expression or body posture, we may miss important signals about how receptive a person is to our approaching at this time. For example, is the person signalling an approach-me or a leave-me-alone stance? Finally, recognizing the difference between a soft pat and a more intrusive touch may result in a completely different meaning for a given interchange.

Children who have difficulties with academics due to weak attention to visual details may readily miss visual details in social situations as well. Errors in visual attention may result in a lack of attention to visual indicators such as subtle changes in facial expression providing clues to a person's present emotional status; changes in body posture can signal fatigue or a high-energy level. Similarly, a child who demonstrates poor listening skills in the classroom may also misinterpret social communication by not tuning in at the correct time or by missing important parts of a message.

### Interpretation of Social Information

Provided that we have recognized the cues appropriately, how can we be sure that we have interpreted the cues in the best way, given the context of the situation?

We learn appropriate social responses through the competency skills noted previously, which are acquired over time through our exposure to social input in the home and in previous social interactions. Interpreting a particular social situation requires that we are able to draw on previous experience to help us sort out what we are dealing with. In order to learn, we need to find predictability in our environment, which results in organizing social responses into categories of successful and unsuccessful attempts. We also need to be able to make comparisons between like or similar situations or to generalize the information from situation to situation, so we don't keep repeating our errors over and over again.

Children with specific learning disabilities often have difficulties in the following areas:

- Organizing information
- Attention span
- Memory and expression
- Sequencing information
- Isolating key elements of information
- Transferring information from one situation to another

Can you see how all these areas could affect your success or lack of success in social relationships? All these elements play a crucial role in the interpretation of social events. The skills necessary for the correct interpretation of social exchanges are the same skills required for problem solving in many academic situations. These abilities allow us to learn from our past experiences by storing information about how we acted and what we did in similar social situations. It also allows us to use our reasoning skills comparing this situation to others in terms of how similar or different it might be and what did or didn't work in the past. Being able to correctly sequence which events came first, and how they unfolded, is crucial in being able to understand and anticipate the consequences of our actions. Children who are impulsive often have considerable difficulty in this area.

## Social Responding

Responses to social situations can cause trouble if the response does not match the situation in terms of timing and/or intensity. Children who are hyperactive or impulsive often overreact to social stimulation. Consequently, their reactions are inflated compared to what triggered the reaction. Extremely impulsive children, such as those with ADHD, seem to bypass the interpretation component completely, as if they go directly from ***INPUT → RESPONSE*** without taking the time to interpret or problem solve.

Children who are passive or hypoactive (slow to respond) may take too long to respond and also miss the appropriate opportunity for reaction. Some children who have expressive language problems take a long time to process information and never really get their verbal responses together quickly enough to participate. These are the children who take so long to answer that people often end up finishing their sentences for them. Children who are overly passive may be the opposite to the impulsive responder in their passive or nonresponsive manner (like providing minimal facial expressions or verbal comments). These children by their passivity give off few social cues to which others can respond. These are the children who are often called "hard to read" and may be avoided by others socially, because people are never sure how to respond to them, since they provide so little feedback.

## Social Responding and the Social Self-Concept

A final word of emphasis on the chain of information that takes place in the building of social self-concept. Other people evaluate us by our social responses, and they in turn direct their responses to us based on their interpretations. It is often from this feedback that our positive or negative social self-concept is formed.

# CHAPTER 14

# A Parent's Guide to Behavior and Discipline

Discipline is essential not only in school but also in the home. It can help your child to understand which behaviors are acceptable and which ones are not. As children mature, they begin to see that their behavior at home is also related to the quality of the social interactions they have with other children. Because of its importance, discipline is a significant contributor to your child's development—at home, at school, and in his social relationships.

This chapter will discuss providing structure in the home, show you how to teach your child appropriate behaviors, discuss what to do when behavior problems arise, and address the different types of effective discipline.

## The Importance of Structure in the Home

All children need structure. Creating a predictable environment for your child will foster his physical growth and mental development. Structure provides a safe environment in which to develop healthy self-esteem. Clearly defined rules and expectations, as well as consistent reinforcement, can limit the need for discipline.

**Did you know?** Structure requires you to establish boundaries, follow routines, adapt rules when necessary, and set limits. Structure provides an excellent framework for appropriate behavior.

### Step 1: Establishing Boundaries

There are many ways in which parents can set boundaries to provide structure for children. These include setting rules, establishing consequences, and providing reinforcement.

**Set Rules**  Just as there are classroom rules, there must be rules at home, too. You and your child should work together to think of rules that can be used in the home. Allowing your child to help create house rules gives him some ownership of them, and it increases the chances that these rules will be followed. No more than five or ten rules should be created; the more rules there are, the more likely your child is to forget them. In order to help your child remember the rules, post them in a few places around your home, such as in the kitchen, play area, and his bedroom. Periodically reviewing the rules also is helpful, just to be sure your child remembers them. If your child's behavior is getting worse in one area, it may be helpful to create a new rule that addresses the behavior.

For older children, it is acceptable to state actual rules. Suggested rules may include: "There is no running in the house," "Toys are to be put away after I play with them," and "I will put all of my clothes in the hamper before I go to bed." The Our House Rules chart in Appendix C can be used to post the rules and the consequences, which we'll talk about next. Verbally reminding your child— "Johnny, remember the rule that says no running in the house"—can help him to remember the rules, a strategy you may need to follow after a new rule is implemented. You can use a check mark or hash mark to indicate whether your child followed the rule. Again, before your child goes to bed, review with him how well he did that day. Encouragement and praise can go a long way in helping your child to change his behavior.

Young children may not fully understand rule following, so it is often better to set positive behavior goals instead of rules. Things such as "I will wash my hands before I eat," "I will put away my toys," and "I will brush my teeth in the morning and before I go to bed" are common goals. You can use our Positive Behavior Chart in Appendix C to record the goals and your child's daily progress. When your child reaches a goal, draw a smiley face in that column. If your child forgets the goal, draw a frowning face. This serves as a visual reminder of your child's daily performance. It is a good idea to review that day's progress so that your child can see how well he did. Verbally praise your child when he does well, and encourage your child when he does not.

**Did you know?** Many children are visual learners and would benefit if you posted one of these charts. Use the chart in this book or create your own. You may want to laminate your chart and use a dry erase marker to monitor daily behaviors. Avoid using a red marker.

**Establish Consequences**  Establishing consequences will help your child understand the relationship between his misbehavior and its consequences. When children break the rules, they must learn there will be consequences if they are to learn right from wrong. We like the idea of using a *consequences jar*. This is a jar that includes different consequences, written on small pieces of paper, which have been created by you and your child. Brainstorming for consequences can be a productive and meaningful activity that promotes creativity and person responsibility. When your child misbehaves and you feel it deserves a consequence, ask your child to choose one of the consequences out of the jar. This also helps to minimize some of the verbal feedback such as "That's not fair!" since the child chose it himself. Examples may include "No dessert," "No TV after dinner," or "Going to bed thirty minutes early."

**Provide Reinforcement**   It is important to praise your child when his behavior has been good that day. If your child has earned several smiley faces on the Positive Behavior Chart, or few negative check marks on the Our House Rules chart, you should tell your child that he did a good job, should keep up the good work, and you are proud of him. There are many ways to provide positive reinforcement to your child, both verbally ("Good job!" or "I like your good behavior") and nonverbally (a smile or hug). As a parent, it is important that you make a conscious effort to provide this type of reinforcement on a regular basis. Positive reinforcement will help your child build self-confidence. Children want to please their parents, and this reinforcement will help to increase the chances that they will continue to exhibit good behavior. Children have both good days and bad days, just like an adult, but the goal is to maximize the number of good days. These good days will serve as a model for positive behavior occurring in the future.

### Step 2: Following Routines

Parents can create routines for children, including routines for the morning, after school, and bedtime. There are instances when routines can be changed, which we will address.

**Morning**   Morning routines should be the same every day so that your child knows what to expect and can learn to get ready with little or no supervision. A typical pattern may be:

- Get out of bed
- Brush teeth
- Wash face
- Get dressed
- Make bed
- Eat breakfast
- Go to school

Once you decide on the pattern that works best for you and your child, you may want to list the tasks and post them in your child's room or the bathroom so that he can follow them more easily. For younger children and those with reading problems, you can use pictures to represent each of the tasks.

**After School/Homework**   Whether your child goes straight home or to after-school care, a routine can still be established. If your child goes home, you should decide whether you want all, some, or none of your child's homework completed before he is allowed time to play. Some parents prefer that their children complete work as soon as they get home, so the day's lesson is still fresh in their minds. Other parents give their children some free time first; they prefer to "let kids be kids" and believe that playtime is more important right after school in order to give their child a break from academics. You must choose the routine that works best for you and your child and follow it consistently each day. The routine for homework will depend on whether your child has homework, how much, and the amount of help and supervision he will require. For younger children and children who have no homework, create a routine that includes a snack, playtime outside for exercise, dinner, TV time, book time, and individual time with you. In establishing homework routines, it is important to set aside a consistent place where homework is to be completed. Based on your physical restriction, if at all possible, it is best to restrict homework to locations that are away from high-traffic areas. For example, doing homework on the kitchen table can be a good thing, unless this area is often where the family congregates to talk and share daily information.

The amount of time your child is expected to spend on homework depends on your school district's curriculum and their own expectations. We recommend the following list as a guide, which is based on a child's developmental level. The time spent on homework may vary depending on the severity of your child's disability.

| | |
|---|---|
| Kindergarten | Maximum of fifteen minutes per night |
| First grade | Maximum of fifteen minutes per night |
| Second grade | Maximum of twenty minutes per night |
| Third grade | Maximum of thirty minutes per night |
| Fourth grade | Maximum of forty-five minutes per night |
| Fifth grade | Maximum of sixty minutes per night |
| Sixth grade | Maximum of seventy-five minutes per night |
| Seventh grade | Maximum of two hours per night |
| Eighth grade | Maximum of two hours per night |
| Ninth to Twelfth grade | Maximum of two to three hours per night |

**Bedtime**   A nighttime routine can help your child prepare for a good night's sleep. As with a morning routine, the bedtime routine should follow a typical pattern:

- Brush teeth
- Wash face
- Take a bath (on days when the child needs one)
- Put on pajamas
- Read book with parent
- Talk about the day's events and what the child learned
- Go to sleep

Giving your child a thirty-minute time period to wind down will help him to relax and fall asleep more easily. A sleep routine is important, and children benefit from positive sleep habits even at an early age. This includes waking up and going to bed the same time each day, including weekends.

**Did you know?** Children need between nine and eleven hours of sleep. Your child may require more or need less. Research shows that minor changes in sleep, such as allowing your child to stay up an hour later to watch a TV show, can impair his learning, memory, attention, and concentration.

### Knowing When to Change the Routine

There are times when a change in routine may be necessary. We will address three instances when you may want or need to change a routine.

**Making Exceptions**  It may be necessary to change the routine because of a special event such as a party, vacation, or sporting event. When this occurs, it is important to point out to your child that it is a special time and you are making this change but that his regular routine will resume when it is over. In certain situations, an exception to a routine may be a reward for good behavior.

**Routine Is No Longer Appropriate**  Most of what you do with a child depends on the child's developmental level. As your child matures, you may find it necessary to change his routine to allow for additional homework time or study time, for example. As your child gets older, bedtime may be extended or he may get up earlier for school. You may also ask your child about his routine, which provides him with an opportunity to give you feedback.

**Not Adapting to Routine**  Some children may have difficulty transitioning from one routine to another. If your child has never had a good routine, he may initially struggle when one is implemented. Give your child some time for adjustment. If, after a reasonable period—say, a month—you find that your child is not adapting well, you will need to adjust the routine accordingly. Maybe your child is not getting enough sleep or needs more free time to play. Again, if you think your child is mature enough, be sure to ask him about it. Older children will be better able to verbalize what they see as not working with the routine.

### Step 3: Setting Limits

Setting limits is another way in which parents can provide structure for children. Examples include time limits, material limits, and behavioral limits.

**Time Limits**  Your child must learn to minimize time spent on certain activities and maximize time spent on others. You may need to teach your child that time for watching TV, talking on the phone, playing video games, and playing on the computer is a privilege, and must be earned by displaying good behavior. Even when earned, we recommend that you limit these activities to a reasonable number of hours per week, and instead maximize your child's time spent on reading, puzzles, games, and creative play.

**Material Limits**  Children tend to think the sky's the limit when it comes to owning things. If they have too many toys, they tend to play only with the new ones and a few select favorites, while forgetting about the rest. Your child does not need all of the latest toys, games, and electronic equipment—a few at major holidays is fine. For some children, having a TV in their bedroom may interfere with good sleep habits. In this case, emphasize books and the importance of reading prior to bedtime and perhaps reading with your child at younger ages, and consider removing the TV from his room. It may also be advisable to spend time with your child in your local library instead of a toy store. It is in your child's best interest to place limits on material items. Limiting the number of toys, games, and other play materials will help your child to learn self-control and promote good habits, as well as conscientiousness and creativity.

**Behavioral Limits**  Children must understand that the appropriateness of their behaviors often depends on the setting and situation. It is acceptable, for example, to yell outside but not inside the house, which leads to a difference between "inside voice" and "outside voice." Learning to control impulses is a complex process, affected by developmental level, personality, and environment. Children must also recognize the difference between requesting something once and asking you for it repeatedly. Requesting a cookie is fine once or twice, but not ten times. The limits imposed on this behavior can have implications for their social interactions, as many children may find this type of behavior annoying.

**Did you know?** Most everything you do, your child sees and does, even if you don't witness it. Children are often a reflection of their parents—the apple really *doesn't* fall far from the tree—which is why you serve as a role model, good or bad, to your child.

*Parent as Role Model*

Distinguishing between appropriate and inappropriate behaviors is only the beginning. It is important that you serve as a role model for good behavior so that your child sees appropriate behavior in action. You can do this by demonstrating appropriate behaviors, thinking before you act, and explaining your behavior when you do something wrong.

**Demonstrate Appropriate Behavior**   Each time your child misbehaves, you are provided with an opportunity to demonstrate how he should have acted differently. Your child will not only understand that this behavior was incorrect, but by your demonstrating the appropriate behavior, he will learn an alternative way to act. For example, rather than grabbing a toy from another child's hand, explain to your child how to ask for the toy ("Johnny, when you are done with the toy, may I please play with it?"), and then discuss why it's important to wait for one's turn (another child may find him unfriendly if he grabs for the toy, and he probably would not like it if another child did it to him). The teaching of social skills and manners will help your child to foster positive social interactions. Role-playing different scenarios with your child, while discussing and demonstrating the appropriate behaviors, can also be helpful.

**Think Before You Act**   Children model their behavior after yours. They observe you, your behavior, and your reactions to different situations. If you want your child to act appropriately in different situations, the best way to teach him is to set a good example.

**Explain Your Behavior**   Although you may be an excellent role model, there may be times when you say or do something you shouldn't. When this occurs, use it as a teaching opportunity. Tell your child that what you did was wrong and what you should have done instead. If you don't, your child will think your behavior was acceptable and will be confused if he gets into trouble later on for exhibiting the same behavior.

**Did you know?** You should consider your child's behavior in the context of several factors. Behavior problems can be complex, and it is important to follow the next five-question assessment to gather enough information about why your child may be misbehaving.

## When Behavior Problems Arise

To better understand your child's behavior, it is important to look at it in the context of several factors, several of which may be occurring at the same time. We advocate a five-question assessment to gather information about the child's behavior. This will not only help you to understand your child a little better, but it can help you to choose appropriate discipline, which we'll talk about in the next section.

### Question #1: Is the Behavior Developmentally Appropriate?

You must first consider whether the behavior is typical for your child's age. Your response to your child's behavior will depend on his developmental level. If the behavior is typical for a child his age, you probably should not discipline him unless he is putting himself or others at risk. Children with cognitive delays often exhibit behaviors typical of children at a younger developmental level, so this must be considered as well.

### Question #2: What Is the Situation?

Situational factors can have an effect on behavior. Everything from medication use to physical/emotional/sexual abuse to situational factors (parental divorce; death of a friend, family member, or pet; social problems) can cause a child to display atypical behaviors. In cases where there is a distinct change in behavior, you should consider whether something different is occurring in your child's life. When in doubt, ask your child. You can say something like, "It seems that you may be feeling really bad about something. What do you think may be bothering you?" Keep in mind that things that bother children often seem trivial to us. Some children will exhibit behavior problems because they were not chosen for a friend's team in gym class, or their friend did not sit next to them at lunch.

### Question #3: When Does the Behavior Occur?

Children behave differently at different times of the day, and the timing of their behavior may provide you with important clues. For example, if your child misbehaves in the morning before leaving for school, it could mean it is school-related, and you need to investigate what may be occurring. Maybe your child has a test and does not feel prepared, or your child is being bullied and is scared. Behavior problems occurring immediately after school are an indication that something happened at school that may be bothering him. In this case, ask. Behavior problems right before going to bed could indicate that your child has nightmares and does not want to go to bed, although it's often related to the fact that what the child is doing before bedtime is more exciting than going to bed itself.

### Question #4: What Is My Child's Emotional State?

Like adults, children behave differently because of changes in their emotional state. When your child misbehaves, you may want to consider things such as whether your child is tired hungry, frustrated, ill, bored, anxious, or depressed. These feelings can often lead to misbehaviors, so take a moment and ask your child how he is feeling, although young children are often unable to express how they are feeling. In the absence of verbal feedback from your child, you may be able to obtain important information from his demeanor and posture.

### Question #5: What Is My Child's Temperament?

Your child's temperament should also be a consideration. Is your child typically shy? Active? Outgoing? Your child's temperament can affect how he reacts to others and to specific situations. What often are believed to be behavior problems may instead be the typical behaviors of an extroverted child. Once you better understand *who* your child is, you can understand *why* your child behaves a certain way.

**Did you know?** A school psychologist can assess your child's temperament. The *Student Styles Questionnaire*, for example, is used to detect individual differences students display in their preferences, temperaments, and personal styles. Results are useful for grouping students for cooperative learning tasks, exploring vocational and prevocational choices, assisting in social and emotional counseling, and planning intervention strategies appropriate to a student's particular style.

## Disciplining Your Child

Child discipline depends on many factors. Parents must consider the age of their child, the nature and severity of the disability, and the behavior he displays, in addition to their own feelings about discipline. Most experts agree, however, that *some* form of discipline is necessary for children to understand the consequences of their behaviors. Let's talk a bit about different forms of discipline, including positive reinforcement, time-out, negative reinforcement, and punishment.

### Positive Reinforcement

Positive reinforcement is one of the easiest, most effective forms of discipline. It involves catching your child "being good"—engaging in good behavior—and rewarding it quickly and often. When you see a behavior you like, point it out to your child. Feedback may include comments such as "I like how you are playing with your brother," "I liked the way you put away your crayons when you were finished coloring," or "I like how you are using good table manners." Rewards you give your child can be a smile, hug, kiss, smiley face on a chart, choosing the movie to watch that night, or special time with you. We don't recommend using material rewards like money because children then have an expectation that they will get a monetary reward each time they are caught being good.

## Negative Reinforcement

You can increase behavior in two important ways: positive reinforcement (reward for good behavior) and negative reinforcement (removing a negative consequence or penalty). For example, if we said to Johnny, "If you do all your work in class, you won't have to do any homework tonight," the predicted response is that Johnny would increase his working behavior at school to avoid having to work at home (negative consequence). In doing so, he does not have to complete it as homework, which would take up some of his playtime. He has learned that he can avoid homework (aversive) by completing his assignments at school (reinforced behavior).

## Time-Out Procedures

Time-out can be an effective behavioral intervention. It involves removing your child from the environment in which he is displaying unacceptable behavior. Time-out involves moving your child to an isolated area—for example, a chair in his room—for a short period of time. In doing so, you are removing the child from the situation and removing an audience. Children will often stop their inappropriate behavior when there is no one around to see it or provide attention to it. In addition, many children benefit from having a cooling-off period. If your child has a temper tantrum, calmly say, "Your behavior is unacceptable. Please go to time-out." This should be said only once, and you can either walk him to his chair or, in cases of extreme behavior, carry him.

What if your child misbehaves in a store? It can be more difficult to implement a time-out, but you can still use it effectively. Once your child starts misbehaving, walk your child to a quiet area and ask him to stand there quietly. Your child will want to engage you in conversation, but there should be no verbal communication while the child is in time-out. Each attempt on your child's part to speak should be followed by repeating, "There is no talking while in time-out." Your child will soon learn that he is not going to get and maintain your attention while in time-out. In cases of severe misbehavior, you may wish to leave the store and use a time-out outside.

**Did you know?** A digital or egg timer has many uses. They are not only helpful during time-out but can also be used for academic drills when your child is completing math problems, to set a limit on TV watching, or indicate the number of minutes until bedtime.

Time-out can reduce behavior problems such as hitting, temper tantrums, biting, spitting, not following directions, and others. It may be used with children as young as 2 and as old as 10 or 11. Once your child is in his room, set a timer (keep it on a shelf or somewhere high so that the child can't reach it) and tell your child that time-out is over when the timer goes off. When it does, go to your child's room to ask if he has calmed down and can display acceptable behavior. The only acceptable answer should be yes (or a variation), and it should not be said in an angry or nasty tone. If your child's behavior has not improved, or if your child says he is not ready, the child shouldn't remain in time-out, but should instead play in his room or another quiet area until he appears ready to leave the room.

> **Did you know?** A rule of thumb is to place a child in time-out for two minutes for each year of their age, but never more than ten minutes. Time-out will lose its effectiveness when the period of isolation is too lengthy for the child's developmental level. A digital or egg timer works well.

## Punishment

While both positive and negative reinforcements work to increase behaviors, punishments work to decrease behaviors. There are different types of punishments. The type of punishment you use may depend on the situation, your child's response to different punishments, or your personal preference. Removing privileges is one form of punishment that is effective. This can also be called a penalty. If your child misbehaves, you may choose to not allow him to go to a friend's house to play, cancel plans to go to the park, or go to the movies. You should make it clear that your child has lost the privilege because he did not have good behavior, and that other privileges may be lost if you do not see an immediate improvement in behavior.

Removing material items is another type of punishment. Taking away a favorite toy or video game when your child misbehaves can be effective. The items you choose to take away must mean something to your child or he won't care that you took it away. Let your child earn the item back with good behavior. If your child's behavior changes, you may want to give the item back in an hour; if there is no improvement in behavior, you may not want to return it until the next day.

Spanking, a form of corporal punishment, remains questionable as an effective type of discipline. When done correctly, it provides an intense, short-term consequence that is negative to your child. It sends a strong message that his behavior was unacceptable. On the other hand, you are modeling aggressive behavior. Plus, it teaches your child that aggression is an acceptable way to deal with issues, and your child may engage in hands-on physical behavior with other children. If you decide to use spanking, it should be used with caution, especially since it can have negative effects on behavior when not done correctly. For example, if there is too much time between your child's misbehavior and the spanking, he may not see the relationship between the two. Spankings that are too rough not only can injure your child, but you must also question whether you are doing it to change your child's behavior or using it as an outlet for your frustration. In the end, the use of spanking remains a personal choice.

**Did you know?** Paddling, a form of spanking, is still in use in American schools. While more than half the states ban it, a few hundred thousand paddlings are administered to children and adolescent each year. The National Association of School Psychologists is opposed to the use of corporal punishment in schools because of its harmful physical, educational, psychological, and social effects on students. The American Academy of Pediatrics also recommends that corporal punishment in schools be abolished in all states by law and that alternative forms of student behavior management be used.

## Summary

We want to emphasize that whatever discipline method you choose, you must be consistent in applying your methods. There several rules of thumb in disciplining children, many of which have been already discussed; however, we want to emphasize that in order for discipline to be effective it must be consistent, predictable, have a definite time limit, and be well suited to your child's developmental level.

# Selected Changes in the Individuals with Disabilities Education Improvement Act of 2004

## Important Changes in IDEA 2004

• Provides for a paperwork reduction demonstration program. Authorizes the Secretary of Education to grant waivers of statutory or regulatory requirements, other than civil rights requirements, under Part A for up to four years to up to fifteen states, based on state proposals to reduce excessive paperwork and staff time. However, it prohibits the waiver program from being used to: (1) affect the right of a child with a disability to receive a FAPE; and (2) permit a state or school district to waive specified procedural safeguards.

• Requires all special education teachers in an elementary, middle, or secondary school to be highly qualified no later than the end of the 2006 to 2007 school year. Highly qualified means the teacher has fulfilled the requirements to teach.

• Revises requirements for academic achievement and functional performance of children with disabilities to conform IDEA 2004 to the state and school district accountability system established under the No Child Left Behind Act. This is defined as how the child's disability affects his involvement and progress in the general education curriculum. For preschool children, as appropriate, it is how the disability affects the child's participation in appropriate activities. And for children with disabilities who take alternate assessments designed to meet achievement standards as set by the IEP committee, it is a description of short-term objectives. Data from children with disabilities will be examined to ensure that each such subgroup of children is making adequate yearly progress (AYP) towards reaching proficiency.

• Revises the requirements for student participation in standardized assessments. Requires alternate assessments to be a part of state and school district assessment programs and accountability systems. Included are additional requirements for developing and administering alternate assessments that are aligned with the state's academic content and achievement standards, and for developing alternate standards for those children with significant cognitive (intellectual) disabilities. States and school districts are required to develop and use universally designed assessments to the extent feasible.

• Requires state policies and procedures to prevent an overidentification or disproportionate representation by race and ethnicity of children as children with disabilities, including identification of children as children with a particular impairment. This means that if Hispanic students make up 18 percent of the general population, they should make up about that same percentage of students in special education. For example, if 25 percent of all students in special education were Hispanic, this would be considered an overidentification. In addition, if African-American students comprise 17 percent of the student population, they should comprise about that same percentage for a particular special education eligibility category based on their disability.

• Requires a state's department of education to prohibit school district personnel from requiring a child, as a condition of attending school or receiving IDEA evaluations or services, to obtain a prescription for a substance covered by the Controlled Substances Act. This means that no one can require your child to take Ritalin, for example, in order to receive a special education evaluation or special education services.

• Revises provisions regarding early intervening services. Allows school districts to use up to 15 percent of their IDEA funds to develop and implement early intervening educational services for students who are not receiving special education services but who require additional academic and behavioral support to succeed in a regular education environment, and who may be likely referrals to special education programs and services at a later time. This includes things such as providing professional development for teachers and other school staff to deliver scientifically-based academic and behavioral interventions and providing educational and behavioral evaluations, services, and supports, including scientifically-based literacy instruction.

• Revises requirements for evaluations, eligibility determinations, IEPs, and placements. A parent, state department of education or other state agency, or the school district has a right to request an initial evaluation to determine whether a child qualifies for IDEA services. A district will not be considered in violation of the FAPE requirement by failing to provide special education and related services to a child with a disability as long as these are refused by the parent.

• Revises additional requirements for school district procedures in selecting and administering tests and other evaluations to determine a child's eligibility under IDEA 2004. Requires tests and evaluations to be provided and administered, to the extent practicable, in the language and form most likely to yield accurate information on what the child knows and can do academically, developmentally, and functionally.

• Revises a special rule for eligibility determination to provide that a lack of scientifically based reading instruction cannot be the determinant factor for deciding whether the child is a child with a disability. School districts, in determining whether or not a student has a specific learning disability, shall not be required to take into consideration whether there is a severe discrepancy between achievement and intellectual ability in specified skills (this is discussed more in Chapter 5). Allows school districts, as part of evaluation procedures, to use a process that determines if a child responds to scientific, research-based intervention.

• Revises exit evaluation requirements. Provides that such evaluations before termination of IDEA 2004 eligibility are not required upon: (1) graduation from secondary school with a regular diploma; or (2) exceeding age eligibility for a free appropriate public education under state law. Requires school districts, in such cases, to provide students with a summary of their academic achievement and functional performance, including recommendations on how to assist them in meeting their postsecondary goals (such as college, technical school, or work).

• Requires IEPs to include a statement of the child's present levels of academic achievement and functional performance (in the previous version of IDEA, a statement of educational performance must have been included). Requires the statement of measurable annual goals to include academic goals and functional goals.

• Eliminates requirements for short-term objectives in IEPs. It requires IEPs to contain descriptions of: (1) how the child's progress toward meeting the annual goals will be measured; and (2) when periodic progress reports will be provided. Requires progress updates to provide parents with specific, meaningful, and understandable information on the progress children are making.

• Revises requirements for accommodations and alternate assessments. It provides for testing of some children that includes certain necessary accommodations, an alternate assessment, or an alternate assessment based on alternative standards for those children with significant cognitive disabilities (mental retardation, for example). Requires a statement of appropriate accommodations to be made for state or district-wide assessments. Requires the IEP team, if it determines that a child shall take an alternate assessment, to state why the child cannot participate in the regular assessment and why the particular alternate assessment selected is appropriate for that child.

• Revises requirements for transition services. Requires IEPs, beginning not later than the first IEP to be in effect when the child is 16, and updated annually thereafter, to contain: (1) appropriate measurable postsecondary goals based on age-appropriate assessments related to training, education, employment, and, where appropriate, independent living skills; and (2) the transition services the child needs to reach those goals.

• Allows a member of the IEP team to be excused from an IEP meeting if: (1) no modifications are being made to that member's area of curriculum or service; or (2) when a relevant modification is made, if the member provides input prior to the meeting. Requires the IEP team member, the parent, and the school district to agree to the member's being excused. Directs school districts to encourage consolidation of IEP meetings and reevaluation meetings. Includes the academic, developmental, and functional needs of the child among factors the IEP team must consider in developing a child's IEP.

• Requires IEP teams to provide positive behavioral interventions and supports for children with disabilities whose behavior impedes their learning or the learning of others.

• Authorizes the Secretary of Education to approve up to fifteen proposals from states to carry out a demonstration program allowing parents and school districts the option of developing a comprehensive multiyear IEP of up to three years, designed to coincide with natural transition points.

• Allows parents and school districts to agree to participate in IEP team and placement meetings via means such as video conferences and conference calls.

• Revises procedural safeguards to provide that school districts, as well as parents, have the right to present complaints. Requires the party filing a due process complaint to send the complaint to the other party, as well as to the state agency. Requires, in the case of a homeless child or youth, the parent's notice to the school district to contain contact information for the child and the name of the school the child is attending. Prohibits a due process hearing unless the requesting party has filed a complaint that meets specified notice requirements. Requires states to develop a model form to assist parents in filing due process complaint notices and complaints. Requires the school to provide a parent with a prior written notice, when learning of a parent's dispute for the first time in a parent's due process complaint. Requires parents to receive the procedural safeguards notice generally only once a year, but also upon: (1) initial referral or parental request for an evaluation; (2) a parent's registration of a due process complaint; or (3) request by the parent. Allows a school district to place a current copy of the procedural safeguards notice on its Web site. Requires the procedural safeguards notice to inform parents regarding specified matters, including: (1) the time period in which parents can file complaints; (2) the school district's opportunity to resolve a complaint before a due process hearing; and (3) the time period in which a party can appeal a hearing officer's decision to court.

• Provides that: (1) parents may request mediation before filing a complaint; and (2) a written mediation agreement is enforceable in court. Authorizes a state agency to establish procedures to offer parents, as well as schools, that choose not to use the mediation process an opportunity to speak with a disinterested party regarding the benefits of mediation.

- Provides for a resolution session to give parents and school districts an opportunity to resolve the complaint before a due process hearing.

- Establishes a two-year timeline for requesting a hearing on claims for reimbursed or ongoing compensatory education services (private school, for example), unless there is an applicable state timeline.

- Requires hearing officers to make decisions on due process complaints on substantive grounds based on a determination of whether the child in question received a FAPE. Authorizes hearing officers, in matters alleging a procedural violation, to find that a child did not receive a FAPE only if the procedural inadequacies: (1) impeded the child's right to a FAPE; (2) significantly impeded the parents' opportunity to participate in the decision-making process regarding FAPE provision; or (3) caused a deprivation of educational benefits.

- Authorizes schools to consider any unique circumstances on a case-by-case basis when determining whether to order a change in placement for a child with a disability who violates a code of student conduct.

- Authorizes schools to order, for children with disabilities who violate student conduct codes, changes of placement to an appropriate interim educational setting, another setting, or suspension, for up to ten consecutive school days, to the same extent such alternatives would apply to children without disabilities, without making a manifestation determination. Manifestation determinations are discussed further in Chapter 10.

- Authorizes schools, upon determining that the student's violation was not a manifestation of his disability, to apply beyond that ten-day period the same disciplinary procedures as for a child without a disability, provided that FAPE requirements are met, with the option of providing such FAPE in an interim alternative educational setting.

- Requires, within ten school days of such a disciplinary decision to change placement, a review of all relevant information by the school district, parent, and IEP team to determine if the child's behavior was a manifestation of disability. Bases such determination on whether the conduct: (1) was caused by, or had a direct and substantial relationship to, the child's disability; or (2) was the direct result of the school districts failure to implement the IEP. Requires the IEP team, if the conduct is such a manifestation, to: (1) conduct a functional behavioral assessment and implement a behavioral intervention plan, if the school district has not done so; (2) if such a plan has been developed, review and modify it to address the behavior; and (3) (except in cases involving weapons, drugs, or infliction of serious bodily injury) return the child to the placement from which the child was removed, unless the parent and school district agree to a change of placement as part of the modification of the behavioral intervention plan.

- Authorizes a school, in cases involving weapons or drugs, or when a child has committed serious bodily injury, to remove the child from the regular classroom setting for up to forty-five school days, regardless of whether the child's behavior was a manifestation of disability. Requires that such children receive continued educational services and appropriate functional behavioral assessments and behavioral intervention services and modifications.

•   Sets forth circumstances in which a party may request a hearing regarding disciplinary decisions or proposed disciplinary actions. Allows requests for such hearings by: (1) parents who disagree with the school district's decisions regarding disciplinary actions, placements, or manifestation determinations, with the hearing officer to determine if the district's decision is appropriate; and (2) school districts that believe that maintaining the child's current placement is substantially likely to result in injury to the child or others.

•   Requires the child, during a parent's appeal, to remain in the interim alternative educational setting chosen by the IEP team pending the hearing officer's decision or until the time period for the disciplinary action expires, whichever occurs first, unless the parent and school district agree otherwise. It requires the hearing to occur within twenty days of the hearing request, and to result in a determination within ten days after the hearing.

•   Allows assertion of IDEA protections for a child not determined eligible for special education and related services who has violated a code of student conduct, if the school district had knowledge that the child had a disability before the behavior that precipitated the disciplinary action occurred. Deems a school district as knowing about a child's disability if: (1) the parent has expressed concern in writing; (2) the parent has requested an evaluation; or (3) a teacher or other school personnel has expressed concern about a pattern of behavior to either the special education director, or to other administrative personnel. Provides that a school district will not be deemed to know that the child has a disability if the child's parent has not agreed to allow an evaluation requested by the district.

•   Revises provisions relating to transfer of parental rights at age of majority to allow a parent of a child with a disability to elect to receive required notices by e-mail communication, if a school district makes this option available.

# A P P E N D I X   B

# Sample 504 Plans

## Sample Section 504 Plan #1

| Lake County Schools: Section 504 Accommodation Plan* | | | |
|---|---|---|---|
| Name: _____ Date of Meeting _____ Initial [ ]<br>                                                  Annual Update [ ]<br>Student ID# _____ Date of Birth _____ CA _____<br>School: _____ Grade _____<br>Teacher: _____ | | | |
| **Meeting Participants:**<br>_____ Administrator<br>_____ Guidance Counselor<br>_____ Teacher<br>_____ Teacher<br>_____ Parent<br>_____ Other | | | |

| √ | Accommodations | Person Responsible | Outcome |
|---|---|---|---|
| | A structured learning environment (example: allows the student to keep desk removed from the other students and provide a written schedule for each day so the student can follow the class) | | |
| | Repeat and simplify the instruction about in-class and homework assignments. | | |
| | Supplement important verbal instructions with visual instructions. | | |
| | Adjust class schedules (in sites where alternative schedules are available) | | |
| | Modify test delivery: _____ | | |
| | Additional time to complete assignments. | | |
| | Tape recorders, computer aided instruction, or other audio visual equipment. | | |
| | Modified workbooks or textbooks. | | |
| | Tailored homework assignments. | | |
| | One-on-one peer tutorial. | | |
| | Classroom peer aides and peer note-takers. | | |
| | Involvement of the school guidance counselor as "service coordinator" to oversee implementation of these accommodations. | | |
| | Accommodations to nonacademic times such as lunch-room, physical education, recess, by: _____ | | |
| | In-servicing teacher(s) about the student's disability. | | |
| | Alerting bus drivers and other support personnel. | | |
| | Other: | | |
| | | | |
| *Used with permission from Lake County Schools, Florida | | | |
| Page 1 of 2 | | | |

## Lake County Schools: Section 504 Accommodation Plan

Name: _____ Date of Meeting: _____

**Discipline:**

[ ]     It is generally considered that this student's Section 504 disability (broken arm, asthma, other) would not cause him to violate school rules.

[ ]     This student's Section 504 disability could cause him to violate school rules. (If this box is checked, fill out the Behavior Plan).

**Behavior Plan:** The following behavior plan is intended to help the student alter his/her behavior. It is not intended to simply discipline the student.

_____

_____

Indicators to determine if the behavior plan is working: _____

_____

**Comments:** _____

_____

**Medical Information:**

Name of Physician _____ Phone _____

Medication _____

Medication Administered _____ At Home, and/or _____ At School

Review Date: _____ Reassessment Date _____

Case Manager Signature: _____

_____

I, the student's parent or guardian, have received a copy of my Section 504 rights and agree to this 504 Accommodation Plan as written.

_____          _____
Parent Signature                   Date

Page 2 of 2

## Sample Section 504 Plan #2

The following sample Section 504 Plan was developed by the American Diabetes Association (ADA). For further information, see the ADA Position Statement, "Diabetes Care in the School and Day Care Setting" (Diabetes Care, Volume 27, Supplement 1, January 2004), and National Diabetes Education Program's *Helping the Student with Diabetes Succeed: A Guide For School Personnel* (June 2003).

Section 504 Plan for _____

School _____

School Year: _____

|  |  |  | Diabetes |
|---|---|---|---|
| Student's Name | Birth Date | Grade | Disability |

| | |
|---|---|
| Homeroom Teacher | Bus Number |

### BACKGROUND

The student has type _____ diabetes. Diabetes is a serious, chronic disease that impairs the body's ability to use food. Insulin, a hormone produced by the pancreas, helps the body convert food into energy. In people with diabetes, either the pancreas doesn't make insulin or the body cannot use insulin properly. Without insulin, the body's main energy source—glucose—cannot be used as fuel. Rather, glucose builds up in the blood. Over many years, high blood glucose levels can cause damage to the eyes, kidneys, nerves, heart and blood vessels. Research has shown that these problems can be greatly reduced or delayed by keeping blood glucose levels near normal.

The majority of school-aged youth with diabetes have type 1 diabetes. People with type 1 diabetes do not produce insulin and must receive insulin through either injections or an insulin pump. Insulin taken in this manner does not cure diabetes and may cause the student's blood glucose level to become dangerously low. Type 2 diabetes, the most common form of the disease typically afflicting obese adults, has been shown to be increasing in youth. This may be due to the increase in obesity and decrease in physical activity in young people. Students with type 2 diabetes may be able to control their disease through diet and exercise alone or may require oral medications and/or insulin injections. Neither insulin nor other medications are cures for diabetes; they only help control the disease. All people with type 1 and type 2 diabetes must carefully balance food, medications, and activity level to keep blood glucose levels as close to normal as possible.

Low blood glucose (hypoglycemia) is the most common health emergency for students with diabetes. It occurs when the person gets too much insulin, is not eating enough, delays eating a meal or snack, or gets more than usual amount of exercise. Symptoms of mild to moderate hypoglycemia include tremors, sweating, lightheadedness, irritability, confusion, and drowsiness. A student with this degree of hypoglycemia will need to promptly ingest carbohydrates and may require assistance. Severe hypoglycemia, which is rare, may lead to unconsciousness and convulsions and can be life threatening if not treated promptly.

High blood glucose (hyperglycemia) occurs when the body gets too little insulin, food is not covered by insulin, or the person gets too little exercise; it may also be caused by stress, injury, or an illness such as a cold. The most common symptoms of hyperglycemia are thirst, frequent urination, fatigue, and blurry vision. If left untreated, hyperglycemia can lead to a serious condition called diabetic ketoacidosis (DKA), characterized by nausea, vomiting, and a high level of ketones in the urine. For students using insulin infusion pumps, lack of insulin supply may lead to DKA in several hours. DKA can be life-threatening and thus requires immediate medical attention.

Accordingly, for the student to avoid the serious short- and long-term complications of blood sugar levels that are either too high or too low, this Section 504 Plan and the accompanying Diabetes Medical Management Plan (DMMP) must be carefully followed and strictly adhered to by responsible school personnel. To facilitate the appropriate care of the student with diabetes, school and day care personnel must have an understanding of diabetes and be trained in its management and in the treatment of diabetes emergencies. Knowledgeable trained personnel are essential if the student is to avoid the immediate health risks of low blood glucose and to achieve the metabolic control required to decrease risks for later development of diabetes complications.

## OBJECTIVES/GOALS OF THIS PLAN

Both high blood sugar levels and low blood sugar levels affect the student's ability to learn as well as seriously endangering the student's health. Blood glucose levels must be maintained in the _____ range for optimal learning and testing of academic skills. The student has a recognized disability, type _____ diabetes, that requires the accommodations and modifications set out in this plan to ensure that the student has the same opportunities and conditions for learning and academic testing as classmates, with minimal disruption of the student's regular school schedule and with minimal time away from the classroom. Steps to prevent hypoglycemia and hyperglycemia, and to treat these conditions if they occur, must be taken in accordance with this Plan and with the student's Diabetes Medical Management Plan, which is attached to this Section 504 Plan and incorporated into it.

## REFERENCES

School accommodations, diabetes care, and other services set out by this Plan and the student's Diabetes Medical Management Plan will be consistent with the information and protocols contained in the following documents:

- American Diabetes Association Position Statement "Care of Children with Diabetes in the School and Day Care Setting," *Diabetes Care*, Volume 27, Supplement 1, January 2004.

- National Diabetes Education Program *Helping the Student with Diabetes Succeed: A Guide for School Personnel*, June 2003.

## DEFINITIONS USED IN THIS PLAN

1. *Diabetes Medical Management Plan:* A plan that describes the diabetes care regimen and identifies the health care needs of—and services to be provided to—a student with diabetes. This plan is developed and approved by the student's personal health care team and family. A DMMP is useful in addressing the requirements of applicable federal laws.

2. *Quick Reference Emergency Plan:* A plan that provides school personnel with essential information on how to recognize and treat hypoglycemia and hyperglycemia.

3. *Trained Diabetes Personnel (TDP)*: Nonmedical school personnel who have basic diabetes knowledge and have received training in diabetes care, including the performance of blood glucose monitoring, insulin and glucagon administration, recognition and treatment of hypoglycemia and hyperglycemia, and performance of ketone checks. This training should include the following content based on current standards of care for children and youth with diabetes recommended by the American Diabetes Association:

- General overview of typical health care needs of a student with diabetes and how these needs are addressed in the student's written care plans
- Explanation/overview of type 1 and type 2 diabetes
- The effect of balancing insulin, food, and exercise upon a student's blood glucose levels
- Procedures for routine care of individual students, including blood glucose monitoring, insulin administration, urine ketone testing, and recording results
- Signs and symptoms of hypoglycemia and hyperglycemia and the short- and long-term risks of these conditions
- Treatment of hypoglycemia and hyperglycemia

- Insulin administration
- Glucagon administration
- Managing nutrition and exercise in the school setting
- Tools, supplies, and equipment require for diabetes care and their storage
- Legal rights and responsibilities of schools and parents/guardians

## ACADEMIC-RELATED ACCOMMODATIONS

### 1. HEALTH CARE SUPERVISION

1.1. At least _____ adult staff members will receive training to be Trained Diabetes Personnel, and TDP will be available **at all times** during school hours, during extracurricular activities, and on field trips when the school nurse is not available to oversee the student's health care in accordance with this Section 504 Plan and the student's Diabetes Medical Management Plan, including performing or overseeing insulin administration, blood glucose monitoring, ketone checks, and responding to hyperglycemia and hypoglycemia, including administering glucagon. A written backup plan will be implemented to ensure that a TDP is available in the event that the school nurse is unavailable.

1.2. Any staff member who has primary care for the student at any time during school hours, extracurricular activities, or during field trips, and who is not a TDP, shall receive training that will include a general overview of diabetes and typical health care needs of a student with diabetes, recognition of hypoglycemia and hyperglycemia as described by the student's Quick Reference Plan, and identity of school nurses and TDP and how to contact them for help. Primary care means that the staff member is in charge of a class or activity in which the student participates.

1.3. Any bus driver who transports the student must be able to recognize and respond to hypoglycemia and hyperglycemia in accordance with the student's Quick Reference Emergency Plan.

### 2. TRAINED PERSONNEL

2.1. The following school staff members (including but not limited to school administrators, teachers, counselors, health aides, cafeteria and library staff) will be trained to become TDP by _____ (date):

_____

_____

_____

_____

## 3. STUDENT'S LEVEL OF SELF-CARE

The student's current ability to perform various diabetes self-management skills is indicated by activities check in the chart below:

|  | Yes | No | N/A |
|---|---|---|---|
| Totally independent management (only requires adult assistance during severe hypoglycemia) | _____ | _____ | _____ |
| Student monitors blood glucose level independently | _____ | _____ | _____ |
| Student needs verification of blood glucose number by school nurse or TDP | _____ | _____ | _____ |
| Blood glucose monitoring to be done by school nurse or TDP | _____ | _____ | _____ |
| Student administers insulin independently | _____ | _____ | _____ |
| Student self-administers insulin with verification of dosage by school nurse or TDP | _____ | _____ | _____ |
| Insulin administration to be done by school nurse or TDP | _____ | _____ | _____ |
| Student can independently program pump (i.e., set temporary basal rates, suspend, etc.) | _____ | _____ | _____ |
| Student needs assistance programming pump from school nurse or TDP | _____ | _____ | _____ |
| Student can independently change infusion sets and refill and prime pump reservoir | _____ | _____ | _____ |
| Student needs assistance with infusion set changes and pump reservoir refills and priming from school nurse or TDP | _____ | _____ | _____ |
| Student can independently change pump batteries | _____ | _____ | _____ |
| Students needs assistance with changing pump batteries from school nurse or TDP | _____ | _____ | _____ |

|                                                                          | Yes | No | N/A |
|--------------------------------------------------------------------------|-----|----|-----|
| Student can independently troubleshoot pump alarms and codes             | ___ | ___ | ___ |
| Student needs assistance with trouble-shooting pump from school nurse or TDP | ___ | ___ | ___ |
| Student self-treats mild hypoglycemia                                    | ___ | ___ | ___ |
| Student requires assistance to treat mild hypoglycemia from school nurse or TDP | ___ | ___ | ___ |
| Student monitors own snacks and meals                                    | ___ | ___ | ___ |
| Snacks and meals to be supervised by school nurse or TDP                 | ___ | ___ | ___ |
| Student checks and interprets own ketones results                        | ___ | ___ | ___ |
| Ketones to be checked by school nurse or TDP                             | ___ | ___ | ___ |
| Student implements universal precautions                                 | ___ | ___ | ___ |
| Universal precautions to be supervised by school nurse or TDP            | ___ | ___ | ___ |

## 4. SNACKS AND MEALS

4.1 The school nurse or TDP, if school nurse is not available, will work with the student and his/her parents/guardians to coordinate a meal and snack schedule in accordance with the attached Diabetes Medical Management Plan that will coincide with the schedule of classmates to the closest extent possible. The student shall each lunch at the same time each day, or earlier if experiencing hypoglycemia. The student shall have enough time to finish lunch. A snack and quick-acting source of glucose must always be immediately available to the student.

4.2 The parents/guardians will pack snacks for each day and will provide a supply of additional snacks to be kept at the school to treat hypoglycemia or for emergency situations.

4.3 All school personnel will permit the student to eat a snack in the classroom or wherever the child is (including, but not limited to classrooms, gym, auditorium, playground, field trips, and school bus) at times designated in the Diabetes Medical Management Plan and whenever needed to treat hypoglycemia or in response to a change in the student's regular schedule. A source of glucose will be immediately available wherever the student is.

4.4 The school nurse or TDP ensure that the student takes snacks and meals at the specified time(s) each day.

4.5 The attached Diabetes Medical Management Plan sets out the regular time(s) for snacks each day, what constitutes a snack, when the student should have additional snacks, and where snacks are kept.

## 5. EXERCISE AND PHYSICAL ACTIVITY

5.1 The student should participate fully in physical education classes and team sports.

5.2 Physical education instructors and sports coaches must be able to recognize and assist with the treatment of hypoglycemia.

5.3 The student's blood glucose meter, a quick-acting source of glucose, and water should always be available at the site of physical education class or team sports practices and games.

5.4 Physical education instructors and coaches will provide a safe location for the storage of the student's insulin pump if the student chooses not to wear it during physical activity.

## 6. WATER AND BATHROOM ACCESS

6.1 The student shall be permitted to have immediate access to water by keeping a water bottle in the student's possession and at the student's desk, and by permitting the student to use the drinking fountain without restriction.

6.2 The student shall be permitted to use the bathroom without restriction.

## 7. TREATING HIGH OR LOW BLOOD SUGAR

7.1 The student shall have immediate access to blood glucose monitoring equipment, insulin and syringes, insulin pump supplies, and to glucose in the form of food, juice, glucose gel or tablets in order to treat hypoglycemia. The student shall be permitted to carry this equipment with him/her at all times.

7.2 When any staff member believes the student is showing signs of high or low blood sugar, the staff member will seek the school nurse or TDP, if the school nurse is not available, for further assistance while making sure an adult stays with the student at all times. **Never send a student with actual—or suspected—high or low blood sugar anywhere alone.**

7.3 High or low blood sugar levels should be treated as set out in the attached Diabetes Medical Management Plan.

7.4 Any staff member who finds the student unconscious will immediately contact the school office. The office will immediately do the following in the order listed:

1. **Contact the school nurse or a TDP, if the school nurse is not available, who will confirm the blood glucose level with a monitor and immediately administer glucagon (glucagon should be administered if no monitor is available);**

2. **Call 911 (office staff will do this without waiting for the school nurse or TDP to administer glucagon); and**

3. **Contact the student's parent/guardian and physician at the emergency numbers provided below.**

7.5 The location of supplies for treating high and low blood sugar levels, including equipment for monitoring blood glucose levels and ketones, glucagon, and snacks, is set out in the attached Diabetes Medical Management Plan.

## 8. BLOOD GLUCOSE MONITORING

8.1 Blood glucose monitoring will be done in accordance with the level of self-care listed in the chart in section 3 above and the attached Diabetes Medical Management Plan.

8.2 Blood glucose monitoring may be done at any location at school, including, but not limited to, the classroom, on school grounds, the cafeteria, at field trips or sites of extracurricular activities, or on the school bus.

8.3 Blood glucose monitoring will be done at the times designated in the student's Diabetes Medical Management Plan, whenever the student feels that her blood sugar level may be high or low, or when symptoms of hypoglycemia or hyperglycemia are observed.

8.4 The student's usual symptoms of high and low blood sugar levels are set out in the attached Diabetes Medical Management Plan.

8.5 The location of blood glucose monitoring equipment is set out in the attached Diabetes Medical Management Plan.

8.6 The school or TDP, if the school nurse is not available, will perform glucose monitoring when the student is unable or chooses not to monitor himself/herself.

## 9. INSULIN ADMINISTRATION

9.1 Insulin will be administered in accordance with the level of self-care listed in the chart in section 3 above and in attached Diabetes Medical Management Plan.

9.2 The location of insulin and equipment to administer insulin is set out in the attached Diabetes Medical Management Plan.

9.3 If student disconnects insulin pump to engage in physical education class or for any reason, appropriate arrangements for the safekeeping and security of the student's insulin pump will be made by school personnel.

## 10. FIELD TRIPS AND EXTRACURRICULAR ACTIVITIES

10.1 The student will be permitted to participate in all field trips and extracurricular activities (such as sports, clubs, and enrichment programs) without restriction and with all of the accommodations and modifications, including necessary supervision by identified school personnel, set out in this Plan. The student's parent/guardian will not be required to accompany the student on field trips or any other school activity.

10.2 The school nurse or TDP, if the school nurse is not available, will accompany the student on all field trips and extracurricular activities away from the school premises and will provide all usual aspects of diabetes care (including, but not limited to, blood glucose monitoring, responding to hyperglycemia and hypoglycemia, providing snacks and access to water and the bathroom, and administering insulin and glucagon).

10.3 The school nurse or TDP, if the school nurse is not available, will be available at the site of all extracurricular activities that take place both on and away from the school premises. The school nurse or TDP must be on the school premises or at the location where the activity is taking place whenever the student is participating in the activity.

10.4 The student's diabetes supplies will travel with the student to any field trip or extracurricular activity on or away from the school premises.

## 11. TESTS AND CLASSROOM WORK

11.1 If the student is affected by high or low blood glucose levels at the time of regular testing, the student will be permitted to take the test at another time without penalty.

11.2 If the student needs to take breaks to use the water fountain or bathroom, check blood glucose, or to treat hypoglycemia or hyperglycemia during a test, the student will be given extra time to finish the test without penalty.

11.3 If the student is affected by high or low blood glucose levels or needs to take breaks to use the water fountain or bathroom, check blood glucose, or to treat hypoglycemia or hyperglycemia, the student will be permitted to have extra time to finish classroom work without penalty.

11.4 The student shall be given instruction to help him/her make up any classroom time missed due to diabetes care without penalty.

11.5 The student shall not be penalized for absences required for medical appointments and/or for illness.

## 12. DAILY INSTRUCTIONS

12.1 The school nurse or TDP will notify parent/guardian _____ days in advance when there will be a change in planned activities such as exercise, playground time, field trips, parties, or lunch schedule, so that the lunch, snack plan, and insulin dosage can be adjusted accordingly.

12.2 The parent/guardian may send the school nurse or TDP special instructions regarding the snack, snack time, or other aspects of the student's diabetes care in response to changes in the usual schedule.

12.3 Each substitute teacher and substitute school nurse will be provided with written instructions regarding the student's diabetes care and a list of all school nurses and TDP at the school.

## 13. EMERGENCY EVACUATION AND SHELTER-IN-PLACE

13.1 In the event of emergency evacuation or shelter-in-place situation, the student's 504 Plan and Diabetes Medical Management Plan will remain in full force and effect.

13.*2*. The school nurse or TDP, if the school nurse is not available, will provide diabetes care to the student as outlined by this Plan and the student's Diabetes Medical Management Plan.

13.3 The school nurse or TDP will be responsible for transporting the student's diabetes supplies, medication, and food to the evacuation or shelter-in-place designated location.

13.4 The school nurse or TDP will remain in contact with the student's parents/guardians during an evacuation or shelter-in-place situation, provide updates about the student's health status, and receive orders and information from parents/guardians regarding the student's diabetes care.

13.5 The student's parents/guardians will be permitted to pick up the student without any unnecessary delays as soon as the student can be safely discharged.

## 14.  EQUAL TREATMENT AND ENCOURAGEMENT

14.1 Encouragement is essential. The student must not be treated in a way that discourages the student from eating snacks on time, or from progressing in doing his/her own glucose checks and general diabetes management.

14.2 The student shall be provided with privacy for blood glucose monitoring and insulin administration if the student desires.

14.3 The school nurse, TDP, and other staff will keep the student's diabetes confidential, except to the extent that the student decides to openly communicate about it with others.

## 15.  PARENTAL NOTIFICATION

### *15.1* NOTIFY PARENTS/GUARDIANS IMMEDIATELY IN THE FOLLOWING SITUATIONS:

• Symptoms of severe low blood sugar such as continuous crying, extreme tiredness, or loss of consciousness.

• The student's blood glucose test results are below _____ or are below _____ 15 minutes after consuming juice or glucose tablets.

• Symptoms of severe high blood sugar such as frequent urination, presence of ketones or blood glucose level above _____.

- The student refuses to eat or take insulin injection or bolus.

- Any injury.

- **Other:**

_____
_____
_____

## *15.2 EMERGENCY CONTACT INSTRUCTIONS*

1. Call the student's home. If unable to reach parent/guardian:
2. Call the student's parent/guardian's cell or work phone. If unable to reach parent/guardian:
3. Repeat same steps with student's other parent/guardian, if applicable. If unsuccessful:
4. Call the other emergency contacts listed above.

EMERGENCY CONTACTS:

| Parent's/Guardian's Name | Home Phone Number | Work Phone Number | Cell Phone Number |
|---|---|---|---|
| Parent's/Guardian's Name | Home Phone Number | Work Phone Number | Cell Phone Number |

**Other emergency contacts:**

| Name | Home Phone Number | Work Phone Number | Cell Phone Number |
|---|---|---|---|
| Name | Home Phone Number | Work Phone Number | Cell Phone Number |

**Student's Physician(s):**

| Name | Phone Number |
|---|---|
| Name | Phone Number |

This Plan shall be reviewed and amended at the beginning of each school year or more often if necessary.

## Approved and received:

_____          _____
Parent/Guardian                                                      Date

_____          _____
Parent/Guardian                                                      Date

Approved and received:

_____          _____
School Representative and Title                                Date

Updated 08/11/04

# Sample Behavior Charts

Our House Rules Chart

## **Our House Rules**

_____

(Day of the Week)

| Rule | Followed | Not Followed |
|------|----------|--------------|
|  |  |  |
|  |  |  |
|  |  |  |
|  |  |  |
|  |  |  |
|  |  |  |
|  |  |  |
|  |  |  |

**Your Totals for Today**          _____          _____

Positive Behavior Chart

# Positive Behavior Chart
# for

_____

(Day of the Week)

| Goal | ☺ | ☹ |
|------|---|---|
|  |  |  |
|  |  |  |
|  |  |  |
|  |  |  |
|  |  |  |
|  |  |  |
|  |  |  |
|  |  |  |

**Your Totals for Today**        _____        _____

# APPENDIX D

# Procedural Safeguards

*Procedural safeguards* must be developed by every state educational agency or local school district receiving assistance under IDEA 2004 and disseminated to parents of children with disabilities. Throughout this book, and most notably in Chapter 10, we have presented many examples of the protections and rights of children under IDEA 2004. For your convenience, information relating to the procedural safeguards is located in this section for easy reference. IDEA 2004 states that these procedures must be established and maintained to ensure that the rights of children with disabilities, including children with disabilities who are wards of the state, and their parents are protected with respect to the provision of a FAPE.

The procedural safeguards can be found in Section 615 of the law, regarding children covered under Part B of IDEA 2004 and Section 639 for infants and toddlers under Part C.

The following discussion represents a general overview of the safeguards as presented in IDEA 2004. Since each state is responsible for developing its own set of procedural safeguards, parents should contact the state department of education or local school district to request a copy of these procedures, as outlined by your state. The procedural safeguards spell out the rights of children with disabilities and their parents with respect to issues such as notice, consent, independent educational evaluations, records, hearings, and appeals. This section will also discuss how parental and student rights regarding access to educational records are protected under the Family Educational Rights and Privacy Act of 1974 (FERPA).

According to IDEA 2004, the procedural safeguards notice shall include a full explanation of the procedural safeguards, written in the native language of the parents, unless it clearly is not feasible to do so, and written in an easily understandable manner, relating to:

- Independent educational evaluation
- Prior written notice
- Parental consent
- Access to educational records
- The opportunity to present and resolve complaints, including:
  1. The time period in which to make a complaint
  2. The opportunity for the agency to resolve the complaint
  3. The availability of mediation
- The child's placement during pending due process proceedings
- Procedures for students who are subject to placement in an interim alternative educational setting
- Requirements for unilateral placement by parents of children in private schools at public expense
- Due process hearings, including requirements for disclosure of evaluation results and recommendations
- State-level appeals (if applicable in that state)
- Civil actions, including the time period in which to file such actions
- Attorney fees

## Notice

Under IDEA 2004, a copy of the procedural safeguards must be made available to the parents of a child with a disability *once each year.* However, a copy of the safeguards must also be provided to parents under the following circumstances: *upon an initial referral or parent request for evaluation; upon the filing of a complaint; and/or upon parent request for a copy of the procedural safeguards.* Regarding notice, parents have the right to:

- *Written prior notice provided in the native language of the parents* (unless it clearly is not feasible to do so), whenever the school district does any of the following:
  - Proposes the identification, evaluation, or educational placement of the child in a special education program
  - Provides a FAPE to your child
  - Proposes to initiate or change the child's program
  - Refuses to initiate or change the child's program
- *Contents of the notice should include:*
  - A description of the action proposed or refused by the school district
  - An explanation of why the school district proposes or refuses to take the action

- A description of any other options that the school district considered and the reasons why those options were not selected
- A description of each evaluation procedure, test, record, or report the school district will use or has used as a basis for its decisions
- A description of any other factors relevant to the school district's proposal or refusal
- A statement that the parents of a child with a disability have protection under the procedural safeguards and, if this notice is not an initial referral for evaluation, the means by which a copy of a description of the procedural safeguards can be obtained
- Sources for parents to contact to obtain assistance in understanding their rights under IDEA

## Consent (Sec. 614 D)

Informed parental consent is required in the following situations:

- Before the school district can conduct an initial evaluation to determine if a child qualifies as a child with a disability under IDEA 2004.
- Parent consent for evaluation is not to be construed as consent for receipt of special education and related services.
- If parents refuse to consent for evaluation, the school can pursue an evaluation through mediation and due process procedures.
- If a parent refuses special education and related services, or fails to respond, the school will not be responsible for providing a FAPE or developing an IEP.
- Parent consent is required prior to conducting a reevaluation for a child with a disability, unless the school district can demonstrate that it has taken reasonable measures to obtain consent and the parents failed to respond.

## Records

FERPA is a federal statute that applies to all agencies and institutions that receive federal funds, including elementary and secondary schools, colleges, and universities. The purposes of FERPA are primarily:

- To ensure that parents have access to their children's educational records
- To protect the privacy rights of parents and children by limiting access to these records without parental consent

Therefore, information in the procedural safeguards pertaining to parent and student rights concerning student educational records will comply with the rights and privacy statements as set out in FERPA. These rights transfer to the student when he or she reaches the age of 18 or attends a postsecondary institution. Some of the topics covered under FERPA include:

- Access to educational records
- Parent rights to inspect and review educational records
- Guidelines for the amendment of educational records
- Guidelines for the destruction of educational records

FERPA protects the privacy interests of parents in their children's education records, and generally prevents an educational institution from disclosing the education records of students, or personally identifiable information contained in education records, without the written consent of the parent. The term *education records* is defined as all records, files, documents, and other materials that contain information directly related to a student and are maintained by the educational agency or institution or by a person acting for such agency or institution.

The following is a summary of important guidelines for release of educational records under FERPA:

•  Parents or eligible students have the right to inspect and review the student's education records maintained by the school. Most times, parents who wish to review the records will be invited to do so at the school, since schools are *not required* to provide copies of records to parents. When a parent does request a copy of the records, schools may charge a fee for copies.

•  Parents or eligible students have the right to request that a school amend records that they believe to be inaccurate or misleading. If the school declines the request to change the record, the parent or eligible student then has the right to a formal hearing. After the hearing, if the school decides not to amend the record, the parent or eligible student has the right to place a statement with the record to voice his or her view about the disputed information.

•  Generally, schools must have written permission from the parent or eligible student in order to release any information from a student's education record. However, FERPA allows schools to disclose those records, without consent, to certain parties, such as:

- School officials
- Other schools to which a student is transferring
- Officials for audit purposes
- To comply with a judicial order or lawfully issued subpoena
- State and local authorities, within a juvenile justice system, pursuant to state law

> **Did you know?** Schools must notify parents and eligible students annually of their rights under FERPA. However, how the notification takes place (special letter, inclusion in a PTA bulletin, student handbook, or newspaper article) is left to the discretion of each school.

Parents who wish to obtain further information about FERPA can contact the Family Policy Compliance Office, U.S. Department of Education, 400 Maryland Avenue, SW, Washington, D.C. 20202-5901

### Disciplinary Hearings and Placements in Alternative Educational Settings

IDEA 2004 has provided local school districts with more authority and guidance in managing students with disabilities who violate codes of student conduct. Disciplinary measures for children with disabilities and children who may be deemed "in the process" of being considered eligible under IDEA 2004 have been discussed at length in Chapter 10. At this time, we will present a brief overview of some of the changes in the law that have had an impact on the decision-making process surrounding disciplinary issues. IDEA 2004 addresses the need for local school districts to balance the need to protect the safety of the student body at-large with the individual needs of students with disabilities in the following ways:

- Schools may address the unique circumstances of students with disabilities and issues of student conduct violations in a *case-by-case basis* when determining whether alternative school placement is advised.

- Schools may discipline students with disabilities who violate codes of student conduct in a manner similar to their nondisabled peers for a period of not more than ten school days, whether discipline involves an alternative educational setting, or suspension.

- If the child is removed to an alternative setting, the child will continue to receive services to allow the child to progress toward meeting the goals of his or her IEP; and a FBA and BIP will be developed, or if they already exist, modified appropriately to address the inappropriate behavior.

- If the alternative placement exceeds ten days, and the behavior is deemed not to be a function of the child's disability, then the child may be disciplined in a manner similar to his or her nondisabled peers (suspension or expulsion); however, under this condition, the FAPE will continue for the student with disabilities.

- A student with a disability who commits a violation involving serious bodily harm to another at school or a weapons or drug violation may be removed to an alternative educational setting for up to forty-five *school* days, without the benefit of a hearing and without parent permission. It is up to the parents to appeal the decision.

- Protective rights for children who are "not yet eligible" under IDEA 2004 extend to those students, whose parents have submitted their concerns to the school district, in writing, stating their child is in need of services under IDEA 2004.

- Protective rights are not extended to children whose parents have refused evaluation, or placement, or who have been declared to not have a disability under IDEA 2004.

For additional information regarding manifest determination and the rights of children with disabilities can be found in Chapter 10.

## Independent Educational Evaluation

Parents have the right to have an independent educational evaluation of their child, at their own expense, at any time. An IEE is an evaluation that is conducted by a qualified person who is not an employee of the school district. As we discussed in Chapter 4, and elsewhere throughout the book, parents should be knowledgeable about what their school district requires regarding an assessment for eligibility determination, and who is qualified by the state to administer the assessment.

If parents do not agree with the evaluation conducted by the school district, they have the right to request an IEE be conducted at the public expense and at no cost to the parent. Under this condition, the school district may ask you to provide a reason for dissatisfaction with the school-based evaluation; however, parents are not obligated to provide a reason. Following receipt of the request for an IEE, the school district must respond with either a due process hearing or ensure that an IEE is conducted at the public expense, provided that district criteria are met, regarding the location of the evaluation and the qualifications of the examiner.

## Mediation

IDEA 2004 requires that parents and school districts have an opportunity for mediation, such that:

> Either party has the opportunity to present complaints with respect to the identification, evaluation, or educational placement of the child, or the provision of a free appropriate public education for the child.

Mediation is an informal procedure that may be used to resolve disagreements between parents and the school district. IDEA 2004 requires that states develop procedures for mediation that ensure the process is:

- Voluntary for both parties
- Conducted by qualified and impartial mediators
- Conducted in a manner that is convenient as to time and access for all parties
- Confidential
- Conducted in a manner that will not delay or obstruct rights to a due process hearing

**Did you know?** Under IDEA 2004, mediation may now be used without having to file a hearing. It also encourages the use of a preliminary meeting that can be used to discuss issues and perhaps reach a consensus and resolution without having to proceed to a due process hearing.

## Due Process Complaint Notice

IDEA 2004 requires that each state develop and disseminate procedures outlining how either party, or the attorney representing a party, render a due process complaint notice to the other party; and forward a copy of the notice to the state educational agency. Furthermore, IDEA 2004 requires the state educational agency to develop a model form to assist parents in filing a complaint and due process complaint notice in accordance procedures that includes:

- The name of the child, address, and the name of the school the child is attending
- In the case of a homeless child or youth, available contact information for the child and the name of the school the child is attending
- A description of the nature of the problem of the child relating to the proposed initiation or change, including facts about the problem
- A proposed resolution of the problem

In addition, under IDEA 2004, *neither party may engage in a due process hearing until notice is filed as outlined above.*

**Remember that** under IDEA 2004, a complaint now must not have occurred more than two years before the parent or school district became aware or should have become aware of the circumstances surrounding the nature of the complaint.

*Response to the Due Process Complaint Notice*

Once a due process complaint notice is filed according to the procedures stated above, the school district shall respond within ten days of the receipt of the complaint, addressing:

- Why the school district proposed or did not take action cited in the complaint
- Other options considered by the IEP team, and why those options were not endorsed
- Evaluation procedures, reports, and all information used by the school district to reach a decision
- All other factors relevant to the decision-making process

*Educational Placement Pending Outcome of Mediation and Hearings*

According to IDEA 2004, during the course of the proceedings, unless otherwise agreed to by parents and the school district, the child shall remain in the educational placement that preceded the complaint procedure.

*Appeals of Due Process Hearings*

Either party (school or parent) may file an appeal and request a trial in the appropriate federal district court if they are not satisfied with the outcome of the due process hearing.

*Attorney Fees*

IDEA 2004 continues to make provisions for awarding attorney fees to a parent who prevails in a hearing. However, under IDEA 2004, the court may also award reasonable attorney fees to the prevailing state or local school against the parent's attorney, or parent, if:

- The complaint is considered frivolous, unreasonable, without foundation, or in the case of repeated litigation that has become frivolous, unreasonable, and without foundation
- The complaint was presented for improper reasons, such as to harass, cause unnecessary delay, or to needlessly increase litigation costs

# A P P E N D I X    E

# Sample IEP Forms

These forms, provided by the Paulding County School District in Dallas, Georgia, are based on those approved by the Georgia Department of Education.

## PAULDING COUNTY SCHOOL DISTRICT
## EXCEPTIONAL STUDENTS EDUCATIONAL PROGRAMS
### 522 Hardee Street
### Dallas, Georgia 30132
## NOTICE OF I.E.P. COMMITTEE MEETING

Dear _____:

On __/__/____, you were notified about an IEP committee meeting for _____. The purpose of the meeting was as follows:

(☐) The purpose of the meeting was to review _____'s recent evaluation and, if necessary, develop initial goals and objectives as part of an Individual Education Plan (IEP). Because you were unable to attend the meeting, the plan was developed and it is enclosed.

(☐) Please read the Eligibility Report(s) and IEP carefully, including the recommendation for service(s) and the amount of time for each service. Contact me if you have any questions. If you are in agreement with the plan, please sign the enclosed Placement Form and return it to me as soon as possible. THE PROGRAM WILL NOT BE IMPLEMENTED WITHOUT THE SIGNED CONSENT FOR PLACEMENT. The program will begin as soon as I receive the Consent to Place Form with your signature.

(☐) The committee determined that _____ is not eligible for _____ service(s) at this time, based upon evaluation results and current functioning. As a result, no goals and objectives were developed.

Please read the enclosed Eligibility Report(s) and Committee Minutes carefully, including the recommendation for no service(s) at this time. These are for you to keep and need not be returned. Contact me if you have any questions. If you do not contact me by _____, I will assume that you are in agreement with the Committee Minutes and decision.
*********************************************************************************

(☐) The purpose of the meeting was to review and update the Individual Education Plan (IEP) for _____. Because you were unable to attend the meeting, the plan was developed and it is enclosed. This information is for you and need not be returned. Please read the IEP carefully, including the recommendation for service(s) and the amount of time for each service recommended. Please contact me if you have any questions.
*********************************************************************************

(☐) The purpose of the meeting was to review _____'s recent evaluation and determine continued eligibility for _____. Because you were unable to attend, the committee reviewed the evaluation, current functioning, and mastery of goals and objectives and determined that _____ no longer meets eligibility requirements for _____. Please read the enclosed IEP carefully, including the recommendation of no service. Please contact me if you have any questions.
*********************************************************************************

Sincerely,

_____
(Teacher Name)

_____
(Title)

_____
(School Telephone No.)

**PAULDING COUNTY SCHOOL DISTRICT**
**DALLAS, GEORGIA**
**PARENT NOTIFICATION FORM**

RE: _____

(Student's FULL Name)

Dear _____:

There will be a meeting to discuss you child's educational program. All important information will be reviewed so that the committee may establish an Individual Education Program (IEP) in the least restrictive educational setting for you child. Placement recommendations for special education and / or related services will be based upon the IEP.

The meeting will be:

(☐) Initial Staffing—IEP Placement Committee    Date: __/__/____
(☐) Eligibility Determination                    Location: _____
(☐) Review of current IEP                        Time: _____
(☐) Transition Plan Review                       (☐) 1st notice
(☐) Reevaluation Planning                        (☐) 2nd notice
(☐) Other

The following persons have been invited to this meeting:

| Name | Title | Name | Title |
|---|---|---|---|
| _____ | Sp. Ed. Teacher | _____ | _____ |
| _____ | Sp. Ed. Teacher | _____ | _____ |
| _____ | Classroom Teacher | _____ | _____ |
| _____ | Administrator | _____ | _____ |

Although your presence is not required, your attendance will be helpful to us in planning for your child. Please try to attend, if it is at all possible. If the time or date is not convenient, please contact us so that we can try to reschedule this conference. You may be accompanied by a third party if you wish: however, it will be helpful if you give us at least two days notice so that we can arrange for the appropriate space. If you have any questions, please contact me at _____ (telephone). Your Rights as Parents Regarding Special Education are enclosed for your information. Please check the appropriate box below, sign, and return both copies to me.

(☐) Parent contacted by phone on: _____

Response: _____    Sincerely, _____

(Name)

_____
(Title)

__/__/____
(Date)

Please indicate if you will be able to attend:
☐ Yes, I will attend the meeting.
☐ I cannot attend the meeting at the suggested time. I would like to reschedule this meeting for __/__/____ (date) at _____ (time).
☐ I will not be attending the meeting, but I would like a copy of the recommendations sent to me.

_____        _____

(Parent / Guardian / Surrogate Parent)        (Date)

## PAULDING COUNTY SCHOOL DISTRICT
## DALLAS, GEORGIA
## INDIVIDUAL EDUCATION PROGRAM

DATE: __/__/____

Student Name: _____ Birthdate: __/__/____ Grade: _____
School: _____ SS#: _____ School ID #: _____
Primary Eligibility Date: __/__/____ Secondary / Related Eligibility Date __/__/____
Primary Eligibility: _____ Secondary / Related Eligibility: _____ Other: _____
Purpose of Meeting:
- (☐) To review the recent evaluation(s)
- (☐) To review existing IEP goals and objectives and develop new ones
- (☐) To develop an initial Transition Plan
- (☐) To determine eligibility
- (☐) To develop an initial IEP
- (☐) Reevaluation Planning

Other: _____

**RECOMMENDED SERVICES**     **IEP TO BE REVIEWED ON OR BEFORE:** __/__/____

| Special Education / Related Services | Service Provider | Amount of Time In Setting | | Projected Duration | | Projected Duration | |
|---|---|---|---|---|---|---|---|
| | | General Education | Small Group | Begin | End | Begin | End |
| | | | | to | | to | |
| | | | | to | | to | |
| | | | | to | | to | |
| | | | | to | | to | |

| Special Education / Related Services | Service Provider | Amount of Time In General Education | | Projected Duration | | Projected Duration | |
|---|---|---|---|---|---|---|---|
| | | General Education | Small Group | Begin | End | Begin | End |
| | | | | to | | to | |
| | | | | to | | to | |
| | | | | to | | to | |

**SPECIAL TRANSPORTATION:**
**P.E.:** (☐) Regular   (☐) Adaptive
**EXTENDED SCHOOL YEAR** (ESY):
**ESY TRANSPORTATION:**
Team Attending:

| SIGNATURE | TITLE |
|---|---|
| | Parent |
| | Classroom Teacher |
| | Special Education Teacher |
| | Special Education Teacher |
| | LSS Representative |
| | |
| | |
| | |

| Parent / Guardian / adult Responses | | Initials |
|---|---|---|
| I was invited to participate in the development of this IEP and understand its contents. Due process rights and procedures have been explained to me. | Yes ___  No ___ | ___ |
| The Individualized Behavior Management Plan for my child has been reviewed. I will support the school district in its implementation. | I agree ___  I disagree ___ | ___ |
| I had an opportunity to write my comments/concerns in this IEP process. | Yes ___  No ___ | ___ |
| I received a copy of IEP and all related forms completed by the team in this meeting. | Yes ___  No ___ | ___ |

| General Education Teacher received a copy of PC 14 | ☐ YES  ☐ NO | Initials: _____ |
|---|---|---|

# PAULDING COUNTY SCHOOL DISTRICT

## DALLAS, GEORGIA
## EXCEPTIONAL STUDENTS EDUCATIONAL PROGRAMS

### IEP COMMITTEE MINUTES

| Student Name: _____ | School: _____ | Grade: _____ | Date: __/__/__ |
|---|---|---|---|

**PARENTAL RIGHTS GIVEN:** ☐ Yes  ☐ Waived

**PARENTAL RIGHTS EXPLAINED:** ☐ Yes  ☐ Waived

---

**EVALUATION RESULTS:**                          Date of Evaluation: __/__/____

Results: _____

Strengths: _____

Weaknesses: _____

Medical Report (if applicable): _____

Reevaluation Considerations (if appropriate): PC15 attached ☐   PC15a attached ☐
                                              Not applicable ☐

---

**ELIGIBILITY ISSUES:** Date of Eligibility: Primary __/__/____, Secondary __/__/____

(Name) _____ ☐ is / ☐ remains / ☐ is not eligible for _____
based on _____

(Name) _____ ☐ is / ☐ remains / ☐ is not eligible for _____
based on _____

| Student Name: _____ | Date: __/__/__ | Page _____ of _____ |
|---|---|---|

IMPACT STATEMENT: _____
CURRENT FUNCTIONING: _____ See attached Current Functioning Form
    Academic: _____
    Behavior / Social: _____
    Strengths / Weaknesses: _____
    Positive Strategies: _____
    Parent Concerns: _____

**SYSTEM WIDE TESTING CONSIDERATIONS (Required for Kindergarten and higher)**
    _____ System Wide Testing Considerations Form Attached
    _____ Georgia Alternate Assessment Plan and Minutes attached
**ALL STUDENTS HAVE THE RIGHT TO THE OPPORTUNITY TO PARTICIPATE IN GRADE APPROPRIATE TESTING.**
    _____ 8th grade & higher: Student working toward Special Education Diploma: No assessment required & minutes attached.
    _____ 8th grade & higher: Student working toward College Prep Diploma: Minutes attached.
    _____ 8th grade & higher: Student working toward Tech Prep Diploma: Minutes attached.
**SYSTEM WIDE TESTING MINUTES:**
    _____ The committee decided, based on current functioning information and classroom accommodations, that no modifications are needed for participation in system wide testing.
    _____ The committee decided, based upon current functioning information and classroom accommodations, that modifications are necessary for participation in system wide testing.
    Modifications are as follows: _____

**CONSIDERATION OF SPECIAL FACTORS:** (If yes, document any special factors needed below.)
Does the student have behavior which impedes his/her learning or the learning of others? Yes _____ No _____
    If yes, does the student have a Behavior Management Plan? Yes _____ No _____
Does the student have limited English Proficiency? Yes _____ No _____
Is the student blind or visually impaired? Yes _____ No _____
Does the student have communication needs? Yes _____ No _____
Is the student deaf or hard of hearing? Yes _____ No _____
Does the student need assistive technology devices or services? Yes _____ No _____

| **Student Name:** _____ | **Date:** __/__/__ | **Page** _____ **of** _____ |

### REVIEW OF PREVIOUS GOALS & OBJECTIVES:
 ☐ Completed Goals & Objectives page (PC08) attached
Mastered: _____
Partially Mastered: _____
Not Introduced: _____

### NEW GOALS / OBJECTIVES WERE DISCUSSED, WRITTEN, AND ACCEPTED.
 ☐ New Goals & Objectives page (PC08) attached.

### TRANSITION PLAN (Required for students age 14 and older):
 ☐ Not applicable
 ☐ Graduation requirements and course descriptions reviewed. (For age 14)
 ☐ Initial Plan Attached     Date: __/__/____
 ☐ Revised Plan Attached    Date: __/__/____

### TRANSFER OF PARENTAL RIGHTS AT AGE OF MAJORITY (Required for students age 17 and older):
 ☐ Not Applicable       ☐ No
Comments: _____

### NOTIFICATION TO PARENTS OF PROGRESS ON GOALS AND OBJECTIVES WITH:
 ☐ Progress Notes       ☐ Report Cards
 ☐ Other: _____

### CLASSROOM MODIFICATIONS:
 ☐ Classroom Modifications Form attached (PC14)

### EXTENDED SCHOOL YEAR SERVICES (ESY):
The IEP committee has considered the need for ESY as part of the student's Individual Education Program for meeting the **currently** established goals and objectives. Some factors which may be considered when making this determination included the student's age, the severity of the disability, progress on goals and objectives, transition planning, rate of progress, rate of regression, importance of IEP goals considered, related services, or any disruption of service.
 ☐ ESY services are not required.
 ☐ ESY services are required
 Goals to be addressed:  1. _____
            2. _____
 Amount of time and duration of services stated on the PC04
 ESY Transportation?  ☐ Yes  ☐ Transportation form attached  ☐ No
**ESY Minutes:** _____
 ☐ ESY Registration Packet sent to ESEP office: _____

| Student Name: _____ | Date: __/__/__ | Page _____ of _____ |
| --- | --- | --- |

PLACEMENT DISCUSSION: Additional options discussed should be included in the minutes which follow:

I.   Option Considered: General Education / No consultative or direct service
                    Accepted
     Reason _____

II.  Option Considered: General Education / Consultative Services
                    Accepted
     Reason: _____

III. Option Considered: General Education / Co-Taught
                    Accepted
     Reason: _____

IV.  Option Considered: General Education / Small Group Instruction
                    Accepted
     Reason: _____

V.   Option Considered: _____
                    Not Applicable
     Reason: _____

Placement Minutes: *Must* **include the extent, if any, to which the student will not participate with non-disabled students in the regular classroom or nonacademic activities.**

| Student Name: _____ | Date: __/__/__ | Page _____ of _____ |

## IF THE PARENT IS PRESENT AT THE IEP MEETING, COMPLETE THE FOLLOWING:

As the parent / guardian / adult student, I was invited to participate in the development of this IEP and understand its contents. Due process rights and procedures have been explained to me. I have received a copy of the following:

☐ Parental Rights regarding Special Education
☐ IEP and Placement Minutes

☐ Eligibility Report(s) dated __/_____, __/__/_____
☐ Evaluation Report(s) dated __/_____, __/__/_____

☐ Eligibility and / or Evaluation Report(s) not appropriate at this time.

Parent / Guardian / Adult Student Signature(s): _____ Date: __/__/_____
Comments: _____

## IF THE PARENT IS NOT PRESENT AT THE IEP MEETING, INDICATE THE ITEMS SENT TO THE PARENT AND INDICATE ANY FOLLOW-UP CONTACTS:

☐ Parental Rights regarding Special Education
☐ IEP and Placement Minutes

☐ Eligibility Report(s) dated __/_____, __/__/_____
☐ Evaluation Report(s) dated __/_____, __/__/_____

☐ Eligibility and / or Evaluation Report(s) not appropriate at this time.

Follow-up contacts: _____

Signature / Exceptional Education Teacher:
    Date: __/__/_____

**Dissenting Member(s):**
Name: _____ Title: _____
Reason(s) for non-agreement: _____
Name: _____ Title: _____
Reason(s) for non-agreement: _____

**FOLLOW-UP TO IEP MEETING:** *Indicate any follow-up action or activity as a result of the IEP meeting:*

| Activity | Person Responsible | Date |
|---|---|---|
| | | __/__/_____ |
| | | __/__/_____ |
| | | __/__/_____ |
| | | __/__/_____ |
| | | __/__/_____ |
| | | __/__/_____ |

## PAULDING COUNTY SCHOOL DISTRICT
### Dallas, Georgia
### Exceptional Students Educational Programs

### PRESENT LEVELS OF PERFORMANCE

Student: _____  Date: __/__/____  Return this form by: __/__/____

IEP Date: __/__/____ Time: __:__

Classroom Teacher: _____  Special Education Teacher: _____

Grade: _____ Period: _____  Subject: _____

**Please rate the student on how he or she performs in your classroom. Mark N/A if you do not observe the student in this area.**

| Academic | Exc. | Good | Fair | Unsat. | N/A |
|---|---|---|---|---|---|
| Preparation for class | ☐ | ☐ | ☐ | ☐ | ☐ |
| Task Completion | ☐ | ☐ | ☐ | ☐ | ☐ |
| Classwork | ☐ | ☐ | ☐ | ☐ | |
| Homework | ☐ | ☐ | ☐ | ☐ | ☐ |
| Ability to Follow Dir. | ☐ | ☐ | ☐ | ☐ | ☐ |
| Verbal | ☐ | ☐ | ☐ | ☐ | ☐ |
| Written | ☐ | ☐ | ☐ | ☐ | ☐ |

| Social | Exc. | Good | Fair | Unsat |
|---|---|---|---|---|
| Peer Interaction | ☐ | ☐ | ☐ | ☐ |
| Adult Interaction | ☐ | ☐ | ☐ | ☐ |

| Behavioral | Exc. | Good | Fair | Unsat |
|---|---|---|---|---|
| On task behavior | ☐ | ☐ | ☐ | ☐ |
| Tolerance for frustration | ☐ | ☐ | ☐ | ☐ |
| Follows Classroom Rules | ☐ | ☐ | ☐ | ☐ |
| Response to correction | ☐ | ☐ | ☐ | ☐ |

**School Attendance:** Days Present: _____ Days Absent: _____ Days Tardy: _____

**Does this student demonstrate adequate skill for your class in:**

Yes No N/A

| Yes | No | N/A | | | | |
|---|---|---|---|---|---|---|
| ☐ | ☐ | ☐ | Reading | Class Grade ___ Level of Materials: ☐ Below ☐ On ☐ Above Grade Level |
| ☐ | ☐ | ☐ | Math | Class Grade ___ Level of Materials: ☐ Below ☐ On ☐ Above Grade Level |
| ☐ | ☐ | ☐ | Writing | Class Grade ___ Level of Materials: ☐ Below ☐ On ☐ Above Grade Level |
| ☐ | ☐ | ☐ | Science | Class Grade ___ Level of Materials: ☐ Below ☐ On ☐ Above Grade Level |
| ☐ | ☐ | ☐ | S. Studies | Class Grade ___ Level of Materials: ☐ Below ☐ On ☐ Above Grade Level |

If you answered "no" for any question, does the student have adequate skills when appropriate modifications are used?   Yes   No

**Strengths** _____
**Weaknesses** _____
**Behavioral Concerns:** _____
**Effective Strategies:** _____
**Comments:**
**Does the student have any obvious physical or communication problems?   Yes   No**
If yes, explain _____
**Is the student on any medication?   Yes   No**   If yes, explain _____

_____    _____    __/__/____
Signature of Person Completing Form          Title               Date

# PAULDING COUNTY SCHOOL DISTRICT
## EXCEPTIONAL STUDENTS EDUCATION PROGRAM
### Dallas, Georgia
## CLASSROOM MODIFICATIONS

Student: _____ Date: __/__/____
General Education Teacher: _____ ESEP Teacher: _____
Grade: _____ Period (Segment): _____ Subject(s): _____
Strengths: _____ Weaknesses: _____

**\*Include modifications that support the student:**
**1. To be involved and progress in the general curriculum. 2. Toward the advancement of attaining goals. 3. To move toward participating in extracurricular and other nonacademic activities.**

**Supplementary Aids and Services** (those services and personnel needed by the child or on the behalf of the child in order to participate in the general curriculum or educational programs):
☐ CCTV          ☐ Sound Field System          ☐ Braille Device
☐ Augmentative Communication Device          ☐ None          ☐ Other (specify): _____

## Instructional Modifications
☐ Small group setting for tests          ☐ Assignment notebooks          ☐ Extra set of books at home
☐ Read assignments / tests to student          ☐ Repeat / review / drill          ☐ Preferential seating
☐ Extended time for assignments / tests          ☐ Visual aids / cues          ☐ Reduced length of assignments / tests
☐ Preteach concepts / vocabulary          ☐ Auditory aids / cues          ☐ Oral and written directions
☐ Study guides for tests          ☐ Word banks on tests          ☐ Resource assistance as needed
☐ Modify tests          ☐ Open notes / book tests          ☐ Concrete materials / manipulative
☐ Reduced reading level of assignments / tests
☐ Take classroom tests in special education room
☐ Reduce paper / pencil tasks (circle): typewriter, computer, tape recorder, word processor
☐ Note taking assistance (circle): tape lectures, NCR paper, copies of overheads, copy of peer notes
☐ Use alternative materials (specify): _____
☐ Call parents if assignments / tests are missing or if student is failing any classes
☐ Access to nonacademic activities (specify): _____
☐ Other (specify): _____

## Grading Modifications:
☐ Modified QCC objectives          ☐ Limited spelling penalty          ☐ Grade for content
☐ Grade completed work only          ☐ Modified amount          ☐ None
☐ Other _____

## Medical Concerns: ☐ None
☐ Allergies (Specify) _____
☐ Medications (specify time and dosage) _____
☐ Other (specify) _____
- - - - - - - - - - - - - - - - - - - - - - - - - - - - - - - - - - - - - - - - -

**I have explained the above instructional modifications for _____ to the general education teacher.**

_____  Date: __/__/____
               Signature of ESEP Teacher
I have received a copy of the classroom modifications for _____. I understand that the above modifications may be necessary for this student to be successful in the general education setting.

Signature of general education teacher(s):

_____  _____  _____  _____

_____  _____  _____  _____

# PAULDING COUNTY SCHOOL DISTRICT

## Exceptional Students Educational Programs
## Functional Behavioral Assessment

Student: _____ Grade: _____ School: _____ Date: __/__/_____

☐ IEP—Dated: __/__/_____          ☐ Attendance          ☐ EPBS
☐ Behavioral Management Plan—Dated: __/__/_____     ☐ Teacher Reports
☐ Administrator Reports     ☐ Discipline Reports / File     ☐ Parent Reports
☐ Psychological Report—Dated: __/__/_____          ☐ Other Information

**I.** Description of Target Behavior(s):
    A. _____
    B. _____
    C. _____

**II.** Parental Response: _____

**III.** Conditions Surrounding Target Behavior(s):
    ☐ When given direction _____     ☐ Involved in academic instruction _____
    ☐ When in proximity of _____     ☐ When provoked by _____
    ☐ Unstructured time _____     ☐ When unable to _____
    ☐ When not observed _____     ☐ Other _____

**IV.** Describe any situation where the target behavior *does not* occur:

**V.** Reasons for Behavior:
    ☐ Vengeance / retaliation          ☐ Attention Seeking          ☐ Frustration
    ☐ Task Avoidance          ☐ Expressing Anger          ☐ Self Gratification
    ☐ An attempt to control situations          ☐ Intimidation
    ☐ Other: _____

**VI.** Results of Behavior:
    ☐ Loss of Privileges: _____
    ☐ Time out—Location: _____ Length: _____
    ☐ Quiet Reprimand (verbal warning)     ☐ Detention     ☐ Peer Attention
    ☐ Teacher Attention          ☐ Administrative Classroom Removal
    ☐ In School Suspension          ☐ Out of School Suspension
    ☐ Other: _____

**VII.** Recommendation for Behavior Interventions:
    A. Teacher Interventions: _____
    B. Administrative Interventions: _____
    C. Parent / Guardian Interventions: _____

**Signatures:**

Parent / Guardian: _____     Student: _____

Case Manager: _____     General Ed. Teacher: _____

Exceptional Ed. Teacher: _____

## PAULDING COUNTY SCHOOL DISTRICT
## DALLAS, GEORGIA
### Exceptional Students Educational Programs

### Behavior Intervention Plan

Student: _____ School: _____ Grade: _____

Date Completed _____ Effective Date: __/__/____ Review Date: __/__/____

Exceptional Education Teacher: _____ Eligibility(ies): _____

A behavior management plan is an integral part of the student's IEP. This plan is expected to be applicable to most situations in which the student will be involved; other interventions may be used if necessary, based upon the judgment of the school district personnel (Refer to attached FBA if appropriate).

I.   Behavior Management System used in the Classroom / School Setting.

☐ In-class or in-school reward system
☐ Home-school reward system
☐ Token economy
☐ Point system
☐ Positive social reinforcement
☐ Consumable reinforcement
☐ Behavior contract
☐ Privileges / responsibilities

II.  Recommended Behavior Management Options

☐ Ignore inappropriate behavior                ☐ OSS (up to 10 days)
☐ Before / After school detention              ☐ Restitution
☐ Special privileges                            ☐ Use of assignment sheet / agenda
☐ Referral to counselor                         ☐ Nonverbal signals
☐ Verbal reminder / reprimand                   ☐ Structured warning system
☐ Student /teacher conference                   ☐ Lunch detention
☐ Redirect                                      ☐ ISS (In School Suspension)
☐ Meet privately with the student
☐ Cool off time
☐ Time out
☐ Parent / Guardian contact
☐ Denial of privileges
☐ Classroom management system
☐ Send home for the remainder of the day
☐ Implement previously agreed behavior contract

**Behavior Intervention Plan**

| Student Name: _____ | Date: __/__/__ | Page _____ of _____ |
| --- | --- | --- |

III.  Positive interventions, strategies, and / or supports that will be used: _____

IV.  The following school personnel may be contacted if needed by the teacher: _____

V.   In accordance with the Paulding County Policy, the student will be the subject of a complaint filed with the police / sheriff's department if the student breaks the law.

VI.  The Individualized Behavior Management Plan for my child has been reviewed. I (parent / guardian) am in agreement with this plan. It is my understanding that this plan has been designed to meet the individual needs of my child and I will support the school district in its implementation.

_____ I am in agreement with this plan

_____ I am not in agreement with this plan because: _____
_____
_____

**Signatures:**

Parent/Guardian _____  Student _____

Case Manager _____  _____

ESEP Teacher _____  _____

General Ed. Teacher _____  _____

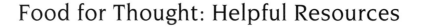

# Food for Thought: Helpful Resources

**The Access Center: Improving Outcomes for All Students K–8**
American Institutes for Research
1000 Thomas Jefferson Street, NW
Washington, DC 20007
202-944-5300
http://www.k8accesscenter.org

**Alexander Graham Bell Association for the Deaf and Hard of Hearing**
3417 Volta Place, NW
Washington, DC 20007
202-337-5220
202-337-5221 (TTY)
http://www.agbell.org

**The Alliance Project**
Box 160
Hill Student Center, Room 101
Peabody College
Vanderbilt University
Nashville, TN 37203
800-831-6134
http://www.alliance2k.org

**American Academy of Child and Adolescent Psychiatry**
3615 Wisconsin Ave., NW
Washington, DC 20016
202-966-7300
http://www.aacap.org

**American Association of the Deaf-Blind (AADB)**
814 Thayer Avenue, Suite 302
Silver Spring, MD
301-495-4402
http://www.aadb.org

**American Association on Mental Retardation (AAMR)**
444 North Capitol Street, NW, Suite 846
Washington, DC 20001
800-424-3688
http://www.aamr.org

**American Brain Tumor Association (ABTA)**
2720 River Road
Des Plaines, IL 60018
800-886-2282
http://www.abta.org

**American Council of the Blind (ACB)**
1155 15th Street, NW, Suite 1004
Washington, DC 20005
800-424-8666
http://www.acb.org

**American Counseling Association (ACA)**
5999 Stevenson Avenue
Alexandria, VA 22304
800-347-6647
http://www.counseling.org

**American Diabetes Association**
1701 North Beauregard Street
Alexandria, VA 22311
800-342-2383
http://www.diabetes.org

**American Federation of Teachers (AFT)**
555 New Jersey Avenue, NW
Washington, DC 20001
202-897-4400
http://www.aft.org

**American Foundation for the Blind (AFB)**
11 Penn Plaza, Suite 300

New York, NY 10001
800-232-5463
http://www.afb.org

**American Occupational Therapy Association (AOTA)**
4720 Montgomery Lane
P.O. Box 31220
Bethesda, MD 20824
301-652-2682
http://www.aota.org

**American Physical Therapy Association (APTA)**
1111 North Fairfax Street
Alexandria, VA 22314
800-999-2782
http://www.apta.org

**American Psychological Association (APA)**
750 First Street, NE
Washington, DC 20002
800-374-2721
http://www.apa.org

**American School Counselor Association (ASCA)**
1101 King Street, Suite 625
Alexandria, VA 22314
800-306-4722
http://www.schoolcounselor.org

**American Society for Deaf Children (ASDC)**
P.O. Box 3355
Gettysburg, PA 17325
800-942-2732
http://www.deafchildren.org

**American Speech-Language-Hearing Association (ASHA)**
10801 Rockville Pike
Rockville, MD 20852
800-498-2071
http://www.asha.org

**Anxiety Disorders Association of America (ADAA)**
8730 Georgia Avenue, Suite 600
Silver Spring, MD 20910

240-485-1001
http://www.adaa.org

**Association for Higher Education and Disability (AHEAD)**
P.O. Box 540666
Waltham, MA 02454
781-788-0003
http://www.ahead.org

**Association of Educational Therapists (AET)**
1804 West Burbank Blvd.
Burbank, CA 91506
800-286-4267
http://www.aetonline.org

**Asthma and Allergy Foundation of America (AAFA)**
1233 20th Street, NW, Suite 402
Washington, DC 20036
800-727-8462
http://www.aafa.org

**Attention Deficit Disorder Association (ADDA)**
P.O. Box 543
Pottstown, PA 19464
484-945-2101
http://www.add.org

**Autism Society of America (ASA)**
7910 Woodmont Avenue, Suite 300
Bethesda, MD 20814
800-3AUTISM
http://www.autism-society.org

**The Bilingual Psychological and Educational Assessment Support Center**
Brooklyn College/CUNY, Queens College/CUNY, and the New York State
    Education Department
Office of Vocational and Educational Services for Individuals with Disabilities
65-30 Kissena Boulevard
Flushing, NY 11367
718-997-5234
http://forbin.qc.edu/ECP/bilingualcenter

**Brain Injury Association**
8201 Greensboro Drive, Suite 611

McLean, VA 22102
800-444-6443
http://www.biausa.org

**Center for Mental Health in Schools**
Department of Psychology
University of California-Los Angeles
P.O. Box 951563
Los Angeles, CA 90095
866-846-4843
http://smhp.psych.ucla.edu

**Center for School Mental Health Assistance (CSMHA)**
University of Maryland, School of Medicine
Department of Psychiatry
680 West Lexington Street, 10th Floor
Baltimore, MD 21201
888-706-0980
http://csmha.umaryland.edu

**Center of Minority Research in Special Education (COMRISE)**
Curry School of Education
University of Virginia
P.O. Box 400273
Charlottesville, VA 22904
434-924-1053
http://curry.edschool.virginia.edu/go/comrise

**Center on Positive Behavioral Interventions and Supports (PBIS)**
1235 University of Oregon
1761 Alder Street
Eugene, OR 97403
541-346-2505
http://www.pbis.org

**Children and Adults with Attention-Deficit/Hyperactivity Disorder (CHADD)**
8181 Professional Place, Suite 150
Landover, MD 20785
800-233-4050
http://www.chadd.org

**Consortium for Appropriate Dispute Resolution in Special Education (CADRE)**
Direction Service, Inc.

P.O. Box 51360
Eugene, OR 97405
541-686-5060
http://www.directionservice.org/cadre

**Council for Learning Disabilities (CLD)**
P.O. Box 4014
Leesburg, VA 20177
571-258-1010
http://www.cldinternational.org

**Council for Exceptional Children (CEC)**
1110 North Glebe Road, Suite 300
Arlington, VA 22201-5704
888-232-7733
http://www.cec.sped.org

**Depression and Bipolar Support Alliance (DBSA)**
730 N. Franklin Street, Suite 501
Chicago, IL 60610
800-826-3632
http://www.dbsalliance.org

**Division for Culturally and Linguistically Diverse Exceptional Learners
     (DDEL)**
Division of the Council for Exceptional Children
1110 North Glebe Road, Suite 300
Arlington, VA 22201
877-CEC-IDEA
http://www.cec.sped.org/dv/ddel.html

**Division for Learning Disabilities (DLD)**
Council for Exceptional Children
1110 North Glebe Road, Suite 300
Arlington, VA 22201
888-CEC-SPED
http://www.dldcec.org

**Educational Resources Information Center (ERIC)**
A national information system funded by the U.S. Department of Education to
provide access to education literature and resources
http://www.eric.ed.gov

**Epilepsy Foundation**
4351 Garden City Drive
Landover, MD 20785
800-332-1000
http://www.epilepsyfoundation.org

**Families of Spinal Muscular Atrophy**
P.O. Box 196
Libertyville, IL 60048
800-886-1762
http://www.fsma.org

**Federation of Families for Children's Mental Health (FFCMH)**
1101 King Street, Suite 420
Alexandria, VA 22314
703-684-7710
http://www.ffcmh.org

**Institute of Education Sciences (IES)**
U.S. Department of Education
555 New Jersey Avenue, NW
Washington, DC 20208
202-219-2239
http://www.ed.gov/about/offices/list/ies/index.html

**International Dyslexia Association (IDA)**
Chester Building, Suite 382
8600 LaSalle Road
Baltimore, MD 21286
410-296-0232
http://www.interdys.org

**International Reading Association (IRA)**
800 Barkdale Road
P.O. Box 8139
Newark, DE 19714
800-336-7323
http://www.reading.org

**Learning Disabilities Association of America (LDA)**
4165 Library Road
Pittsburgh, PA 15234
412-341-1515
http://ldaamerica.org

**March of Dimes**
1275 Mamaroneck Avenue
White Plains, NY 10605
888-663-4637
http://www.modimes.org

**Muscular Dystrophy Association (MDA)**
3300 E. Sunrise Drive
Tucson, AZ 85718
800-572-1717
http://www.mdausa.org

**National Alliance for the Mentally Ill (NAMI)**
2107 Wilson Boulevard, Suite 300
Arlington, VA 22203
800-950-6264
http://www.nami.org

**National Alliance of Black School Educators (NABSE)**
310 Pennsylvania Avenue, SE
Washington, DC 20003
800-221-2654
http://www.nabse.org

**National Association for Bilingual Education (NABE)**
1030 15th Street, NW, Suite 470
Washington, DC 20005
202-898-1829
http://www.nabe.org

**National Association for the Education of African American Children with
    Learning Disabilities (NAEAACLD)**
P.O. Box 09521
Columbus, OH 43209
614-237-6021
http://www.charityadvantage.com/aacld

**National Association of School Nurses (NASN)**
1416 Park Street, Suite A
Castle Rock, CO 80109
866-627-6767
and
163 U.S. Route #1
P.O. Box 1300

Scarborough, ME 04070
877-627-6476
http://www.nasn.org

**National Association of School Psychologists (NASP)**
4340 East-West Highway, Suite 402
Bethesda, MD 20814
301-657-0270
http://www.nasponline.org

**National Association of the Deaf (NAD)**
814 Thayer Avenue
Silver Spring, MD 20910
301-587-1788 Voice
301-587-1789 (TTY)
http://www.nad.org

**National Brain Tumor Foundation (NBTF)**
22 Battery Street, Suite 612
San Francisco, CA 94111
800-934-2873
http://www.braintumor.org

**National Center for Culturally Responsive Educational Systems (NCCRESt)**
1380 Lawrence Street, Suite 625
Denver, CO 80204
303-556-3990
http://www.NCCRESt.org

**National Center for Learning Disabilities (NCLD)**
381 Park Avenue South, Suite 1401
New York, NY 10016
212-545-7510
http://www.ncld.org

**National Center for Special Education Accountability Monitoring (NCSEAM)**
Human Development Center
Louisiana State University Health Sciences Center
1100 Florida Avenue, Building 138
New Orleans, LA 70119
504-942-8212
http://www.monitoringcenter.lsuhsc.edu

**National Center on Education, Disability, and Juvenile Justice (EDJJ)**
Department of Special Education
University of Maryland
College Park, MD 20742
301-405-6462
http://www.edjj.org

**National Center on Secondary Education and Transition (NCSET)**
University of Minnesota
6 Pattee Hall
150 Pillsbury Drive SE
Minneapolis, MN 55455
612-624-2097
http://www.ncset.org

**National Down Syndrome Society (NDSS)**
666 Broadway, 8th Floor
New York, NY 10012
800-221-4602
http://www.ndss.org

**National Dropout Prevention Center for Students with Disabilities (NDPC-SD)**
Clemson University
209 Martin Street
Clemson, SC 29631
864-656-2599
http://www.dropoutprevention.org

**National Early Childhood Technical Assistance Center (NECTAC)**
University of North Carolina
Campus Box 8040
Chapel Hill, NC 27599
919-962-2001
http://www.nectac.org

**National Education Association (NEA)**
1201 16th Street, NW
Washington, DC 20036
202-833-4000
http://www.nea.org

**National Fragile X Foundation**
P.O. Box 190488

San Francisco, CA
800-688-8765
http://www.fragilex.org

**National Dissemination Center for Children with Disabilities (NICHCY)**
P.O. Box 1492
Washington, DC 20013
800-695-0285
http://www.nichcy.org

**National Information Clearinghouse on Children Who Are Deaf-Blind
   (DB-LINK)**
Teaching Research Division
Western Oregon University
345 North Monmouth Avenue
Monmouth, OR 97361
800-438-9376
http://www.dblink.org

**National Institute on Deafness and Other Communication Disorders
   (NIDCD)**
National Institutes of Health
31 Center Drive, MSC 2320
Bethesda, MD 20892
301-496-7243
http://www.nidcd.nih.gov

**National Mental Health and Education Center**
4340 East-West Highway, Suite 402
Bethesda, MD 20814
301-657-0270
http://www.naspcenter.org

**National Mental Health Association (NMHA)**
2001 N. Beauregard Street, 12th Floor
Alexandria, VA 22311
703-684-7722
http://www.nmha.org

**National Mental Health Information Center**
Substance Abuse and Mental Health Services Administration (SAMHSA)
800-789-2647
http://www.mentalhealth.org

**National Multiple Sclerosis Society**
733 Third Avenue
New York, NY 10017
800-344-4867
http://www.nmss.org

**National Neurofibromatosis Foundation (NNFF)**
95 Pine Street, 16th Floor
New York, NY 10005
800-323-7938
http://www.nf.org

**National Organization on Fetal Alcohol Syndrome (NOFAS)**
900 17th Street, NW, Suite 910
Washington, DC 20006
800-666-6327
http://www.nofas.org

**National Research Center on Learning Disabilities (NRCLD)**
Vanderbilt University
P.O. Box 328
Peabody College
Nashville, TN 37103
http://www.nrcld.org

**National Resource Center for Safe Schools**
101 SW Main Street, Suite 500
Portland, OR 97204
800-268-2275
http://www.safetyzone.org

**National Spinal Cord Injury Association**
6701 Democracy Boulevard, Suite 300-9
Bethesda, MD 20817
800-962-9629
http://www.spinalcord.org

**National Stuttering Association (NSA)**
119 W. 40th Street, 14th Floor
New York, NY 10018
800-937-8888
http://www.nsastutter.org

**National Urban Alliance for Effective Education (NUA)**
One Hollow Lane, Suite 100
Lake Success, NY 11042
800-682-4556
http://www.nuatc.org

**Obsessive-Compulsive Foundation (OCF)**
676 State Street
New Haven, CT 06511
203-401-2070
http://www.ocfoundation.org

**Office of English Language Acquisition, Language Enhancement & Academic Achievement for Limited English Proficient Students (OELA)**
2121 K Street, NW, Suite 260
Washington, DC 20037
800-321-6223
http://www.ncela.gwu.edu/oela

**Office of Special Education Programs (OSEP)**
Office of Special Education and Rehabilitative Services
U.S. Department of Education
400 Maryland Avenue, SW
Washington, DC 20202
202-205-5507
http://www.ed.gov/about/offices/list/osers/osep/index.html

**Parent Advocacy Center Coalition for Educational Rights (PACER)**
8161 Normandale Boulevard
Minneapolis, MN 55437
952-838-9000
http://www.pacer.org

**Prader-Willi Syndrome Association (PWSA)**
5700 Midnight Pass Rd.
Sarasota, FL 34242
800-926-4797
http://www.pwsausa.org

**Recording for the Blind & Dyslexic (RFB&D)**
20 Roszel Road
Princeton, NJ 08540
866-732-3585
http://www.rfbd.org

**Research and Training Center on Family Support and Children's Mental Health**
Portland State University
P.O. Box 751
Portland, OR 97207
503-725-4040
http://www.rtc.pdx.edu

**Schwab Learning**
1650 South Amplett Boulevard, Suite 300
San Mateo, CA 94402
650-655-2410
http://www.schwablearning.org

**Special Olympics**
1325 G Street, N.W., Suite 500
Washington, DC 20005
202-628-3630
http://www.specialolympics.org

**Spina Bifida Association of America (SBAA)**
4590 MacArthur Boulevard, NW, Suite 250
Washington, DC 20007
800-621-3141
http://www.sbaa.org

**Tourette Syndrome Association (TSA)**
42-40 Bell Boulevard
Bayside NY 11361
718-224-2999
http://www.tsa-usa.org

**United Cerebral Palsy Association (UCP)**
1660 L Street, NW, Suite 700
Washington, DC 20036
800-872-5827
http://www.ucp.org

# Acronyms 101—Educational Abbreviations and What They Mean

Every profession has its own set of acronyms, or *shortcuts*, that are used to communicate information. Education is no different. While they can be a time-saver for school professionals, acronyms can be overwhelming to people who are unfamiliar with the lingo. This automatically puts you at a disadvantage, because if you do not know what is being said, you will not completely understand all that is being planned for your child.

When we sat down to write this book, we brainstormed about the acronyms we've used ourselves with parents and school personnel. More than one hundred popular acronyms later, we decided that we had compiled enough to give you with a good start. Our goal is to prepare you for some of the acronyms you will hear from school personnel, see in school paperwork, and read about in this book.

## A

**AAD   adaptive/assistive devices:** assistive technology devices designed or altered for special use by children with developmental delays.

**ABA   applied behavior analysis:** an intervention technique that may be used to teach children with autism. It breaks down skills into very small components, which are then taught systematically. Each skill builds the foundation for the next one.

**ADA   Americans with Disabilities Act:** Enacted in 1990, it gives civil rights protections to individuals with disabilities similar to those provided to individuals on the basis of race, color, sex, national origin, age, and religion. It guarantees equal opportunity for individuals with disabilities in public accommodations, employment, transportation, state and local government services, and telecommunications.

**ADD**   see ADHD

**ADHD   attention deficit/hyperactivity disorder:** developmentally inappropriate behavior, including poor attention skills, impulsivity, and hyperactivity. A person can be predominantly inattentive (often referred to as ADD), predominantly hyperactive-impulsive, or a combination of these two.

**ADL   activities of daily living:** personal care activities necessary for everyday living, including eating, dressing, bathing, grooming, and toileting.

**AEP   alternative education placement:** an alternative classroom setting used to improve classroom behavior and address needs that cannot be met in a regular classroom setting.

**AFDC   Aid to Families with Dependent Children:** provides transitional financial assistance to needy families. In order to be eligible for AFDC, a family must have a dependent child who is under age 18 (a state may elect to extend the age limit to include 18-year-olds who are expected to complete secondary school or the equivalent level of vocational or technical training before turning 19); deprived of parental support or care because of a parent's death, continued absence, incapacity, or the unemployment of the principal family earner in a two-parent family under the AFDC-Unemployed Parent (UP) program; living in the home of a parent or other specified, close relative; a resident of the state; and a U.S. citizen or an alien permanently and lawfully residing in the United States. Along with the dependent child, an application for AFDC includes any eligible natural or adoptive parent and any eligible blood-related or adoptive sibling with whom the child is living. Current eligibility requirements are available at *http://www.acf.dhhs.gov/programs/afdc/afdc.txt.*

**AG   annual goal:** used in an Individualized Education Program (IEP), it is a goal that a student will strive to achieve in a twelve-month period. An example would be: "David will read at a second-grade level by the end of the next school year."

**AI   auditorily impaired:** an inability to hear within normal limits because of physical impairment or dysfunction of auditory mechanisms.

**AP   assistant principal:** an administrator who assists the principal of a school; may also be called a vice principal.

**APD  antisocial personality disorder:** a psychiatric condition characterized by chronic behavior, often criminal, that manipulates, exploits, or violates the rights of others. This diagnosis must be made after 18 years of age, and prior to that, teens may be categorized as conduct disordered.

  **auditory processing disorder:** an inability to accurately process and interpret sound information. Students with APD often do not recognize subtle differences between sounds in words (such as "hit" versus "hat").

**APE  adaptive physical education:** alternative physical education for students who cannot participate in the regular program.

**ASD  autism spectrum disorders:** one of several disorders characterized by varying degrees of impairment in communication skills, social interactions, and restricted, repetitive, and stereotyped patterns of behavior.

**ASL  American Sign Language:** a form of communication used among deaf persons. The system uses signs to communicate based on specific movements and shapes of the hand and arms, eyes, face, head and body posture.

**AT  assistive technology:** technological devices used by children with developmental delays (see AAD).

**AUT  autism:** the category of special education services for students with autism. (Also, as a disorder, see ASD.)

**AYP  adequate yearly progress:** Required by the No Child Left Behind Act (NCLB), all public school campuses, school districts, and the state are evaluated for AYP. Each is required to meet AYP criteria on three measures: reading/language arts, mathematics, and either graduation rate (for high schools and districts) or attendance rate (for elementary and middle/junior high schools).

**B**

**BD  behaviorally disordered:** the category of special education services for students with a behavior disorder.

  **brain damage:** damage that can occur as a result head trauma, infections, bleeding into the brain, lack of oxygen, failure of the brain to develop properly, or neurological damage.

**BIL  bilingual:** the ability to use two languages with equal or nearly equal fluency.

**BIP  behavior intervention plan:** a plan that includes positive strategies, program modifications, and supplementary aids and supports that address a student's disruptive behaviors and allows the child to be educated in the least restrictive environment (LRE).

**BMP   behavior management plan:** see BIP.

## C

**CA   chronological age:** a student's actual age in years and months, or birth age. It is calculated when intelligence and achievement measures are administered to your child, since these tests are scored using chronological age.

**CAI   computer-assisted instruction:** drill-and-practice, tutorial, or simulation activities used alone or in conjunction with classroom instruction.

**CAP   central auditory processing:** skills used to interpret and store information that is received orally. Examples include auditory discrimination (being able to distinguish between similar sounds (a, e, i) or being able to attend to some sounds, while purposefully ignoring other sounds.

**CAPD   central auditory processing disorders:** difficulty understanding speech or auditory instructions in the presence of normal hearing sensitivity. Although the child has normal hearing, he cannot understand oral communication at the same level as other children his age.

**CBA   curriculum-based assessment:** an ongoing assessment of a student's ability to meet expected performance standards for behaviors in the developmental areas of cognitive, communication, social, motor, and adaptive behaviors.

**CBM   curriculum-based measurement:** a method teachers use to find out how students are progressing in basic academic areas such as math, reading, writing, and spelling. These measures are based on how well a student masters the curriculum goals. When using CBM, the teacher will give the student brief, timed samples (called probes), which are created from material taken out of the school curriculum. To keep things standard, the teacher will read the same directions every time that he gives a specific probe. These probes are timed and may last from one to five minutes, but this will depend on the child's age and the skill being measured. The child's performance on a probe is scored for speed and accuracy of performance. Used repeatedly as practice drills, the student's results are charted to monitor the rate of academic progress.

**CD   conduct disorder:** a group of behavioral and emotional problems in children and adolescents that result in great difficulty following rules and behaving in a socially acceptable way. Behaviors may include aggression to people and animals;

destruction of property; deceitfulness, lying, or stealing; and serious violations of rules.

**CHI    closed head injury:** an injury occurring when a head sustains a blunt force by striking against an object (an example is a concussion).

**CLD    culturally and linguistically diverse:** refers to students who come from a different culture and whose background includes a different language.

**COTA    certified occupational therapist assistant:** a trained professional who works under the direction and supervision of an occupational therapist (OT).

**CP    cerebral palsy:** a term that encompasses many different disorders of movement and posture.

## D

**DAP    developmentally appropriate practices:** practices that are age appropriate and individually appropriate for each student.

**DB or DBL    deaf-blind:** students who are both deaf and blind.

**DD    developmental disabilities:** a diverse group of severe chronic conditions due to mental and/or physical impairments.
   **developmentally delayed:** a child with delays in cognitive development, communication development, social/emotional development, physical/motor development, and/or adaptive/self-help development. Some districts place a limit on the age that a child can retain this categorical label. For example, in some districts, a child can only be designated as DD prior to their sixth birthday. After that time, further assessment is required to provide a more appropriate designation.

**DSM-IV    Diagnostic and Statistical Manual of Mental Disorders:** a book that includes diagnostic criteria for the most common mental disorders including description, diagnosis, treatment, and research findings. Now in its fourth edition, a text revision (DSM-IV-TR) occurred in 2000; no diagnostic criteria were changed.

## E

**EBD    emotional and behavioral disorders:** the category of special education services for students with both emotional and behavioral problems.

**EC    early childhood:** the early stage of growth or development.
   **exceptional children:** children who have special needs; often used to refer to those receiving special education services.

**ECE   early childhood education:** the education of a child in grades K–3 (age range of birth through 9 years of age).

**ECI   early childhood intervention:** programs designed to provide assistance to preschool-age children with physical or developmental problems.

**ED   emotionally disturbed:** the category of special education services for students who demonstrate emotional problems, as described below.
    **emotional disturbance:** students with severe emotional disturbance at various times can feel extremely sad, angry, worthless, anxious or worried, fearful, and afraid that they are not in control of their minds or behavior.

**ELL   English language learner:** someone who is learning to speak and understand the English language.

**EMH   educable mentally handicapped:** the category of special education services for students with mental retardation (mild impairments in intelligence and adaptive behavior).

**EMR   educable mentally retarded:** see EMH

**ESE   exceptional students education:** refers to special education services to students who qualify for such services

**ESL   English as a Second Language:** English learned in an environment where it is the predominant language of communication.

**ESOL   English for Speakers of Other Languages:** English instruction for persons who speak a language other than English.

**ESY   extended school year:** students receiving special education services may qualify for ESY services, which extend beyond the regular school year (summer school). The IEP team determines eligibility for ESY services.

**F**

**FAPE   free appropriate public education:** as required by IDEA, all disabled children must receive special education and related services at no cost.

**FBA   functional behavioral assessment:** a problem-solving process for addressing student problem behavior that relies on techniques and behavioral strategies to identify what precipitates or triggers a given behavior and to select interventions that directly address the problem behaviors.

**FERPA Family Educational Rights to Privacy Act:** a federal law that protects the privacy of student education records.

**FY fiscal year:** a twelve-month period used for calculating yearly financial reports. Most schools use a July 1 to June 30 fiscal year.

## H

**HI hearing impairment:** a category of special education services for students with an impairment in hearing, whether permanent or fluctuating.

**HS Head Start:** a child development program for children ages 3 to 5 and their families that focuses on increasing the school readiness of young children from low-income families by increasing opportunities for learning.

   **high school:** a secondary school offering the final years of high school, usually grades 9 through 12.

## I

**IDEA Individuals with Disabilities Education Act of 2004:** a federal law mandating that all children with disabilities have available to them a free, appropriate public education that emphasizes special education and related services designed to meet their unique needs and prepare them for employment and independent living. (See also Chapter 1.)

**IED intermittent explosive disorder:** a disorder that is characterized by frequent and often unpredictable episodes of extreme anger or physical outbursts. Between these episodes, there is typically no evidence of violence or physical threats.

**IEE independent educational evaluation:** an evaluation conducted by a qualified examiner, who is not employed by the school district, at the public's expense.

**IEP Individualized Education Program:** a document written for each child who is found eligible for special education services. It addresses each child's unique needs and includes, among many other things, goals and measurable objectives a child will strive to achieve. (See also Chapter 9.)

**IFA individualized functional assessment:** an assessment that examines whether a child can engage in age-appropriate activities effectively.

**IQ intelligence quotient:** a measure of someone's intelligence as indicated by an intelligence test, where an average score is 100. An IQ score is the ratio of a person's mental age to his chronological age multiplied by 100. For example, if the mental age of a child is 130 months, and he is exactly 10 years old (120 months), the child's IQ is 108 (130/120 x 100 = 108).

**ISS   in-school suspension:** an alternative placement program that allows students to come to school, but they are not allowed to attend regular class. They are placed in an isolated, supervised, small-group setting where they can still complete their school work.

**ITP   individualized transition plan:** transition services begin when a student is ready to transition from high school to postsecondary education, vocational training, independent employment, supported employment, continuing and adult education, adult services, or independent living. When transition services begin for students with an IEP, they will complete a transition planning interview to identify their needs. The IEP team will use this information to develop an ITP, which is designed to accomplish the student's goals.

## L

**LD   learning disability:** a neurological disorder that affects the brain's ability to receive, process, store, and respond to information. A person may have difficulties in the areas of reading, writing, mathematics, listening, and/or speaking.

**LEA   local education agency:** a school district, for example.

**LEP   limited English proficient:** a student who is not fully proficient in English, speaks a language other than English at home, and does not demonstrate English language skills of comprehension, speaking, reading, and writing at a level that would allow him to be placed in a mainstream class setting where only English is spoken.

**LRE   least restrictive environment:** for most students, the least restrictive environment is the regular classroom, but the IEP team must determine the LRE for each student based on his or her individual needs.

## M

**MA   mental age:** the level of intellectual development as measured by an intelligence test. For example, if an 8-year-old is only able to successfully answer questions that the average 6-year-old could do, then his mental age would be 6 years.

**MDT   multidisciplinary team:** a group of school professionals that conducts an in-depth evaluation of the psychological, academic, behavioral, communication, health, hearing, and vision of a student because of a perceived disability.

   **manifest determination team:** a group of school personnel who meet to review the case of a student receiving special education services whose behavior has resulted in expulsion or a change in placement. The team determines whether the behavior is related to the disability.

**MI   multiple intelligences:** Dr. Howard Gardner's theory, which states that our conception of intelligence, based on I.Q. testing, is too limited. Gardner proposes there are eight different intelligences: linguistic intelligence ("word smart"), logical-mathematical intelligence ("number/reasoning smart"), spatial intelligence ("picture smart"), bodily-kinesthetic intelligence ("body smart"), musical intelligence ("music smart"), interpersonal intelligence ("people smart"), intrapersonal intelligence ("self-smart"), and naturalist intelligence ("nature smart").

**MMR   mild mental retardation:** the category of special education services for students with mild mental retardation. This category falls within the IQ range of roughly 55 to 70, although this varies from state to state.

**MR   mentally retarded:** someone who has mental retardation.
   **mental retardation:** the category of special education services for students with mental retardation. As a disorder, someone with significantly below average intellectual functioning and significant deficits in adaptive behavior. Mental retardation is classified in three different ways by three different sources: the DSM-IV; the American Association of Mental Retardation; and the educational system. See Chapter 7 for an in-depth discussion of how different organizations define MR. Although the cause for most people with mental retardation cannot be explained, it may be due to trauma before or after birth (lack of oxygen to the brain before, during, or after birth, severe head injury), infectious diseases (meningitis, encephalitis), chromosomal abnormalities (Down's syndrome, fragile X syndrome, Angelman syndrome, Prader-Willi syndrome), genetic abnormalities and inherited metabolic disorders (Tay-Sachs disease, PKU, Rett syndrome), metabolic (Reye's syndrome, hypoglycemia), toxic (lead poisoning, intrauterine exposure to alcohol, cocaine, amphetamines, and other drugs), nutritional (malnutrition), and environmental (poverty, low socioeconomic status).

# N

**NCLB   No Child Left Behind Act of 2001:** its purpose is to ensure that all children have a fair, equal, and significant opportunity to obtain a high-quality education and reach, at a minimum, proficiency on challenging state academic achievement standards and state academic assessments.

# O

**O&M   orientation and mobility:** instruction that teaches individuals who are visually impaired, blind, or deaf-blind to move about safely and independently in a familiar or unfamiliar environment.

**OCD   obsessive compulsive disorder:** a disorder characterized by recurrent obsessions (thoughts/ images) and/or compulsions (actions) that are unwanted and cause anxiety. Obsessions are recurrent and persistent thoughts, impulses, or images that are unwanted and cause a great deal of anxiety. Compulsions are repetitive behaviors or rituals (like hand washing, keeping things in order, or checking to make sure a light is turned off) or mental acts (like counting or repeating words silently). Often the actions serve the purpose of attempting to reduce the anxious thoughts and/or images.

**OCR   Office of Civil Rights:** the federal agency that serves student populations facing discrimination and the advocates and institutions promoting solutions to civil rights problems. An important responsibility is resolving complaints of discrimination, as well as developing creative approaches to preventing and addressing discrimination.

**ODD   oppositional defiant disorder:** a disorder characterized by an ongoing pattern of uncooperative, defiant, and hostile behavior toward authority figures that seriously interferes with a student's daily functioning. A high percentage of children with ODD also are diagnosed with ADHD.

**OH   orthopedically handicapped:** the category of special education services for students with severe orthopedic impairments.

**OHI   other health impairments:** the category of special education services for students with limited strength, vitality or alertness, due to chronic or acute health problems (such as asthma, ADHD, diabetes, or a heart condition).

**OSEP   Office of Special Education Programs:** part of the U.S. Department of Education, its goal is to improve results for infants, toddlers, children, and adolescents with disabilities ages birth through 21 by providing leadership and financial support to assist states and local districts.

**OT   occupational therapy:** a rehabilitative service to persons with mental, physical, emotional, or developmental impairments. In the school setting, OT can reduce barriers that limit student participation within the school environment and can use assistive technology to support student success. Some examples of OT include helping a student with his pencil grip, physical exercises that may be used to increase strength and dexterity, or exercises to improve hand-eye coordination.
   **occupational therapist:** a trained professional who provides occupational therapy.

**OT/PT   occupational therapy/physical therapy:** receiving both occupational and physical therapy services.

# P

**PDD   pervasive developmental disorder:** the category of special education services for students with delays or deviance in their social/language/motor and/or cognitive development.

**PLOP   present level of performance:** a statement that describes how the child is performing currently.

**PRE-K   pre-kindergarten:** the year of education that occurs before kindergarten. The goal of pre-K is to promote school readiness so that children have a better chance of later success in school.

**PT   physical therapy:** instructional support and treatment of physical disabilities provided by a trained physical therapist, under a doctor's prescription, that helps a person improve the use of bones, muscles, joints, and nerves.
   **physical therapist:** a trained professional who provides physical therapy.

**PTA   physical therapist assistant:** a professional who works under the direction and supervision of a physical therapist and provides rehabilitative services to students with physical or developmental impairments.
   **Parent-Teacher Association:** a school district–based group that is part of the National PTA.

**PTSD   posttraumatic stress disorder:** a DSM-IV psychiatric disorder that can follow the experience or witnessing of life-threatening events such as natural disasters, serious accidents, or threat to life. Persons suffering from PTSD often relive the experience through nightmares and flashbacks, have difficulty sleeping, and feel detached or estranged. Children with PTSD often reexperience trauma through play.

# R

**RAD   reactive attachment disorder:** the failure of a child to bond with a caretaker in infancy or early childhood. It is often precipitated by severe attachment trauma (such as previous child abuse or neglect), as children develop they may either treat all people as if they were their best friend or show mistrust of nearly everyone.

**RTI   response to intervention:** the response-to-invention (RTI) model is also often called the Three-Tiered Model. Under IDEA 2004, school districts can use this model as an alternative to the discrepancy model, as a process of determining whether a student has a learning disability.

## S

**SAT   Student assistance team:** see SST

**SDD   significant developmental delay:** a category of special education services for younger students experiencing a delay in a child's development in adaptive behavior (daily living skills), cognition (learning), communication, motor development (walking, running), or social development.

**SEBD   serious emotional and behavioral disorder:** a category of special education services for students experiencing significant emotional disturbance (see ED).

**SED   seriously emotionally disturbed:** a category of special education services for students experiencing significant emotional disturbance (see ED).

**SI   speech impaired:** the category of special education services for students with a speech impairment.

**SIB   self-injurious behavior:** self-inflicted wounds from behavior that can cause tissue damage, such as bruises, redness, and open wounds. Examples of behaviors include hand-biting, head-banging, and excessive scratching or rubbing.

**SLD   specific learning disability:** a category of special education services for students with one or more of the basic psychological processes involved in understanding or in using language, spoken or written, that may manifest itself in an imperfect ability to listen, think, speak, read, write, spell, or to do mathematical calculations.

**SLP   speech-language pathologist:** sometimes referred to as speech therapists or speech teachers, these professionals assess, diagnose, treat, and help to prevent speech, language, cognitive, communication, voice, swallowing, fluency, and other related disorders.

**SPED   special education:** services offered to children that possess one or more of the following disabilities: specific learning disabilities, speech or language impairments, mental retardation, emotional disturbance, multiple disabilities, hearing impairments, orthopedic impairments, visual impairments, autism, combined deafness and blindness, traumatic brain injury, and other health impairments.

**SST   student study team:** student support team, can also be called student assistance team (SAT): a team of school professionals (including classroom teachers, curriculum specialist, school psychologist, speech-language therapist, and principal or assistant/vice principal,) and parents who meet to discuss problems a child is having in regular education classes. The goal of SST is to discuss ways in which to assist a child so that his learning or behavior problems minimize the effect they have on his or her education.

# T

**TBI   traumatic brain injury:** the category of special education services for students with a traumatic brain injury (TBI), which occurs when a sudden physical assault on the head causes damage to the brain.

**TDD   telecommunication devices for the deaf:** special telephones with typewriter keyboards and visual displays that provide people who are deaf with access to telephones.

**TMH   trainable mentally handicapped:** a category of special education services for students with moderate or severe mental retardation (see MR).

**TMR   trainable mentally retarded:** a category of special education services for students with moderate mental retardation (see MR).

**TPP   transition planning process:** helping a student transition from school to adult life. This requires effective planning, school experiences, services, and supports so that he can achieve his desired outcome.

# V

**VI   visually impaired:** a category of special education services for students with an impairment in vision (including blindness).

# References

**Johnson, Jean, and Ann Duffett.** "When It's Your Own Child: A Report on Special Education from the Families Who Use It." New York: Public Agenda, 2002 (http://www.ecs.org/clearinghouse/37/06/3706.pdf).

**Rosenthal, Robert, and Lenore Jacobson.** *Pygmalion in the Classroom: Teacher Expectation and Pupils' Intellectual Development.* New York: Crown House, 2003.

**Wilens, Timothy E.,** *Straight Talk About Psychiatric Medications for Kids,* rev. ed. New York: Guilford Press, 2003.

# Index